A Fez of the Heart

'Entertaining, witty and original, Jeremy Seal's is an extraordinarily informative and sympathetic account of modern Turkey's dilemmas – illuminated by the author's compendious knowledge of Turkish head-gear. Superbly written and fascinating' – PAUL MICOU

'Seal's history of the fez is a brilliant idea, a mock-serious investigation of the all but forgotten headgear, as a way of illuminating the tensions of Turkish life . . . very engaging' – JUSTIN CARTWRIGHT, *The Times*

'A truly beguiling book' – HARDY AMIES, *Literary Review*

'There are a thousand reasons for writing a book, many of them more bizarre than Jeremy Seal's notion that he might discover the soul of Turkey through a pursuit of her national hat – the fez. But seldom will they produce a book so charmingly eccentric . . . No ordinary travelogue, the book is more an entertaining mix of history, politics and conversation . . . It's also very funny' – *Marie Claire*

'A magical journey through the many contradictions of modern Turkey' – *GQ*

'He weaves into the tale such lively, frank and touching descriptions of country life that it ranks as the best travel book on Turkey this decade' – *Cornucopia*

'Jeremy Seal has produced what any fair-minded reader would simply call a modern travel classic . . . Good title. Good book' – *Herald Express*

'It is with a noble spirit of myth-breaking that Jeremy Seal takes us through modern Turkey . . . *A Fez of the Heart* is well worth reading . . . It works for Seal (as it did for V. S. Naipaul in India), as he pursues his quietly metaphorical hunt for the lost fez' – TOM HINEY, *Spectator*

JEREMY SEAL has worked in publishing, taught in Turkey and now writes travel articles for publications including the *Daily Telegraph*, *The Times* and the *Sunday Times*. This is his first book. He lives in Gloucestershire.

JEREMY SEAL

A Fez of the Heart

✸

TRAVELS
AROUND TURKEY
IN SEARCH
OF
A HAT

PICADOR

First published 1995 by Picador .

This edition published 1996 by Picador
an imprint of Macmillan Publishers Ltd
25 Eccleston Place, London SW1W 9NF
and Basingstoke

Associated companies throughout the world

ISBN 0330 34362 9

5 7 9 8 6

A CIP catalogue record for this book is available from
the British Library.

Typeset by CentraCet Limited, Cambridge
Printed and bound in Great Britain by
Mackays of Chatham plc, Chatham, Kent

To Dad

acknowledgements

I AM INDEBTED to the staff of the Turkish National Tourist Office in London, particularly Ayşen St Clair Abbot and Mustafa Türkmen. The advice, assistance, and considerable knowledge of Ghislain Sireilles at specialist tour operators Simply Turkey in London was invaluable.

Philip Mansel was an inexhaustible source of information. Thanks too to Professor Anthony Bryer, Mary Burkett, Dr Celia Carslake, Peter Lane, John Norton, Sir Mark Russell, Khalil Sara, Jennifer Scarce, Sarah Searight, and Roddy Taylor. Thanks also to the library staff at the Royal Asiatic Society, the British Library, and the National Art Library at the V&A.

In Istanbul nobody was more generous in their assistance and good company than the staff of the admirable *Cornucopia Magazine*: John Scott, Berrin Torolsan, and Arzu Musa. I would also like to thank Guldenir Kurtar, Mary Işin, Ziyad Ebbuzia, Oya Eczacabaşı, Gullum Yalcintepe, and Ahmet Kayikci. Particular thanks go to Erdoğan Akyuz for barely prompted, tireless research on my behalf.

Jane Bradish-Ellames at Curtis Brown and all at Picador, particularly Peter Straus and Rachel Heath, have been model agents and publishers respectively, and excellent company as well.

Love and thanks to Conrad Bird, Sophie Cottrell, Tom Owen Edmunds, Katie Hickman, Nick Tudball, and Pete Moller, who slave-drove damaged minds on the morning of New Year's Day 1992 in Northumberland. This book was their idea. Also to Justin Creedy Smith, for the author photo and his friendship and enthusiasm on numerous trips to Turkey. And, as ever, to Ash.

✹

author's note

The Turkish letter 'ş' is pronounced as *sh*, 'ğ' is silent. Umlauts on 'o' and 'a' simply serve to skew the pronounciation of the vowel. In some cases, the conventional anglicization of Turkish words has been retained. The correct Turkish 'inşallah' appears as the more familiar *inshallah*, 'haç' appears as *haj*, 'hoca' as *hoja*. (The Turkish 'c' is pronounced like *j*.) This inconsistency should help readers avoid confusions of pronunciation.

'I think it is that you are trying to be something
which you never can be, something which nobody
with any sense would wish to be – a European.'

British traveller Marmaduke Pickthall
in conversation with a 'gloomy' Turk

If the cap fits, wear it
English adage

✳

prologue

> 'When you make a world for tourists you make a lie, a
> patchwork from all the coats you have shed.'
>
> Mary Lee Settle

BY THE SHORES of the Turkish Mediterranean they once built
a city beyond reproach. Such a city that nothing, it was said,
could steal from its grandeur. And then they named it Pomegranate, or Side in the Turkish.

And so, as the city dwindled to a village over the centuries
and only passing armies gave any indication that new empires
were afoot, the people made an unremarkable living – the
fishermen from mullet and the farmers from lamb – among
the fallen capitols and pilasters, plinths and pediments, col-
umns and statuary of the ruined city of their forefathers.
Among the masonry, coins from the second century featuring
Nike, Goddess of Victory, lay in dust-strewn profusion.
Children might dig up the coins as a temporary distraction
while the years passed in uneventful succession, people grew
old, and the poppies bloomed and died. The catch was landed
in the small port, the muezzin sounded mournfully from the
minaret five times a day. So life unravelled, and the meaning
was revealed in its pattern, and for two thousand years the
pattern was enough.

By the 1980s, however, the sons of those same fishermen
and farmers had discovered the value of the coins and sold
them to the local museum. Old Nike for new, they spent their
earnings on shedding themselves in the latest trainers and set
about running hotels and restaurants where the menus offered
fisherman's *mallet* and farmer's *lamp*. They touted *boot* trips
to those interested in boots, hired out deck chairs, sold

3

paragliding experiences, chased young girls from Southend through Pomegranate's discotheques in the hope that they might lie down with them, and whispered sweet *bitte schöns* at fat women from Dortmund that they might buy a leather jacket or a bag to remind them of their time here, in this place of labels whence the echoes of the past had long since fled.

I am left with a man I never met, a few stonings fuelled by outrage, and a purple hat they no longer wear.

Mustafa Yildirim saw little of the 1980s. In 1982, he would die in Pomegranate, the village where he had been born and had lived his entire life. Mustafa could tell his children nothing of his origins, only that a Greek family had taken pity on an orphan boy and assisted by providing him with a donkey to set him on his way through life. By dint of hard work and an orphan's instinct for survival, Mustafa graduated from donkey owner to farmer while his benefactors vanished in the Greco-Turkish population exchanges of the 1920s.

In the reforming, Westernizing years of the 1930s, a decree went out that all Turkish citizens were to be counted. Everybody was to stay at home and usefully occupy themselves on census day. How the injunction was widely interpreted only became clear nine months later when a previously unknown first name – Nufus, meaning population or census – enjoyed a popularity as widespread as it was short-lived.

So countless, however, were the Ahmet Son of Mehmets and the Mehmet Son of Ahmets, the patronymics by which Turks were then known, that the census largely fell into confusion, and in 1935, before a further census was attempted, another decree went out that all Turkish citizens were first to find themselves a surname.

After eighteen months, the warning went, those families which had failed to find themselves a surname to their liking would be fined and supplied with one of the district official's choosing. Many citizens needed no such incentive. Admit-

4

tedly, some, such as the Turks arriving from Crete in the population exchanges who often called themselves Giritli, or Mr and Mrs From Crete, were unimaginative in their choice. But others adopted names such as Overthrower of Mountains, Eagle-eyed, Pure Turk and Lion-hearted. Army officers named themselves after victories for which they believed themselves to have been solely responsible, ministers after rivers which they had helped establish as national frontiers. The country's President chose Father of the Turks to add to his first names, Mustafa Kemal, while Pomegranate's rather more humble Mustafa ended up with the surname Lightning.

Mustafa Yildirim could not remember much about the genesis of his surname. He could not remember paying a fine. Nor, unlike the President, could he ever quite explain what the name meant. It may have been a fanciful reference to orphan origins so obscure that he could only have come from the sky. Or perhaps it referred to the legendary speed at which he worked his fields – and certainly the same nimble energy is evident in the inherited movements of his son, Halil. But the surname always makes Halil think of something else, an abiding childhood memory of his own. He remembers being commanded to stand near his industrious father in those pre-electricity nights, protecting with his child's frame and cupped hands from buffeting gusts of sea-blown wind the flickering naked flame of the torch by which his father guided the furrow of his plough.

Halil is now a successful Pomegranate hotelier, but he has not forgotten his father. The tools of the old man's trade such as the wooden ploughs and the threshing sleds – horse-drawn slabs of walnut from whose base diagonal lines of flints protrude to separate wheat from chaff – have been tidied up, varnished, and displayed around the hotel, along with photographs of an ancient face, to commemorate the man and his way of life. Even the baggy *shalvar* trousers of Mustafa *amja* – old man Mustafa – have been loving patched, washed, and ironed, and draped over one of the ploughshares.

The tools of Halil's trade are fax machines, tour operators, a facility with profit margins and exchange rates, charm, and foreign languages. No son will build such a memorial to Halil – a wall adorned with his typewriter, Filofax, and a sheaf of holiday brochures above beach shorts and sunglasses – and not only because it would look ridiculous. Halil knows that there never were, nor will be, such differences in Pomegranate livelihood and lifestyle as existed between him and his father, and their respective generations. There is a yawning gulf between their lives that cannot be closed, only recognized. The shrine is testimony to a time when life in Pomegranate changed so fast that the tools of working men were museum pieces before those who once had used them had had time to die.

It was hard to imagine a more achingly beautiful place than Pomegranate in the early seventies. The pioneering trickle of independent tourists certainly thought so. The locals, who took such scenic magnificence for granted, were struck instead by these visitors whose behaviour was quite as strange as their clothes, colourful and entirely absent below knee and elbow. In July and August, when the villagers were indulging in lengthy recesses from the heat of the day, these people could be seen pottering around the ruins of ancient temples and the amphitheatre, puzzling over fallen friezes before taking themselves off to undress – as well as men, women! – on the long beach that fringes the peninsular where Pomegranate stands. According to the sleepy but indignant village commentary that raised a cloud of drowsy wasps as it issued from beneath the shady vine trellises of homes and tea houses, the ruins had been there as long as anyone could remember and hardly merited exploring in the baking heat of high summer, while even the infidel Greeks in the old days, the oldest villagers readily confirmed, had never undressed on the beach.

Not that it was for the villagers to wonder why. Turkey had long been host to the unpredictable tidetables of invasion that had thrown up the Hittites and Mongols, Romans and Persians, Selcuks and Ottomans, and countless others besides. On the great Eurasian land bridge unsolicited visits from passers-by were largely considered to come with the territory, and the people of Pomegranate were habitually sympathetic to requests for billeting or a glass of fortifying tea.

So some Pomegranate families were prompted to clear spare rooms and offer them to the latest arrivals as *pansiyon* accommodation. The more enterprising among them even dared, having heard the practice was acceptable, to charge a few lira at the end of the visitors' stay.

But the first signs of trouble were not long in coming. Some visitors started to wander back from the beach in their bikinis, and so caused grave offence among a profoundly traditional Muslim population. For whatever else the Mongols had done, they had kept out of bikinis. Signs in atrocious English and German – 'Bikini in village No' – were erected on street corners in an attempt to stem the offence. Unsurprisingly, these signs proved incomprehensible as much in concept as language to French visitors who had been largely brought up on nude sunbathing and doubtless thought slipping on a bikini for a jaunt through town might label them as puritan killjoys. As a result, several of them were stoned by incensed villagers.

Bruised and bemused, the French were driven back to the beach, but the influx of tourists was not discouraged. Pomegranate's twenty-five-bed capacity soon doubled, and doubled again, setting a pattern for the years to come. *Pansiyon* owners even started requisitioning the rough notice-boards which had recently railed against bikinis on which they might advertise their bed and breakfast rates. Suddenly, there was a new livelihood called *turizm*, predicated on the astounding discovery that foreigners seemed happy to pay for the things – accommodation, meals, and even visits to ruins – that the local people had always marked down under hospitality. It was not surprising then that Halil Yildirim should wake up early one spring morning as a young man and decide he no longer wanted to be a farmer.

By the spring morning in 1992 when I arrived, it was obvious that there were very few farmers indeed left in Pomegranate. I had set out for the village at dawn from a nearby town on a minibus crammed with men and women employed in servicing Pomegranate's shops and restaurants, and its hotel beds, now estimated to be anywhere in number between forty and a hundred thousand. The minibus came to a premature halt when the engine emitted a valedictory thud, wheezed a bit, and abruptly died. Then the improvised tow-rope by which we continued soon frayed and gave within a mile of the town while our tow disappeared round the corner, quite unaware of our parting.

By the time we had reached the new tourist bus station on the village outskirts, the fleet of tractor-hauled trolleys was in service shuttling European visitors, dressed in yellows and pinks above fat-dimpled, sun-fried flesh, through the shimmer of the red poppies among the unkempt fields into town.

I dressed to the sight of Pomegranate putting out flags, the white crescent and star on a red background of the Turkish Republic. The flags hung from every house, carpet shop, and kebab stand, draped fragments of a heraldic solar system. It was May 19, a public holiday commemorating the day in 1919 when a gallant young Turkish officer called Mustafa Kemal landed on a distant Turkish Black Sea coast, far from the White Sea as the Mediterranean is locally known, at a town called Samsun.

At Samsun, Mustafa Kemal set about assembling opposition to the proposed dismemberment of what remained of the Ottoman Empire in the aftermath of the Great War. With the compliance of a cowed government, an international treaty had condemned the defeated empire to a carve-up that would satisfy the territorial interests of her enemies, Russia, France, Italy, Britain, and Greece, and also grant nationhood to numerous subject peoples of the former empire. 'Turkey', as my *Philips New Handy General Atlas* (1930) details the treaty clauses, 'to cede the greater part of Thrace to Greece together with Smyrna [now Izmir] and its hinterland. Turkey to recognize the independence of Armenia, Kurdistan, Mesopotamia, Syria, and the Hejaz, the British Protectorates over Egypt, the Anglo-Egyptian Sudan, and Cyprus, that of France over Tunisia and French Morocco, and Italian sovereignty over Libya and the Dodecanese.' All that the Turks would retain was a pitiful shred of Black Sea littoral, an Anatolian Gaza Strip.

But in brackets below the atlas' treaty details are the two words 'never ratified'. May 19 celebrates the emergence of Turkish nationhood and of an attendant national identity against the longest odds. Without heroism, a long war, plenty of luck, and Mustafa Kemal Atatürk, the belief has often been expressed, Turkey would not now exist.

By 1923, Atatürk had driven the Allies into the sea. The massive paradox that I walked straight into as I set out to explore was that they might as well not have bothered, for despite that Turkish victory and excepting the ubiquitous Turkish flag, Turkey did not seem to exist in Pomegranate that morning.

On the main street, the incursions of English and German had rendered Turkish a minority language. Turkish food had been replaced by 'handburgers', and even the ubiquitous döner kebab was being advertised as 'authentik Turkische cuisine', as if this staple of Turkish food could only hold its own by being touted as a gastronomic heritage experience. Here was the grilled red mallet, the lamp chops, even a distinctly unappetizing fried squit, something called stew of bot, bolloknese and cold drings. You could have your potatoes French freud regardless of psycho-Austrian objections. The music that drowned out the muezzin in the village's one mosque was Euro-pop. On the beach, serried ranks of oiled European breasts jiggled in the sun while the postcards on the nearby stands brazenly endorsed them with complementary images of topless girls and voluptuous buttocks ornamented with the briefest of G-strings above the bald statement: *No Problem in Turkey*.

One thing was clear: that underdressed Gallic retreat, a beachwards scuttle in a hail of traditionalist stones, had at some point been halted. The bikini signs had been taken down, the locals had come up with a new message in tidy English, and relaunched it on postcards as the slogan of a radically reinvented society, one that claimed to have gone from stonings to toplessness in twenty years. The retreat which had once seemed headlong was now exposed as a canny French feint; bikinis had established a bridgehead in town, and bared breasts were dug in on the beach. Where the Anzacs had failed, the mammarial brigades of package-holiday Europe had triumphed. 'I do not command you to obey me,' Mustafa Kemal had told his troops at Gallipoli in 1915. 'I command you to die.' And so they had gone to Paradise in such numbers that the sheer weight of their discarded bodies alone prevented the Allies from securing the Dardanelles, the very key to Constantinople, now Istanbul. Surveying the beach below me, the entire heroic exercise seemed pointless.

The Turkish tourist office recently screened a promotional film in London. Images of mosques and markets, fresh vegetables and leather jackets were punctuated by insistent close-ups of naked breasts until it seemed that Turkey's beaches were nothing but a kind of bosomy paradise. When the film throttled itself mid-reel, our quick-thinking host blamed Saddam Hussein for the film's demise, but those who incline to a belief in ouside agencies might have looked instead to the inflamed spirit of Turkey herself, courteous, traditional, and above all Islamic, where a good many women will not show their faces, let alone their breasts.

All afternoon, I wandered through Pomegranate's avenues of boutiques that sold Naf-Naf and Chanel, Moschino and Lacoste, T-shirts and sun-hats, sun cream and perfumes, leather jackets and foreign currencies, bags, jewellery, and carpets. Indolent young men wearing shades, purple Italian suits, and manelike hairstyles, long ashes drooping from the cigarettes clamped between their fingers, prowled outside their shopfronts, whispering their siren *bitte schöns* to the bulging shadows of passing women. Tulip-shaped glasses of dark tea, that indiscriminate gesture of Turkish goodwill, had been withdrawn from the streets to lurk in strategic reserve among the weaponry of the Pomegranate sales arsenal in case the semblance of generosity that the offer of tea suggested might be deployed to banish any lingering doubts from the mind of a prospective buyer. In Pomegranate, sales were the priority, with sex shaded into second – but a close second which meant buying ruinously expensive drinks for impressionable young foreign girls in Pomegranate's discotheques. Stratonicus, quite a card in his time, was once asked whom he regarded as the most rascally of people. 'In Pamphylia,' he replied, 'the men of Phaselis; in the whole world the men of Pomegranate.' Pomegranate, you see, was also in Pamphylia.

Not that you would have guessed by the 1990s, when Pomegranate had travelled so far towards a European ideal, modern and liberal, that the old names had fallen away, such associations with the past no longer sustainable, terminally broken by the sheer weight of Naf-Naf and fried squit.

Since I had not been in Pomegranate long enough to make a seasoned judgement, I made the quite unseasoned one that the town was on the wrong end of nothing less than a Faustian pact with the worst aspects of the twentieth century. 'Life used to be fun,' Halil told me: 'Now it's just business.' In its twenty-year transformation, it seemed that Pomegranate had lost more than it had gained, and it was hard to see what could reclaim it. For Mustafa Yildirim was dead ten years now, the signs signifying outrage were long gone, and there was no more talk of stonings in Pomegranate.

Then I noticed the fezzes, and in them was a reminder taking me back to a family attic and the accumulations there of a family history, far from the noise of an everyday foreign culture being strangled by the sound of holidaymaking. I remembered dust and slanted sunshine, old cardboard boxes and yellowing newsprint, powdered cobweb and desiccated spiders. I saw an old sewing machine, a chipped vase, sepia photographs, and mildewed leather suitcases, and sea charts rolled together for so long that they remained tightly furled long after the elastic that once bound them had perished and given way. And in the midst of it all was the red felt fez, tasselled and conical, which seemed to have been in that attic for ever.

The fezzes were piled forlornly in a shop corner, gathering dust. I lifted one from the pile and as I ran a hand across the felt the dust retreated ahead of my fingers, furling up like a reefed sail into a discernible line of grey fluff. Now the felt appeared as a deep, lustrous maroon, and the tassle gleamed snake-black. A young man, who had just attended to a woman wearing an 'I love Dortmund' T-shirt, sidled over. 'All night long,' he cooed tentatively to the half-understood lyrics of the Lionel Richie song playing in the background.

'I understood these hats were forbidden in Turkey,' I told him, vaguely remembering that Atatürk had outlawed the fez in 1925.

'For us, they are forbidden,' he replied in halting English. 'For tourists, they are – ' he searched for the word in vain – 'bidden. But we don't like fezzes anyway. They are not modern. Fezzes are *Ottoman*. Fezzes are *Islam*.'

The young man directed me through the trinkets. 'I think you prefer one of these,' he said and placed a baseball cap on my head. A supine, scantily clad girl had been embroidered above the peak below the old refrain, *No Problem in Turkey*. The full force of her rounded buttocks weighed upon my brow.

'No,' I replied. 'I'll take a fez, thank you.'

'I think you are not modern,' pronounced the shopkeeper, making my predicament sound like a will-making condition.

Ashamed that he stocked such things, he wrapped my illicit headgear in a brown paper bag and saw me on my way.

'But I am happy,' I replied as I walked out into the warm spring sunshine, fez under my arm, and down through the throbbing disco-beat to the sea.

My fez was cheap, and not very well made, as if to accord with its banal trinket status. How had it come to such a pass, this once grand hat, the hat of the greatest empire of the East, of the Sultan and of Allah? What was the untold thread of history that had led to this humiliation, now serving as a brief distraction for tourists? Hearteningly, however, I recognized that my fez had embarrassed the young shopkeeper. Evidently, the old associations still clung to it, enough of them at least so that it sounded a tellingly discordant note in the glossy melody that was modern Pomegranate. Like the stoning parties, the badly written signs, the life of Mustafa Yildirim, it was an awkward reminder that Pomegranate had changed, and a key to a past that the village had washed its Pilate hands of. Perhaps, it occurred to me, I could use this hat.

In Pomegranate, an exhaustive search turned up a single fez wearer. I peered through windows, glanced into the backrooms of shadowy grocer's shops, hung around the mosque, and searched the most back-street – although Pomegranate didn't get that back-street – of the bars, only to find him standing outside a restaurant above the beach. For a moment, I dared to hope that his taste in headgear indicated an inclination to reactionary subversion, but his greeting put me straight.

'Fried squit?' he asked.

'I've eaten,' I lied, and pointed at his fez. 'I thought it was illegal to wear that.'

'My boss like me to wear it,' he replied in English. 'He think to bring tourists.' From his disgruntlement, it was apparent that he was an unwilling fez wearer. In as much as it struck me that there were easier ways to attract custom, like making a few spelling amendments to the menu, I sympathized.

'But it's not illegal?' I persisted.

'Not illegal to wear for the tourists, but in normal life . . .' He brought his wrists together to indicate handcuffs. 'Big problem in Turkey.'

His words, a pointedly juxtaposed echo of the postcard slogan, highlighted a curious fact; by law, you could go topless in this Middle Eastern and almost exclusively Muslim country but you could not wear a fez. These reflections set me off at speed and without brakes down a metaphorical cul-de-sac to arrive at an unavoidable comparison of breasts and fezzes. Little, it struck me, was more quintessentially Turkish than the fez; little was less representative of the country than breast-covered beaches. Was one to be banned while the other was encouraged? Was Turkey really more at ease with breasts than fezzes? It was as if the country's enduring search for its own identity – Eastern or Western, Islamic or secular, traditional or liberal – was encapsulated in these two contrasting objects and their symbolic payloads that even in shape had a certain resemblance. Pink flesh or purple felt?

Mustafa Yildirim would have been a young boy when fezzes were last legal in Turkey. It was too late to ask him what he had made of his life. I only had the son's recollections of a man who knew nothing of fake Moschino bags and of fried squit and who had never tried to learn the lyrics of Lionel Richie songs. He had ploughed his fields during the night and wandered breast-free beaches, offered his spare room to passing travellers and shared his bread and water in the shade of an olive tree.

Perhaps it is only the privileged outsider that can afford to do so, but I recoiled from what Pomegranate had become and sided with the remnants, the memory of Mustafa, the outrage of the stoning parties, the badly written signs, and the outlawed fez. In them I detected a reminder that the truth could not be denied. The truth was that far from being fairly representative of Turkey, Pomegranate was unrecognizable as such. Pomegranate had tried to drag the Turkish hinterland into the modern world and not yet turned round to discover that under a strain that could not be borne the tow-rope had long since broken.

For in the hinterland beyond the poppies that Pomegranate had left behind, the veil was said to be widespread. An intensive mosque-building programme had been under way in the country for several years. The number of Turks making the *haj*, or pilgrimage to Mecca, was increasing annually. Journalists with secular views were routinely murdered by shadowy terror groups. And the fez, symbolic of a general orthodoxy that would have been scandalized and saddened by what Pomegranate had become, had not simply gone out of fashion. Those who persisted in wearing the fez had been marched to the gallows in a ruthless attempt to hasten its eradication. No Problem in Turkey?

It might even be, it struck me, that the fez clung on in the mountainous, suspicious hinterland. For if it only survived as a tourist trinket devoid of meaning, then why the discomfort of the young shopkeeper who had sold me my fez? I preferred to believe it still had the power to remind Pomegranate's Turks of a past they preferred to deny, a kind of amulet against Turkish self-deception. So when I set off down the Turkish road in search of the end of a broken tow-rope, I took my fez with me.

Winter

chapter one

IT WAS JANUARY 1993 when a kindly but disbelieving Turk in an ill-fitting suit and a homburg approached me as our flight was called at Heathrow Airport.

'Why are you going to Turkey?' he asked, without unnecessary preamble. This rhetorical question was partly prompted by the fact that it was the middle of winter, but I did not doubt that it also harboured residual traces of a belief prevalent among Turks for hundreds of years; that I was travelling in the wrong direction.

West has been best for Turkish ideologues and leaders ever since the eleventh century when they and their people upped their Central Asian sticks and relocated to Anatolia. What with the scorched earth chic inspired by the Mongols, you could do that in those days, and with the capture of Constantinople in 1453 the Turks could make the first of many claims to be European. These, they might have felt in a far-sighted moment, would one day lend substance to their applications for EC membership. The fact that they would be competing for World Cup places alongside Italy and Germany instead of soft touches like Afghanistan and China may have been considered a price worth paying.

Eventually, this western impetus carried them to the very gates of Vienna where the Ottoman army encamped during the great sieges of 1529 and 1683, setting down a fabulous image that has at once haunted and enthralled Christendom ever since. The camp was pitched in front of the city in the form of a huge half-moon Islamic crescent, the thirty thousand tents visibly overshadowed by those of the Sultan and his

Grand Vizier, which were covered in hangings of richest tissue coloured green and striped with gold. Gold too, great knobs of solid gold, were the pinnacles above their tents, while carpets, cushions, and divans within were studded with jewels. Deep inside was a sanctuary housing the sacred standard of the Prophet, and baths, fountains, flower gardens, and menageries. At the entrance, five hundred archers of the Royal Guard kept watch while thousands of turbaned infantrymen and black eunuchs passed among the field harems and their concubines, the Ottoman military kitchens filled with bejewelled silverware, the Turkish baths and bedrooms hung with priceless satins and velvets. And beyond them grazed the twenty thousand mules, horses, and camels of the baggage trains, and the four hundred ships of the Imperial flotilla moored upon the grey depths of the Danube.

On the other side of the walls was no such extravagance. Beef in Vienna was twelve times its price prior to the beginning of the sieges. Poultry could not be bought at any price. Cats, no longer exempted from the dinner table, were chased through cellars and over roofs until the Viennese came to know them as *dachshasen*, or roof hares.

A besieged, desperate population of cat eaters quivering at the Islamic scourge outside the walls is thus imagined, and doubtless there were plenty of Turks ready to confirm the worst of such fears. Even so, this bewitchingly forceful image may yet be misleading. Listen carefully, it seems to me, and rather than the merciless proclamations and chants of an army intent on malevolence one may actually hear among the tents and the majesty the muted 'Can we join you?' of a people pleading to belong. On Turkey's summer beaches, in the bars and by the backgammon tables where the Europeans can be found, it is a request the Turks are still making.

For the Turks never did get into Vienna. As European armies got stronger, further Westernization by simple geography became increasingly expensive on soldiery. So they by and large stayed where they were and consolidated their empire by incorporating weak neighbours to the south while their leaders introduced new hats of an increasingly Western tint every century or thereabouts. The march which had been foiled on the ground would continue in the mind. If they couldn't get there in their boots, then they'd do so in hats instead.

In the defining moments of their national history, the British have their Magna Carta, Agincourt, Trafalgar, Waterloo, Reform Bill, Battle of Britain. The Turks have their hats.

In 1826, the turban was abolished in Turkey and replaced by the fez. In 1925, the fez was outlawed and replaced by Homburgs, panamas, bowlers, and flat caps. And so a series of hats have provided the stepping-stones, the caravanserais on the central theme of Turkish history, her great march westwards towards the promised land represented by that ultimate measure of Westernization – the bare head.

There was the rest, of course; the rise of a splendid empire and the passing of Sultans, an endless succession of wars, the fall of the Ottomans and the rise of the republic, and a series of coups, but always there were hats. In Turkey, headgear has since time immemorial had a symbolic significance inconceivable in the West. In Turkey even today, you are largely identified by what you wear on your head. Your headgear acts as your badge of cultural and religious affiliation. The problem comes when your choice of hat is prescribed. Rather than a complex expression of your own personality, your headgear may now originate in a simple memo sent by the head of state to his ministry responsible for hats. The cap that once fitted becomes the hat permitted, and leads to headgear that may not be of your choosing.

For many Turks, then, the march westwards has been a forced one. In 1950, the election defeat of the avowedly secular Republican People's Party at the hands of a party promising extended religious freedoms led to an outbreak of illegal fez-wearing in eastern Turkey; and in 1989, the 'turban affair', when female students flouted legislation banning Islamic head-gear in Turkey's educational establishments, led to demonstrations, civil disorder, and assassinations.

In 1993, Turkey had been embarked for several years on her third European siege. Only this time her forces were encamped not in tents outside Vienna but in the international hotels of Brussels, with showers where they once had Turkish baths, mini-bars where they once had field kitchens, portable telephones where they once had envoys, and bare heads where they once wore turbans, lobbying for full membership of the European Community. They claimed that Turkish democracy – something of an oxymoron during the coup-ridden sixties, seventies, and eighties – had finally come of age.

Certainly, the voices of dissent, which once had been lost in interminable prison terms and torture chambers, could now be heard. Refah, the Islamic Welfare Party which advocates the restitution of the *sheriat*, or Islamic law, was garnering an increasing number of votes. There was a growing disenchantment with the West, not only because its various promises were coming to sound increasingly hollow but more specifically because it was considered to have been criminally negligent in its attempts to relieve the plight of the Bosnian Muslims, with whom the Turks feel an acute sense of kinship not only as brothers in Islam but also because the Bosnians were conspicuously loyal Ottomans in the days of empire. The ten-million-strong Kurdish minority, while learning to take pride in a language which had finally been recognized by the state, was busy expressing its increasingly insistent sense of nationhood in whatever language the audience would listen to. Into the struggle for the soul of modern Turkey a degree of fairness had finally crept, but social liberalization had only served to highlight the factional currents of ideology running counter to the ebbing tide of westward national direction.

And so in spite of the government's best efforts, Turkey has not yet been permitted to belong. The phones ring ceaselessly, the mini-bars are emptied late at night, the lobbyists squeeze and cajole those who matter, but Europe observes

Turkey's growing pains through suspicious eyes, seeing a country that walks a geographic, ethnic, and cultural tightrope, balanced uneasily between two worlds; a bridge between East and West with a foot in both camps, but with her heart in neither.

Stalled by the EC, pragmatic Turkey has flaunted her clubby charms elsewhere. But membership committees have tended to wince at her applications. Bridges by their very nature have feet in two camps – and that's not what leagues, clubs, and associations are all about.

So Turkey remains only an associate member of the EC. She is on the Council of Europe but then so is Liechtenstein. NATO, of which she is a member, is rapidly losing any coherent sense of its post-Soviet function. She is a member of the Islamic Conference Organization but since she is the most avowedly secular state in the Islamic world she is marginalized by definition. Topless bathing in Pomegranate was never going to go down a storm in Mecca. She is now considering a league of her own wherein she will head the Turkic republics of former Soviet Central Asia. She is a member of the Black Sea Co-operation Council along with Bulgaria, Romania, and Russia. All at once, she is looking for companionship to all four points of the compass. And she probably has a sore diplomatic neck.

Later that same wintry day in January 1993 I would catch a news report on the television in my Istanbul hotel room showing the then Turkish Prime Minister at prayer in Mecca, Saudi Arabia, wearing traditional white holy robes while the then President (and they change fast), dressed in a pinstripe suit, was addressing prominent businessmen in Washington. The Prime Minister, for the rather confusing record, was regarded as the avowed secularist while the President was the devout Muslim. The country's two leading political lights seemed to be dividing their people's cultural affiliations by example.

But I still had to get through immigration. In front of plywood kiosks long queues had formed, comprised chiefly of returning Turks, entrepreneurial Russians, and a few European journalists dispatched on editors' hunches that Saddam was about to hit out at his Kurds while the world's attention was focused upon the Clinton inauguration. On the wall above passport control Mustafa Kemal Atatürk's bareheaded portrait was framed in gilt. A man stopped me at customs, gestured for my passport, and read it at length.

'And what is your business in Turkey?' he asked as one hand unzipped my holdall and made a cursory journey through my spare underpants. I was about to answer when his eyes narrowed in a manner that indicated he had either had a compelling experience with those pants or discovered something that was less to his taste. From my holdall, he withdrew a hat, maroon, tasselled, conical, and made of felt.

'And what is this?' he asked – the question whose answer is self-evident of the type beloved by petty schoolmasters.

'My fez,' I replied dutifully. 'I am researching a document about the history of Turkish hats,' I told him, hiding behind the low-profile activities of academia.

It was as if I were in Pomegranate again. With this reminder of the past, I had offended the customs officer. I had questioned the version of Turkey that held sway at the country's airports and at resorts such as Pomegranate. And in so doing, I had buried my own doubts. I was here in search of my own version, a Turkey that was not so certain that its future was European and a people who had been hanged less than a lifetime ago for refusing to relinquish their fezzes.

He gave me a long, cool look, dropped the fez into my holdall, zipped it up, and returned it to me. 'You are ridiculous,' he said. 'Welcome to Turkey.'

chapter two

'From thee, dear friend, of other days I part,
Ah! Who can speak the anguish of my heart?
My turban! long thou didst these temples bind,
Now, torn from thence, around my soul entwined;'

> From English traveller and painter Thomas Allom's
> rendition of an 1830s protest ode lamenting the
> abolition of the turban, as heard in a Constantinople
> café.

ON A MORNING made of low skies and skittering pigeons I shouldered my way up the path above Eyüp. As I climbed, the wreckage of a view clambered out above the cypresses and the stunted forest of headstones. An exotic history and a decrepit present had evidently collided here; an Istanbul winter had then shunted into the back of what remained.

I turned at the sound of bells. A shepherd was herding his flock through the cemetery.

'*Memleket?*' he asked. Country? England, I told him, looking beyond him to the view. 'What happened here? They say this was a beautiful place under the Sultans.'

'Sultans.' He spat out the word across the mean flanks of his sheep.

'Atatürk changed our country. You don't like Atatürk?'

'Of course I like Atatürk,' I replied, bowing to the Turkish paradox which enshrines the nation's commitment to the modern in the memory of a man who died fifty-five years ago, before space travel, before the last war, before even the Beatles.

The image of the great Turkish Gazi, the warrior Atatürk, still adorns every Turkish coin and banknote and his bust dominates the country's every town square. His name honours airports and football stadia, streets and boulevards, dams and farms, schools and bridges, cultural centres and forests, villages and ships, lakes and hospitals. Back in the twenties, it was even proposed that they rename Constantinople not Istanbul, but Gazi Mustafa Kemal. Admiring the modernizing Father of the Turks is what you do in Turkey. And if you sense you have not yet been forgiven for doubting it, you engage whomsoever you have offended on the subject of his pride and joy. Sheep in this case.

'Where are you taking them?' I asked, and it was sufficient. The shepherd winked, ran a surreptitious finger across his throat as if to preserve his flock in blissful ignorance, and smiled so that deep crevices in which all suspicions were finally banished broke out all over his face. 'Last view of Istanbul, my dear hearts,' he told his sheep, took a deep drag on his cigarette, nodded, and was gone.

The sheep trailed after him, leaving me alone with the view. The slope fell sharply away below where a jumble of brambled and broken graves gave way to the road and the water beyond it. A rim of still scum lacquered the waterline in a ruff of black flecked with mercury. Beyond it lay a palette of putrid greens, greys, and browns. Fishing boats lined the waterfront and occasional freighters lay broken-backed in the mud, seeping coiled gouts of rust. To the west, where hills hemmed in the water on all sides, mudbanks shrugged out of the murk to punctuate the poisoned shallows. Far to the east, the water eddied into the Bosphorus and lapped at the fringes of Asia. But I could not see so far, only a succession of bridges shrouded in mist, whited-out echoes of bridges that bound Istanbul across her legendary waterways, each like a fainter impression of Turkey herself spanning land masses, continents, even beliefs.

I was looking down at the western extent of the fabled Golden Horn which was known to the Ottomans as the Sweet Waters of Europe. In the eighteenth century, there were tulip shows along these banks where the Sultan's guests wandered through the gardens and along the marble quays drinking sherbet, while candle-bearing tortoises clambered among the flowerbeds, throwing lumbering flickers of light. Now, there was a cold, snow-laden wind, and a shepherd driving his sheep through a graveyard to the butchers, and all those who had seen the tulips and the tortoises were dust at my feet. I remembered a line from Pierre Loti: 'In no other country have I seen so many cemeteries, so many tombs, so many dead.'

Loti, a young French romantic and adventurer, often returned to this sprawling, hilltop cemetery in the late 1800s to dream of an Orient that even then was fast disappearing. The tulips and the tortoises were long gone, and cobwebs were beginning to ravel up the Ottoman Empire in a cocoon of decay as the last of the Sultans languished in their palaces while the great powers collected at the deathbed of the Sick Man of Europe.

At the top of the hill, Loti's memory had been press-ganged into service at the Pierre Loti Shop, Bazaar, and Café. Where once he had sat and conjured up quixotic visions, the modern world had wreaked vulgar revenge until all that remained of him was now swathed in trinketry.

'Excuse me,' I asked the café owner. 'Can you point me to Loti's grave?'

'France,' came the reply, the head remaining firmly below the counter so I was looking down on thinning whorls of scalp hair scattered with a light dusting of dandruff that resembled the snowfall threatening outside.

'I see.' My muttered reply probably did not disguise the fact that I had been expecting directions of a less national nature. I had always assumed that this romantic orientalist would have insisted on being buried in his beloved Constantinople. But by the time of his death in 1923, I reasoned, Turkey's official rebirth as a secular, Westernized republic was months away. Loti, who had come here for the allure of Constantinople's past, for the fabulous Orient, and for veiled, forbidden, and thus irresistible harem girls, can only have been disenchanted by Turkey's unswerving march towards the Europe he had long since rejected. And at the time of his death; the indifferent embrace of French soil and wretched thoughts haunting him of another French citizen who had first come to Constantinople eighty years before him to energize Imperial commitment to the ideas of the West: Aimée, the French Sultana, influential mother of Mahmud II, the greatest reforming Sultan of them all.

I walked through the colourless winter grass and among the headstones. Some were chipped, cracked, and broken; others ran green with lichen and brown with rust. Squat stones arched to a rounded point while minor mausoleums were ringed with low rusty chain fences. There were delicately engraved tablets and tall cylindrical steles, topped off sometimes by stone turbans gathering lichen, but mostly by Mahmud II's innumerable stone fezzes. They were everywhere, these fezzes, large and small, some with carved tassles, some tapering dramatically to the crown. A number of stones had been decapitated so that the fezzes lay in the mulch at their feet or had rolled away until the trunk of a cypress tree or another headstone had finally brought them to rest above the remains of another.

It all dated from a morning in 1826 when Grand Admiral Koja Husrev Mehmed Pasha of the Ottoman Imperial Fleet dressed with unusual care. Having just returned from naval exercises off Tunis, he was bound for an audience with the Sultan. He had with him his naval report, but would also deliver to His Highness an unprompted package containing some articles he had chanced to pick up in the markets of Tunis. Word had reached the Grand Admiral that the Sultan was looking to abolish the turban. Widely known as the 'crown of the Arabs', the turban had strong Islamic and Eastern associations: its continued use represented a stubborn bulwark against Mahmud's reform programme, and the Sultan wished to see it removed.

Mahmud did not greatly care for Muslims, and less so for

Arabs. His cultural outlook had been actively shaped by his mother, a French Creole dead some years now who had been taken by corsairs from a ship off Majorca, dispatched to the Ottoman authorities in Algiers, and finally presented to Sultan Abdul Hamid in Constantinople as a glittering prize for his harem. Mahmud's beloved mother had come from western North Africa, and the Grand Admiral had high hopes that his own package from Tunis might find favour with the Sultan – to his reputation's lasting enhancement.

It was the tradition of the harem that concubines were chosen not from the Ottoman heartland of the Anatolian steppes but from outlying provinces such as Circassia and Bulgaria, and from further afield whenever a corsair captain in control of his baser instincts and looking to recommend himself at the highest level happened across a defenceless and beautiful girl such as Aimée. Officially, it was considered below a Sultan's status as Allah's vice-regent on earth and Emperor of all Ottomans to lie with Turkish women. The more practical reality was the urgent need to encourage imperial issue. Firing the jaded sexual palettes of overweight and undersexed sultans was the aim of the exercise, and experience had proved that exotic foreigners often provided the spark.

In Adbul Hamid, Aimée ignited a lasting conflagration, and she soon conceived. But Aimée was different. At the time of her kidnap, she had just completed eight years in France and was returning to Martinique an educated and highly European-ized young woman. To the reactionary elements in the Otto-man Imperial Court, she was a cultural time bomb charged with a high explosive called change.

Aimée raised Mahmud much as she might have raised a boy in France. He learned French and French ways, ate French cooking under French chandeliers, and grew up amongst French furniture. The Janissaries, the powerful and ultra-conservative Imperial Guard, had long understood it to be their function to guard not the Sultan himself – especially if he harboured alien notions of progress – but rather the time-honoured and unalterable institution of the Sultanate as *they understood it*. Which made Mahmud a despised *giaour* or foreigner, and a threat to the old orthodoxies that had guaranteed the Janissaries unbridled influence for centuries. Specifically, here was a man who had already expressed heretic interest in the three-cornered hat then popular in Europe before it was pointed out to him that the hat's three points represented the Christian trinity. On learning this, Mahmud was politician enough to abandon the three-cornered hat without a murmur. He might make his subjects less Muslim; he would never make them Christian.

Mahmud was still pondering the thorny question of his subjects' headgear when the Grand Admiral returned from Tunis with the answer. In the package were a number of felt hats, brimless, red, and tasselled. As they were unpacked before him, Mahmud recognized them as the compromise which, with a little persuasion, the influential religious authorities might be prepared to endorse. And if these fezzes were not perhaps as Western as he had hoped, they at least would provide him with a clean break from the burdensome turban.

A revised costume for selected corps of the Ottoman military was introduced on June 10 1826. It included a prototype fez. Two days later, guessing only too well what new hats signalled – a crash course in Westernization – the Janissaries rebelled in support of the old order, but were routed by forces loyal to Mahmud in a single day. The Sultan put the word about that the corpses of the slain Janissaries had become vampires and were lurking in the night-time streets of Constantinople. As their graves were broken open and stakes driven through the corpses' hearts by the more impressionable of his subjects, Mahmud prayed that the forces of reaction would trouble him no more.

Mahmud was soon to discover, however, that a few stakes would not still them. His suggestion that the military fez be fitted with a peak to shield against the sun met with the stony disapproval of the religious authorities, who countered by pointing out that such a peak would prevent the wearer from touching his forehead to the ground at prayer time. In a bid to press his point, Mahmud ensured that the recalcitrant religious leaders were directed to seats in the full glare of the sun at the next Imperial audience, and he kept them there for far longer than was customary. But mere sunstroke did not dislodge the religious leadership, and a non-peaked fez was introduced in 1827 – with a further Islamic accoutrement, the silk tassle, the single hair by which devout Muslims were effortlessly raised to Paradise by Allah.

The result was that the Ottoman infantryman went to war not with a helmet to protect him but with an article of headgear whose primary design feature was to resemble a prayer mat, with heavenly emergency exit in the form of a tassle attached. And since the likelihood was that the prescribed headgear prevented the soldier from effectively seeing his enemy, pray he might. There will doubtless have been much frantic squinting at the enemy during the Ottoman summers on campaign in the nineteenth century, squinting which continued into the twentieth century; even at Gallipoli, sunstroke was still endemic among the Ottoman soldiery.

In the late 1820s, it was decreed that all Ottomans were now to wear the fez. The people were acquainted with this headgear, but only in its exclusively ancillary role as a humble chassis or foundation around which the beloved turban had long been wound. Originally a kind of covered skullcap marginally larger than a saucer, it was as if the fez had now returned after hideous tinkerings, grotesquely enlarged and uncovered like a surfacing tumour. The Sultan might next expect them to wear their underpants outside their trousers. Only a *giaour* would so treat his subjects.

One summer in the mid-1830s, Thomas Allom came to Constantinople from England to sketch and write 'while the brightest skies of the East looked down upon the work of the painter'. Allom described the abolition of the turban as 'the unkindest cut of all, and one which has certainly excited the unfavourable sentiments of the Mahometans towards their sovereign in a greater degree than any of his more important changes'. Allom sketched a café in a quarter of the city 'where the inhabitants still refuse to regulate their costume by direction of the Sultan; they refuse to doff the cherished turban, the "crown of a Mussulman", for the recently introduced fez'. In the sketch, the turbans of the men defy the infidel Sultan on every side. A single fez is depicted in the background on a man whose singular expression indicates that he has obeyed his Sultan – and in so doing betrayed both God and tradition – with the profoundest misgivings. The murmur of Allom's 'protest' ode drifts among the scattered plumes of pungent Turkish tobacco that frame the sketch.

Such, in spite of Mahmud II, his mother, the routing of the Janissaries, and even the existence of French furniture, was the enduring influence of traditional Islam in the nineteenth-century Ottoman Empire. The Empire ruled much of the Islamic world at that time and led the rest of it by consent. The Sultan was automatically the Caliph, the undisputed supreme religious head of all Muslims. The Islamic symbol itself, the crescent, derives from the legend of a Macedonian king whose attempts to take Constantinople (then Byzantium) in 340 BC were thwarted by Hecate, Goddess of the Moon, when she veiled herself and denied him the required moonlight for the attack. Even in those distant origins lie two ideas which continue to stalk contemporary Islam: the enduring threat of, and the belief in divine protection, from, the Christian West.

I left the cemetery of broken fezzes and walked down into Eyüp. A narrow maze of overhanging houses enclosed me where stove pipes emerged through walls and billowed brown coal smoke over washing which had been hung out to dry one floor above. Ahead of me, a young man ducked into a small shack fronted by stacks of fresh marble headstones. I peered through the grimed windows and watched him hand a piece of paper to an elderly man who perused it and ran a hand across his white beard. Guessing that the words on the paper could only mean one thing, I waited respectfully until the young man left before taking his place in the shop.

'A foreigner,' the elderly man exclaimed on my entrance and directed me to a stool by the stove.

'You're not too busy?' I asked, inclining my head sympathetically to indicate the bereaved young man who had just left.

'Him?' the old man asked. 'He only brought me a quote for a television. Certainly, we're busy. People are always dying here. But in Turkey these days people are always buying cheap televisions as well.'

'He looked a bit sad, though.'

'That's because I didn't like his price. Did somebody die or have you got a television to sell?'

The stonemason was called Fehmi. I would call him Bey, the routinely respectful form of address for Turkish men of any standing. His crisp blue eyes were set in a sea of wrinkles run amok. He had run the business here, just below Eyüp cemetery, for fifty years. He was currently working on the headstone of a young woman who had recently died of tuberculosis. She would be remembered in the standard modern style, an engraved garland of tulips picked out in green and red below the epitaph on a simple marble headstone. 'I used to do bigger, more complicated jobs for the rich but they don't seem to come here any more,' said Fehmi Bey. I asked him about the old Ottoman headstones, the turbans and the fezzes.

'Holy men and often those who had gone on the pilgrimage to Mecca were accorded the turban on their gravestones while the fez was for everybody else of any standing – good Ottoman Muslims.'

'Everybody?'

'Everybody in the cities anyway, a little less so in the country. Not women, of course.'

'What did women get?'

'Flowers; the big slabs of stone with the tulips engraved all over them. It's harder to carve a veil on a gravestone than a fez or turban.' Which was true, but did not convincingly explain the preference for flowers. For while the fez and turban were pointers to public status, the veil has always functioned as nothing but a concealment, a negation of the female public presence. After a life in hiding, what could Ottoman women have expected from their menfolk but flowers and an inscription commending them to Allah as the wife of their husband?

'Since we're no longer allowed to wear turbans and fezzes,' said Fehmi Bey, pouring me a glass of tea from the pot boiling on the stove, 'everybody gets tulips these days.' The tea came hot and strong, and the shape of the glass made me mindful of a connection. Turkish tea glasses, opening with a delicate curve at the top as if towards the sun, are said to take their shape from tulips, in which word the origin of the Turkish word for turban is said to lie. Was the tulip emblem on gravestones a conscious echo of the banned turban? Did it remember the defiance of the smoke-wreathed men in the Allom sketch, a codified expression of a more overtly Islamic yearning than was tolerated in Turkish life? Was it a kick against Turkey's march since Mahmud II towards a modern, godless world? Did even the shape of the Turkish tea glass mourn the old order?

'We like tulips,' Fehmi Bey replied with a shrug. 'We also like Atatürk.' For the second time that morning, I felt as if I had caused offence by casting conversational glances towards the past. But the discomfort was soon dispelled as the first notes of the muezzin sounded in the cold morning air, and the stonemason answered a call far more ancient than a reverence for Atatürk.

'I must go to prayer,' announced Fehmi Bey as he rose rapidly to his feet, heading for the one Turkish public institution which has never carried the name of Atatürk. Together, we walked through the streets of Eyüp to the sounds of old Turkey – a whip streaking across a horse's flank, the shrill of endless voices above the muezzin – colliding with the new – distant pop and the low revs of motor cars. Small grimy children took my hand and asked for lira. 'Always, always you say tomorrow,' a young boy with snot plastered black around his nostrils said in English, pre-empting my answer as he approached me with his box of shoe polishes and brushes, and I laughed.

Ranks of men, mostly in unrimmed skull caps or thicker woolly hats, were gathering at the water fountains in the mosque courtyard to wash hands, feet, and faces. They had come to pray at Istanbul's holiest shrine; the mosque at Eyüp and the area itself take the name of Mohammed's faithful companion whose mausoleum lies in an annexe to the mosque. Such was its significance that the Sultans used to come here upon their succession to receive the Imperial Sword of sovereignty, the crown of coronation. Pierre Loti wrote in 1876 that 'access to the shrine has always been forbidden to Christians, for whom even its immediate precincts are none too safe'.

It felt safer by 1993, but even now there could be traced in the air an attitude deriving from that same exclusive ancestry. For Fehmi Bey shook my hand in some haste as if to dissociate himself from me in preparation for Muslim fellowship. Perhaps he did not feel entirely comfortable standing by the water fountains with a man who was at once probably Christian, evidently foreign, and definitely wearing a rucksack.

I stood in a cloud of disturbed pigeons and waited until the long file of men had removed their shoes and disappeared into the mosque before removing my own shoes and slipping inside the shrine-annexe. In the half light I could make out a rail, and the raised sarcophagus beyond it draped in green. Eyüp Himself lay there surrounded by candlesticks, old volumes in alcoves, and Arabic inscriptions on the walls while veiled women stood swaying before his sarcophagus, arms outstretched as they murmured devotions. Mindful of the swaying which occasionally increased to a dangerous degree, I kept to the back. Eyüp had led Islam's early campaigns against infidel

Byzantium and I did not wish to raise the ire of any veiled, swaying zealot who might wish Eyüp had been more thorough. Furthermore, early accounts suggest a stone thrown by an infidel had killed Eyüp, and although other sources concede he might in fact have died from a quite secular bout of dysentry, there was that certain sense of the old gods staring down the new beliefs of the foreigners with undisguised intolerance.

I weaved my way out of the annexe, collected my shoes, fended off a couple of loitering shoeshiners, and walked through the litter of brittle leaves towards the Golden Horn. Thin strips of sunlight were falling over Istanbul but did not pierce the low cloud above Eyüp's mosques and cemeteries just as the city itself, engulfing outlying villages on all sides, had advanced to Eyüp's periphery, and abruptly stopped. It was as if the predatory maw of development, of shops, tower blocks, and advertising hoardings had picked at Eyüp and turned away from a taste too rich even for its indiscriminate palate.

I was leaving Eyüp's graveyards and dusty cypresses when a rusty street sign surprised me. It read *Feshane Caddesi*; I was on Fez Factory Street. 'Oh, it still stands,' a tailor told me from the gloom of his shop, what light there was catching on the array of pins stacked alarmingly between his teeth. 'But they no longer make fezzes there, you know. Fezzes are banned these days.'

His directions led me to a large square building, squatting low roofed on its haunches and staring out across the murk of the Golden Horn. On the waterfront decrepit fishing smacks were beached. A pair of earthmovers stood in the mud. The roof of the building gleamed with fresh green paint.

I walked the building's considerable perimeter until I surprised a man standing in a back doorway, smoking.

'Hello, tourist,' he addressed me in English. 'You want to see inside?'

When I replied that I spoke Turkish, he looked relieved

and impressed, and by way of welcome took me firmly but mutely by the forearms. His introduction was typical. Many Turks possess a single line of English which is invariably buffed by constant use to such a shine that visitors to Turkey merely assume from the subsequent smiles, nods, and conspicuous lack of English that their new, evidently fluent friend is only touchingly shy.

He was called Osman, and was the site foreman, keeping an eye on the project until work resumed in the spring.

'So they used to make fezzes here?' I asked him.

His dismissive expression, a glance over his shoulder, graphically painted a past safely out of reach. 'But now,' he said with enthusiasm, 'it is a modern art museum,' and he offered to show me round.

The interior was largely finished and comprised white expanses of space where paintings would soon hang. 'Gallery,' intoned Osman respectfully, 'conference centre,' or 'store room,' as we wandered among the old cast-iron pillars made in Belgium early in the last century, passing random bags of cement looking like suitably experimental artistic statements, thoughtfully positioned in emptiness.

Our footsteps fell heavy in the silence. All that remained was the shell of a building, a lifeless blank prepared for the display of modern art from which the slightest echo of Mahmud II's imperial fez factory had been erased. The absent builders had repaired the roof and the windows, repointed the walls and relaid the floors, rewired and repainted until the building was cleansed of its history, the one thing that might properly be said to belong to it.

'Now, let me show you something more interesting,' said Osman proudly as he took my arm. 'My office.' Steering me away from my interest in the past, he took pleasure in telling me how they had ripped the old fez-making machinery from its fixings in the floor two years earlier to make way for the wide white spaces that modern ideas and representations would soon inhabit. But in attempting to describe progress, he had given me a link, an imagined glimpse of mouldering machinery, damp scraps of discarded felt and old threads of tassle, and evocative images escaped from the grasp of the blank white walls.

I saw how, for the best part of a century, over three thousand workers had turned out tens of thousands of fezzes a month here. Fine wool from Spain and Russia was prepared, spun into balls, and then distributed among the fez-making women of the city, Turks, Jews, Armenians, and Greeks. Once knitted, the fezzes were returned to the factory, washed in soap and cold water, scoured and dried, and clipped and pressed until the knitted wool was felted. They were then dyed in large coppers before being stretched over fez-shaped moulds. Next, they were taken to a drying room and once dried, loose hairs were removed with the spiky teasel head of a bullrush and finally clipped for the last time before the tassles · were attached.

Then there had been those intriguings in the dyeing rooms: the greatest problem that confronted the staff at Eyüp had been to produce a strong and lasting dye; many of the factory's early attempts had resulted in a washed-out raspberry pastel which bestowed disgrace upon the fez makers. Tunisian experts were drafted in to provide urgent remedy, but their efforts were in vain. More precisely, their efforts were non-existent. Naturally enough, the Tunisians were loath to surrender the financial and social advantages their knowledge afforded them, a fact finally recognized when the management planted a shrewd Armenian chemist disguised as a simple labourer in the Tunisians' midst. When the Armenian was able to report not only what the Tunisians were doing – surreptitiously sabotaging their own process so as to extend as long as possible their thoroughly enjoyable stay in the Sultan's employ – but also to describe the precise manner in which they were doing so, the secret was finally revealed, the Tunisians dismissed, and the Armenian appointed Head Dyer and charged with the honour of deciding the exact colour tint of the fez that Mahmud II, the Light of the Universe, would grace by wearing.

Once these teething problems had been resolved, Ottoman fezzes generally came in a spectrum of strong shades either side of purple. They could be scarlet, crimson, vermilion, maroon, cerise, purple, mauve, or red. When I came to ask a friend in Istanbul to list the Turkish words for these colours, she replied that the word *fezrengi* covered the entire spectrum. To the Turks, all these tones were simply 'fez coloured'.

In the office which Osman had proudly claimed as his own (the winter absence of the architects and senior foremen had, I rather suspected, persuaded him to temporarily promote himself without consultation), a single fez lay alongside a paper stapler on a bookcase. A chair, desk, and telephone made a weak fist at filling the rest of the room. Osman steered me into the chair while he made tea on a small gas stove in the corner. I took the fez in my hands. It reminded me of a flower pot with a black silk tassle attached at the point where the pot would drain. I put it on my head.

Osman laughed. 'You are not a modern man,' he told me.

'And you are?' I replied. 'With a name like yours?' Osman is the Turkish word for Ottoman.

'A name does not matter,' Osman replied. 'I am modern because I go bareheaded.'

'Even in weather like this?' At the window, occasional flurries of snow whipped across the building site.

Osman nodded. 'I am a modern Turkish man,' he repeated. 'With modern Turkish problems,' he added ruefully. Osman earned one and a half million lira a month, the equivalent of £110. He lived in a small house in the Istanbul quarter of Fatih where the rent cost him two-thirds of his salary, leaving him with about £40 to sustain a wife and four children. The biggest problem, Osman explained, was affording prescriptions when the children got ill, as invariably they did in the bronchial coal-smoke smogs of Istanbul winters. When the museum was finished, Osman would be out of a job, and in the manner of the Tunisian fez dyers, I imagined him dismantling walls and digging up floors as fast as he clandestinely could in an attempt to extend a contract that he could not afford to lose.

'Still,' he insisted, sipping at his tea, lighting another cigarette, and looking disdainfully at the fez, 'it is still better than it was under the Sultans. As you foreigners say, the Sick Man of Europe died.'

'And the Sick Man's hat with him,' I replied.

Later, I walked along the edge of the Golden Horn in the freezing afternoon. Puddles of ice lay in broken lattice across the mud. A pair of brown dancing bears stood chained to their owner, a farouche gypsy character with glaze-dark eyes. Huddling against a raw wind laden with particles of dust and snow, they looked as if they would never dance again. A crippled woman nudged along the pavement on her bottom, lifting herself with her arms to edge forward. On her hands she wore a child's wooden clogs as protection against the cold, rough ground. As I passed, she raised an arm to ask for money. But it was a clogged hand, a hand she could not cup. She rapidly withdrew it in an attempt to preserve her dignity, and the bears looked on with watery eyes.

I looked back and saw, in the shadow of the great mosque where the remains of the Prophet's companion lay, the green-roofed building that since the time of Mahmud II had pointed towards a Western future. The setting was doubtless designed to shock. When in 1835 the Sultan ordered the manufacture, not four hundred yards from Constantinople's holiest shrine, of radical and Western-oriented fezzes, he was deliberately confronting Eyüp's old gods with the fact, whether they liked it or not, that the Empire was now set fair for the West. So it was appropriate that the artistic heterodoxies of Western Europe should convey the selfsame inclination from the walls of the old fez factory one hundred and fifty years later.

I was walking east towards the centre of the city when I came across huge sections of floating pontoon moored at random by the waterside. A tangle of twisted metal infrastructure like that of a wrecked battleship reared up from the water. Along the top ran the various sections of a tarmac road which had collapsed in a rollercoaster swoop. The pieces clearly once fitted together, but it was impossible to see how. You could recognize that it once had been a jigsaw puzzle, but only that much was certain. Among the crushed supporting struts below the twisted road surface were tables, chairs, old fridges, torn pieces of wallpaper, broken pipes, old partitions latticed with oriental curlicues, and lavatories exposed indecently to the air. Everywhere there was dust and the dung of passing seagulls, the sound of water slapping indifferently at the pontoons, and the blackened evidence of fire.

Suddenly, however, I could picture it as it had been, and in my mind I was able to straighten the struts, right tables and chairs, return these pontoon sections to their place at the heart of the city, and fill them with the sound of human life meeting to eat and drink on the old Galata Bridge. The bridge had stood at the confluence of the Golden Horn and the Bosphorus. It had by no means been Istanbul's biggest bridge; it had not spanned the Bosphorus, that wide waterway which divides continents and so is automatically assumed to demarcate the two cultures of East and West. Instead, the Galata Bridge had spanned the Golden Horn. This had caused no great problems for the structural engineers, but those who crossed it took a cultural leap into the unknown.

For, rather than the obvious Bosphorus, here was the dividing line that defined Turkey, the long inlet of water cutting across the middle of the city's geographical west. To the south was Stamboul and Beyazit, the old imperial city where, with its mosques, harems, the tombs of the Sultans, and the barracks of the Janissaries, one nineteenth-century writer said there was nothing European save the ground. And to the north were Pera and Taksim, the original foreigners' mercantile districts where even today the embassies, the luxury hotels, and the night clubs can be found.

And linking the two was the bridge where Turkey had met until old age and fire had done for it and it had been towed away to rust down in this neglected backwater. The country that was said to bridge East and West had done away with its premier bridge, had scrapped the very symbol of itself, the bridge that had known the processions of Sultans and the funeral cortège of Atatürk above the eating houses of men who laughed to describe themselves as restaurateurs. This was ominous indeed, and it didn't take a particularly sophisticated feel for metaphor to see that.

An unbroken line of traffic stretched across the stark lines of the new bridge, free of the chaotic life that had colonized the underbelly of the old one. As I approached I discovered, with a sense of relief, that a few hardy fishermen had already made the new bridge their own. One man, casting an expert line between the passing cars at his back, turned and nodded at my approach.

'A pity about the old bridge,' I muttered.

He wrapped the fishing line round a railing and dug his hands into his pockets, looked out across the water to Asia, and shrugged. 'It got rusty,' he said. I had uncovered a breed of Turks who worried about rust. After that discovery nothing could be the same again.

❉

chapter three

THERE WAS NO sign of Ahmet that January morning, a morning so cold that any sign of him and the warmth of his car would have been welcome. What light there was reflected weakly off grey potholes of crushed ice. Refrigerated wind blew in pulses off the street as if timed to signal the arrival every half-minute or so of another overnight bus from Anatolia. They swung into Istanbul's bus station from Trabzon, Konya, and Amasya, distant cities of the Turkish interior and the Black Sea coast. Glimpsed faces at the windows stared out at the blear dawn, and what they saw was concrete, skittering litter, and unfamiliarity at the beginning of a new life.

They clambered from the buses, these families, gathered their shapeless coats around them, and started to unload their belongings. There were old cardboard boxes bound by string that once held cartons of soap powder. There were blankets and rolled-up mattresses. There were suitcases straining with necessity. There was an ironing board and a small table and an empty bird cage, and piles of pots with impolite bottoms seared by cooking.

A thousand people were moving to Istanbul today, just as a thousand people had done so every day for the last ten years, turning the city's outlying villages into sprawling suburbs housing hundreds of thousands. Not long before, I guessed, the day had come when these families had finally realized that there was nothing for it but to leave, the cruel, indifferent processes of economics and history turning the screw tight until it could no longer be borne. Such was their situation that the things which mattered, their friends, perhaps a tree, a courtyard, or a scrubby hillside, views from a window that they and their grandparents had known as long as they could remember, had become sentimental luxuries that they could no longer afford. Today, economic necessity had defeated a thousand more Anatolians, and the old life became the past as they shouldered their ironing boards and empty bird cages and took the only chance remaining at the jostling margins of the big city.

Ahmet's parents, newly married, came this same way and took such a chance in 1946. They left their village and their families for the city; a common story of the twentieth century. But they were lucky. Ahmet's father did well, making cakes and pastries from honey, walnuts, and pistachios. He sold them to sweet tooths across the city, became rich while dentists prospered on the teeth he had ruined, and then he grew old. Now Ahmet was running the family business.

A group of migrants were arguing the price of a cart.

'We could get a truck for that!' a man exclaimed disgustedly at the price mentioned.

'Where are you from, brother?' replied the carter, hugging himself repeatedly to keep warm. 'Trabzon? Ordu? You might get a truck for that price in Ordu. Here, you get this.' And he pointed to the broken horse standing patiently between the withers. Carter and migrants stood round making comments about Ordu and the horse respectively of a desultory, unflattering kind that hardly seemed designed to lubricate the negotiations. One of the younger women stood back from the group. Dressed in a headscarf, she looked over her shoulder at the departing buses and perhaps only now realized what it had meant, that last glimpsed view of the village on a winter afternoon before it disappeared among tucks in the hills.

A car drew up and hooted. When I reached Ahmet, he was watching the negotiations intently but from the warm cocoon of a car all his own while he listened to Turkish pop and to Right Said Fred. He wore an expensive tweed jacket. On the back seat lay a newly savaged carton of two hundred Marlboro. I asked him how he was, and Ahmet tugged ruefully on a cigarette. Last night's hangover, it transpired, came courtesy of Chivas Regal. Twenty-eight-year-old Ahmet lived a European life on the fringes of geographical Europe. Except that his car, jacket, and taste in whisky were more expensive, he was very like me.

'Sandwiches,' said Ahmet, thrusting a packet towards me. 'Rose petal jam.' Only in Ahmet's sandwiches, it seemed, traces of his past lingered. We gunned our way through the murky streets. Grimy concrete buildings disappeared in low cloud around the second floor. Grey figures milled along the pavements, skirted around tarpaulins where salesmen had spread their wares – bundles of sheeny-grey socks piled like catches of fresh fish, a neat stack of paper tissues, a pile of worry beads shiny like viscera – and spilled across the road in breaks between the traffic. 'Life is hard,' said Ahmet sententiously. I nodded, thinking that but for a brave decision by his parents in their youth, Ahmet might now be a new arrival in Istanbul standing in the cold arguing the price of a horse and cart. Or he might be persevering with life in the same Anatolian village where his grandparents and several uncles' families still lived – six hours away if we drove fast. As the migrants poured in from Anatolia, Ahmet was taking me back to the world they had forsaken. Sentiment and memory were luxuries that Ahmet could now afford.

As we crossed the Bosphorus Bridge, coal smoke rose from countless houses beneath us to be lost in the haze above a litter of roofs, brown and broken. Minarets gleamed in the morning, a broken bed of nails above the city. Then the bridge was behind us and we were in Turkey in Asia; in Anatolia.

Beneath the cigarettes and the music, Ahmet seemed preoccupied. 'My family, you understand,' he eventually explained, 'are very poor people. Very simple.' There was instinctive pride in this, but a stronger, tragically learned element of apology. 'Poor!' As if he feared me to exclaim, 'I didn't come here to see poor bloody people, even if they are your family. Haven't you got any rich friends I can sponge off, sleep with?' Ahmet looked relieved when I said something trite about the privilege of meeting them, and my apparent lack of concern encouraged him to emphasize the point. 'I mean, really poor,' he insisted.

We climbed gently on to the high Anatolian plateau, flat and interminable, a kind of underfunded Holland on stilts where the lorries were always breaking down. Engine guts and various tools lay scattered round stricken vehicles while their defeated drivers warmed themselves by roadside fires and wondered how miracles worked. Low horizons appeared on all sides with occasional dun hills streaked with old snow. There were broken fence lines and unnaturally precise stands of poplars protecting more featureless dun hills from the wind. Unfinished buildings regularly appeared, as illogically situated as the poplars.

'What are the buildings for?' I asked.

'Maybe for watching the poplars.' Ahmet was clearly feeling better.

Poplar Progress Observation Posts, we agreed, abandoned when it was recognized that poplars do the growing themselves. Unlike buildings. And so brick or breezeblock constructions which would never finish their growing stood beside piles of bricks or breezeblocks topped in snow. Steel rods protruded from each roof, buildings condemned to know nothing but neglect, the wind, and the memory of confused builders' voices.

At the small town of Düzce, where our road caught on and became unfinished, we left it for a minor one leading into the mountains. Ahmet was now smoking at a ferocious rate; something else was worrying him. 'One more thing,' he eventually said. 'My family. They do not use toilet paper.'

'Toilet paper?' I replied dismissively. 'Toilet paper's for sissies.' But although we laughed together, you could tell whose was the laughter that did not ring hollow.

46

'When in Rome' is all right up to a point, and that point is generally accepted to be well passed when it comes to, say, headhunting with the natives of Papua New Guinea. Nor, in my view, does the point extend to smearing one's fresh droppings over the left hand. Nothing had been more firmly impressed upon me in my journey through life than the signs along the way saying *Do not touch the kaka*, and on this at least I had been a quick learner. I hid my discomfort with the thought so successfully, however, that Ahmet's mood was transformed, changing gear with extravagantly dramatic flourishes that left his arm hanging in the air with open hand long after the new gear had been found. I kept thinking he was releasing doves in the confined space of a small car going fast.

Early that afternoon we reached Karabük where a great iron foundry stood against the mountains in dystopic grandeur.

'What does Karabük mean?' I asked, leafing through the possibilities in my mind. Anvil? Blacksmith? Forge? Fritz Lang?

'Blackberry,' replied Ahmet.

One of Ahmet's uncles had come to live in Blackberry ten years ago. Less intrepid than his brother, he had chosen to compromise at a dusty little house on a hill an hour and a half from the village that would always be home. He had found work as a security guard at the foundry and was not at home. But his aunt was there, along with a selection of Ahmet's cousins. Among the younger girls was Emine. She greeted Ahmet – with his car, his wealth, and the sheen of the big city – by touching his outstretched hand first with her lips and then her forehead before rising to kiss his proffered cheeks. Emine, who was fourteen, had lost her father six months earlier when he shot himself to escape gambling debts.

We sat wreathed in smoke, drinking tea and discussing cousin Mustafa's appendix. He had complained of stomach pains on Tuesday night, been admitted to Blackberry General the next day, and was operated on the same night. Light snow was falling on Blackberry and coal smoke from the foundry turned the night sky mocha at the window. Dogs fell silent as the muezzin started singing from a nearby minaret.

For much of the evening, a black and white television chirruping away in the background was affectionately ignored like a senile senior of the family. But everyone came to attention with the main news item. One of Turkey's most highly regarded journalists, known for his democratic and secular views, had been blown into a hundred pieces by a car bomb in Ankara one hundred and fifty miles to the south. An organization called Islamic Jihad was first to claim responsibility. Emine turned away from the television and the reminders of loss that it served, hoping that her retreat into sorrow would not be noticed.

Before we left the next morning, Ahmet distributed money on the instructions of his father. Distance had not undone the family bonds, bonds otherwise expressed in the manner that the family referred to the village where they all had their origins. They spoke of it not by name but in the possessive, referring to 'our village' long after they had moved away. It was a kind of yearning constantly expressed in spite of the townie haughtiness they had consciously adopted in its place; people have been taught that big city life confers a respectability, but village rhythms are not easily unlearned.

Ahmet's evident excitement grew as we drove through a bright and cloudless morning. I could detect it in the way he hummed indistinct tunes and changed gear in that elaborate manner of his. Orchestral conductors could have learned something from Ahmet.

'Where the Bee Lands,' he said, announcing the name of a village where the metalled road gave way to track, and broken ribs of ice straddled the deep tyre tracks. We climbed steadily through hazel and pine woods, and slalomed our way up north-facing slopes where ice and snow lay unbroken among the shadows. That morning, I had noticed Ahmet sling two shotguns on the back seat.

'So what are we hunting?' I asked him.

'Kurds,' he replied.

I knew something of Turkish–Kurdish enmities, and of the persisting troubles in the south-east of the country. But I did not know that young men from Istanbul had them in their sights when they packed their shotguns for a weekend's sport in the north-west.

'You often shoot Kurds, do you?'

'Oh yes, there are many about in the winter. They take our chickens.'

Taking chickens struck me as an arcane separatist gesture.

'And you're allowed to shoot them for taking your chickens?'

'Oh yes. Deer are rare so we don't shoot them.'

'But you shoot Kurds.'

'Yes.'

'Why?'

'I told you!' Ahmet exclaimed in exasperation. 'The chickens!' And as we followed the rutted track round a corner, the village finally came into view. But since it was not my village, I refer to it by its proper name of Sabuncular, or Soapmakers.

Soap has not been made in Soapmakers for as long as the villagers can remember. So to suggest that Soapmakers has remained unaltered for five hundred years is not entirely accurate. Equally, change hardly encapsulates the prevailing mood in late twentieth-century Soapmakers. While the rest of the world is being transformed, change meanders into Soapmakers, makes the vaguest of gestures at the future, and then goes away again. Seasons pass much as they always do; it gets hot, it gets cold, but the village spring continues to run.

Something did happen in 1962 when the village mosque was restored by Ahmet's father, flush with new cash when his cakes went down a storm in distant Istanbul. But since there were no shops, no school, no police station, just a room in the mosque building where the village elders gathered to make their decisions, the restoration of the mosque served only to reinforce the influence of the past.

We drew up in a small yard before the mosque. Below us, tracks threaded their way between a cluster of some fifteen houses where smoke rose in orderly plumes. Chickens pecked between rafts of ice and dogs skulked against stone walls larded with old snow.

Ahmet's grandparents lived opposite the mosque. We pushed our way through an old wooden door and found a man bent double by age, tending to his two donkeys in the stable on the ground floor. Grandfather was known as Haji Baba and wore a beard in recognition of the fact that he had made the *haj* to Mecca. He wore a brimless woollen cap and puzzled over my interest in his donkeys.

'Donkeys,' he said simply, frowning as I scratched their ears. Perhaps, I reflected, I would have been equally puzzled by his disproportionate interest in my Flymo.

The living quarters were upstairs. Grandmother was tending to the stove in the middle of the kitchen. On my appearance, she hugged, kissed, and patted me more like a lover – and not so long lost – than a friend of her grandson's.

'It's your blue eyes,' Ahmet told me. Eighty-eight-year-old Grandmother had not seen many blue eyes.

She was as hunched as her husband. In fact, one could have inserted extra floors on every level and neither resident would have been in the least danger of bumping heads. Like Haji Baba, Grandmother's face was gnarled, knotted, and lined, and the colour of old wood, and their eyes were similarly bright. It was as if in the course of their long lives together the differences between them had been gradually eroded. The brightness of their eyes were important for without those spots of light I would have struggled to locate their faces against the ancient woodwork of the panelling around them. Whenever I met their eyes, hers were always smiling and his expressed something which I took to be a vague fear for the welfare of his donkeys.

They gave us lunch at ten o'clock in the morning, soup, bread, and a salad of fresh onions and eggs, wheeling out a wooden table that stood six inches from the floor and making space for us around it.

'So who is this man?' Haji Baba asked his grandson.

'He's a friend from England, Haji Baba.'

The old man nodded vigorously. 'England, where's that?'

'Europe, Haji Baba.'

'What does he want?' Haji Baba could be a trifle suspicious.

'Nothing. He's here as a guest.'

'Oh, that's good.' Haji Baba thought a moment. 'Does he need any chickens?'

Haji Baba had once run a farm of six hundred sheep. But as his sons moved away or found more easeful ways of making money, the old man sold his land and sheep until all that remained were his chickens. In the summer, he would take the donkeys to the higher ground and gather wood for the winter. In his old age, he had more time for his God, had been to Mecca three times, and was often to be found reading his battered copy of the Koran in the light of the window as the snowmelt dripped off the roof. Haji Baba was the *agha*, the head of the village. He was in his eighties now. And for a few short years, I calculated, he would have been a fez-wearing Ottoman.

When the muezzin started, Haji Baba hunched off to find his boots bemoaning the latest village priest's inability to sing straight. Ahmet grabbed the shotguns and took me hunting. I was uncomfortable about this, but was enough of a shot to know I could always make sure I missed any chicken-stealing Kurd we happened upon.

We walked among young Turkish oaks and pines, trunks surrounded by scraps of snow. The earth at our feet was a wet mulch of red-brown earth and pine needles warmed by a weak sun. The criss-crossed patterns of animal tracks in the remnant snow indicated dogs, wild pigs, small deer, and rabbit. There were also bears in these mountains, although Ahmet had never seen one. At one point he stopped suddenly and gestured me over. 'Kurd,' he said with authority. But he was pointing at a large paw mark, and no Kurd has paws. But a *kurt*, the Turkish word for a wolf, does. In fact, we did not encounter so much as a rabbit. Ahmet unleashed his frustrations by loosing off the two rounds of his shotgun. The echoes resounded round the hills, returning to us with the distant noise of alerted dogs and alarmed cattle.

By the time we got back to Soapmakers, night was falling. In the mosque, the men were finishing prayers. The door was eventually opened by a small boy with a plastic machine-gun who sprayed Ahmet, me and a couple of nearby dogs with imaginary lead. I wondered what he'd been learning for the last ten minutes. Happily, he took a tumble on the ice in his attempts to finish us off.

'You just shot yourself in your manhood,' Ahmet told the boy, helping him to his feet as the congregation emerged.

They were seven elderly men and a much younger, gangly man who turned out to be the tuneless village priest, or *hoja*. They mostly wore woollen caps in the style of Haji Baba. One wore a turban in the wild style once favoured by British washerwomen. Later, Ahmet told me that its wearer felt safe from those who might disapprove, but would be unlikely to wear it on a visit to Blackberry. There was not a fez in sight, but nor was there a brim. The men of Soapmakers wore hats designed for prayer. Only the *hoja* was bare headed. As an employee of the secular government, he was not expected to wear anything other than Western hats.

'I prefer,' the *hoja* would tell me theatrically, 'to wear nothing.'

In the manner of Emine, Ahmet touched his lips and forehead to a number of wrinkled hands. Familiar with villager statuses, he chose the major players and left me to follow his lead. In the confusion, I ended up bowing and scraping to a short man with a round face and trouser legs that hardly reached his shins. A hand on my shoulder alerted me.

'You are honouring the village idiot,' said Ahmet.

The village idiot, who had never known anything more than affection, was now receiving a foreigner's respect. In the shine of his eyes, I could see that he would not forget me.

The approaching lights of the lurching village *dolmush* jabbed crazily through the darkness, illuminating stroboscopic sections of wall, earth, and sky. *Dolmush* derives from the word to stuff, most vividly expressive in its frequent use to describe peppers or vine leaves stuffed with rice. But as I looked in at faces, limbs, vegetable sacks, and livestock squashed against the glass in jumbled proximity, I was reminded of nothing so much as bottled preserves.

As the *dolmush* came to a halt and the contents piled from the doors, the natural order in Soapmakers was rapidly restored. Women who moments before had been crushed out of necessity against all manner of male anatomy slipped away into the night, as if to reinstate the demarcation lines between the genders that should properly exist in Soapmakers, dragging their vegetables behind them. Meanwhile, the men joined us to stand in the cold and smoke cigarettes. When we had finished, Mehmet, another of Ahmet's uncles, led us back to his house.

A stove dominated the front room. The floor was covered by pieces of random carpet and linoleum. A cuckoo clock was stopped at two fifteen; the cuckoo had slumped forward lifeless between its little open shutters amidst a spill of visceral mechanisms, as if the victim of an irritable sniper. In the corner stood a small table covered in plastic red-check gingham on which a solitary plastic salt cellar stood. A postcard from Istanbul featuring the Bosphorus Bridge was wedged between the wall and the electricity cabling. As men filed into the room – the *dolmush* driver, the *hoja*, a baker from a neighbouring village, and a number of farmers – Mehmet lit a pine cone with his lighter, opened the stove door, and tossed it in.

As young boys ferried back and forth from the kitchen with bowls of chicken stew, rice, and meat pastries, the villagers started to talk.

'We got electricity twelve years ago.'

'No, it was fifteen.'

'It was two years before Ali got the telephone.'

'But six months ago, we got direct lines. Now, we've got six telephones in the village.'

'And televisions.'

'And in England,' asked Mehmet, apropos of little, 'what yield do fields give?'

'I'm afraid I'm not a farmer,' I replied.

But even tourists know about yields, the expression of a man too polite to say so protested before telling me about theirs. 'Ours give between seven and ten times depending on the weather.'

'Good,' I replied lamely.

'I once met some tourists in Istanbul,' said Mehmet. He had worked there for two summers in the seventies. He opened a cupboard, removed an object with great care, and handed it to me.

It was a calendar dated 1976 and featuring pastoral scenes from Bavaria, complete with statutory lederhosen and foaming pints of beer in lidded pewter tankards. There were neat stacks of firewood and light filtering through the linden trees. Everybody crowded round for a glimpse of this otherworld.

'It is England?'

'If only,' I replied. 'It's Germany.'

'It looks like the village,' said somebody else.

'Except for the mugs,' came another voice.

'And the silly trousers.'

'And the beautiful women.' And everybody laughed. Then the man in the kalpak walked in.

I noticed his hat before I noticed him, and not only because I was becoming increasingly hat-obsessive. I had seen such a hat before, a kind of astrakhan associated with the Turkish military in the early years of the twentieth century, in a portrait of Atatürk that often featured on the walls of Turkish shops and homes. In it, the great man leans forward as if into a merciless headwind, intent on direction. The picture portrays Atatürk in action during his famous victories at Gallipoli in 1915 and the Independence War four years later. But there is perhaps more to the picture than martial glorification, for it struck me that these victories were characterized not so much by going forward in the manner suggested by Atatürk's posture but by crucially holding the line. Modern Turkey's emergence, in military terms anyway, was founded on heroic defence. So I read the picture's meaning as figurative, a heroic representation of his political charge against the forces of reaction, a grim determination to advance whatever the cost. In the picture, Atatürk is in mud-brown military fatigues, and he too is wearing a kalpak.

The kalpak reminded me of fading daguerrotypes of the Young Turk officers who had opposed the Sultan in 1908 and forced him to concede significant constitutional reforms. Historians have called the actions of these officers a revolution but in truth it was little more than a modification, for all these young men in kalpaks had wanted to do was tinker with a system that they largely accepted. They could not accept that the confederation of anarchies that comprised the late nineteenth-century Ottoman Empire was unsustainable. The Young Turk position on hats was similarly indecisive. In shape at least, the kalpak was no more than a tinkering with the Sultan's hat, the fez. For although the kalpak was made of black lamb's wool, although it did not sport a tassle and widened to the top rather than the bottom, it was nevertheless conical and, most importantly, brimless, identifying the Young Turks with those who put prayer before practicality.

Mustafa Kemal had been a young officer at the time of the Young Turk Modification and quickly took to wearing a kalpak. He was sympathetic to the aims of the Young Turks, but only in as far as they went. Fifteen years later, he would embark on a radical transformation of Turkish society that mocked the Young Turks' notions of revolution, and outlawed their hat along with the fez. In the mean time, the kalpak provided him with a stepping-stone, another sartorial caravan-serai, an initial means of breaking free from adherence to the Ottoman orthodoxies symbolized by the fez. Use of the kalpak expressed disenchantment with the old system, but moderate disenchantment, and for a young officer looking for prefer-ment, the appearance of moderation was all.

The man in the kalpak was called Ali Bey. He had round mournful eyes, a great stomach for ballast, and a moustache that continually drooped despite the repeated efforts of his fingers to twist it into horizontal obedience. A young child was soon clambering all over him and reaching for something in the area of Ali's pocket.

'Ali Bey is my uncle,' Ahmet explained, 'and will be *agha* when my grandfather dies.' Clearly, Haji Baba had sired many sons. The child eventually emerged from the folds of Ali Bey's jacket brandishing a pistol. Then he aimed it at me. Ali Bey slapped him down and apologized. I asked him why he carried the gun.

He shrugged as if the answer were obvious. 'There are no police for miles and we don't know what trouble might come our way. Besides, there are wolves in the winter. You'll hear them tonight. Leave the gun alone, child. Where's your water pistol?' The child backed off to gaze enviously at Ali Bey's holster.

The gun-toting, kalpak-wearing village lieutenant turned to me. He was fondling a medal which hung from his left lapel in so manifest a way that my next question was prompted. He sat back, trying to appear surprised when I asked him about it.

'It's my War of Independence Medal,' he replied. 'Atatürk's war against the Greeks.'

'But Ali Bey, you look much too young,' I said admiringly, and since he was referring to a seventy-year-old war I wasn't simply being polite. Ali Bey, it transpired, was indeed much too young. The medal had actually been awarded to his wife's grandfather. But in this village, medals won in distant wars filtered down through the generations like the ownership of fields.

The fact that the medal was borrowed did not seem to trouble the villagers, who gathered reverently for one more look before Ali Bey insisted on slipping it into his top pocket, as if he'd been obliged to boast against his modest will. Nor did it matter to me, for Ali Bey looked every inch one of Atatürk's brave irregulars. He told me that he wore his kalpak as he was wearing it now, along the head so that it fanned out at the top when he stood in profile, in the course of his ordinary working life. On special occasions such as *bayrams*, or religious holidays, he would wear it across his head like a bishop's mitre. Then he would buff up his medal and revel in the glory of 1919 to 1923 when Atatürk and his soldiers carved a Turkish motherland out of their heroics, even if only because he had happened to marry a valiant bandolier's granddaughter.

'I am Atatürk's greatest admirer,' Ali Bey told me.

But Ali Bey also told me that he was not a rim-wearer, unlike Atatürk. Nor, in this alcohol-free village, did he drink alcohol; Atatürk had drunk raki, the local Pernod with muscles, to distraction if not to death. Like most of the men in the village, Ali Bey supported Refah, the Islamic Welfare Party, and its call for the restitution of the *sheriat* or code of Islamic law. He would not brook the notion of the women of the village voting or even holding political views although they had been granted the vote in 1934 – by Atatürk. Ali Bey seemed to revere Atatürk in spite of himself.

But that was the elastic appeal of the Turkish icon. Multiple distinct incarnations of the man seem to exist in the Turkish mind, the product perhaps of numerous Atatürk images not only in the portraits and pictures gracing walls throughout the land but also in the thousands of statues in town squares from the borders of Greece in the west to those with Iraq and Iran in the east. Atatürk has fractured and multiplied until every aspect of his character and achievement stands alone and distinct. He has become the pick 'n' mix icon; everything from the doughty fighter, the national father, the great educator, to champion of women, of panama hats, and of Western coat-tails. As such, every Turkish constituency can find something in the man of which they approve. It may be imagined that further manifestations of his personality and achievements will be manufactured to soak up other constituencies as they emerge so that if existing versions of Atatürk do not fit to his world view then the Turk can tailor-make him in other images until one does. Atatürk in the kalpak was the one that appealed to Ali Bey, no matter that Atatürk's kalpak period was merely a piece of politicking, a transitional period on the way to a hatless future free of kalpaks.

Another image, conspicuously popular in government offices and in westernized parts of Turkey, depicts Atatürk in tails, wing collar, and hatless. In this picture, which unsurprisingly I did not see in Soapmakers, he has considerable poise and looks like a cross between the Duke of Edinburgh and Fred Astaire. Of the images in widespread use in Turkey, this is probably closest to the true spirit of the man. But for Ali Bey and many of the villagers of Soapmakers, it was Atatürk at his most unrecognizable. From his reading of the Koran, Haji Baba had doubtless warned the villagers about the dangers of bare heads: *The wicked man will be dragged down to hell by his exposed, lying, sinful forelock.*

I wondered then how versatile the Atatürk icon could be. Was the elastic beginning to perish? Ali Bey, who had fallen with the help of his grandfather-in-law's medal for the image of the brave Gazi forging a nation by force of arms, could soon look no closer at Atatürk for fear of the complications that might rise up to undermine a simple, stirring image.

Ahmet lit a cigarette and leaned across. 'Refah,' he said dismissively. 'My uncle is crazy. Uncle,' he shouted. 'Our visitor wants to know why you vote Refah.'

Ali Bey paused to consider a moment. 'Because Refah will

make our village rich,' he replied. 'Refah will pay for tractors and farm machinery and new buildings.'

'Dreams, dreams,' murmured Ahmet. 'You know, Uncle, politicians aren't like that.'

'Tractors,' Ali Bey insisted.

'Tractors,' Ahmet mocked him quietly.

'And they'll tidy things up – stop the fucking on the streets of Istanbul,' Ali Bey added, warming to his theme.

'Do they really do that?' asked the village idiot, appearing at the back of the room behind ranks of villagers. 'Can I go sometime?'

But for once, the Turkish sense of humour was not tickled. Uncle and nephew stared at each other with a mutual lack of comprehension. They clearly felt too much love for each other to be truly at variance, but the differences between their lifestyles and beliefs was all too apparent. Uncle believed himself to be Turkish and thus Islamic; Ahmet believed himself Turkish and thus European. Families have divided over less. A Turkish journalist called Uğur Mumcu had died in a car bomb in Ankara the previous day for championing the essentials of Ahmet's instinctive convictions.

Refah has existed in various guises through the turmoils of Turkish political life, but at no time has it enjoyed its present levels of support. Nor has it ever been so effectively organized. The party receives significant funding from Saudi Arabia, which it ploughs into communities at grass-roots level to fund the construction of new schools and hospitals. The Welfare Party can afford to live up to its name, and deliver promises which other parties can only hope will be conveniently forgotten.

As the evening grew late, the conversation was steered into safer waters. The villagers wanted to know where I was next headed, and hearing my destination was two hours to the east, imagined me entering another world where none of them had ever been. The *dolmush* driver wanted to know about prices in England.

'Well,' I said, short of conversation and noticing a pile of discarded husks in a corner of the room. 'Pistachios are very expensive in England.' A whispered command woke a young boy and sent him scurrying from the room. The foreigner who could not afford pistachios would take a large bag of them from Soapmakers the next morning.

Ahmet and I skirted the village dogs which stirred malevolently at our presence, slipped into Haji Baba's house, and threw mattresses down as waves of heat blurred off the stove.

'Refah,' murmured Ahmet dozily. 'Bah!'

There was moonlight at the window and, as I fell asleep, the distant howling of wolves.

I awoke early to a similar sound; Haji Baba was right about the new *hoja*'s singing. After breakfast, I washed and then went with misgivings into the lavatory. I looked through the hole in the floor, looked at my left hand, and promptly left.

Haji Baba found me looking at the old farming gear in his shed. Strange how little the foreigner knew; only this morning, Mehmet Bey had told Haji Baba that the Englishman did not know what yields his fields gave. 'A *döven*,' he explained patiently. 'A horse drags it across cut wheat to separate the ears from the chaff.'

It was a large wooden sled, similar to the one I'd seen on the wall of Halil Bey's hotel in Pomegranate. But this one was covered in winter cobwebs, not coated in shiny display varnish. It would be some time before the *dövens* of Soapmakers slipped from the present to serve as a nostalgic reminder of the past.

When the time came to leave, Haji Baba received my kisses and handed me a plastic bag. Inside was a chicken roughly plucked. I thanked him as convincingly as I could.

'He always does that,' muttered Ahmet in an attempt to placate him as we drove away. 'What's a man supposed to do with a chicken in this day and age?' He glanced at me, irritated. 'Your hair,' he exclaimed. It was damp from a cursory wash that morning. 'You should have borrowed my hairdryer.'

'It's wonderful, your village,' I told Ahmet in an attempt to placate him as we bumped along the track.

'Your village too,' he replied, 'now that you've been here.'

After a few hundred yards we drew up opposite the village cemetery. Ranks of simple stones topped with snow abutted a ploughed field.

'A fine place to be buried,' I mused.

'Yes,' replied Ahmet. 'I'm almost looking forward to it.'

'But you live in Istanbul.'

'And this is my village. Refah or no Refah.'

I tried to picture how they would one day bring Ahmet here and lay him down alongside his forebears to return to the earth where his heart – in spite of his absence – had always been. But vague recollections of a recipe that somehow incorporated both chicken and pistachio to spectacular culinary effect kept nagging at me, and Ahmet's final scene eluded me.

chapter four

AHMET DREW UP where the Soapmakers track met the road. Before returning to his cakes in Istanbul, he would see me on to the first bus to pass.

'Goodbye,' he said as I thanked him and clambered aboard. 'When you arrive,' he instructed me, 'find a hotel that's not too cheap; you don't want to get robbed. But not too expensive either. And remember to dry your hair. You'll catch a cold otherwise. Perhaps you can find a hairdryer there.' Really. Having just clambered over two goats and a sack of turnips, I thought to have put myself beyond hairdryers.

One spring day in 1925, Mustafa Kemal Atatürk had summoned his advisers and asked them what was considered the most fanatical part of Anatolia. After retiring to consult, they returned to report that the most fanatical part of Anatolia, exalted Gazi, was generally held to be the town of Kastamonu. 'Good,' said Atatürk. 'Prepare a presidential visit for Kastamonu later in the year.'

I too was on my way to Kastamonu, a town far from the tourist routes where dissident Turks had traditionally been exiled. As the bus passed through a monochrome winter landscape, I doubted there was another European within a hundred miles of me. But the pioneering feeling did not last; intrepid journeys in cold and distant countries are fatally undermined by hairdryers. 'Watch your cakes,' I muttered to myself vengefully, resentful of Ahmet's mothering. 'Not too much flour. They won't rise, you know.'

I soon forgot Ahmet, however, as I began to pay the price for spurning his grandfather's lavatory. By the time we reached

Kastamonu, every single rut and bump of the two-hour journey was recorded as a distinct and separate tremor upon the seismograph of my bowels. I subjected the chicken to an inelegant dash to the nearest hotel.

And when I could concentrate once more on my surroundings, I saw that I had arrived in a town at the back of nowhere. I had checked into a hive of cramped rooms fetid with the transactions of small-town businessmen dreaming of tawdry mischief. The view from my window was of a breeze-block wall three feet away, a canvas of grey across which occasional snowflakes strayed. If I craned my neck, I could see low, dirty clouds that hung in bloated bags around the town's minarets, brown slush rising in malevolent arcs from the wheels of passing vehicles, and snow slithering from warm roofs to snuggle down the backs of passing collars. The radio buried in the wall above my bed came on at random, supplying scraps of Arabesque music before falling silent. Later, I would find that if I crept up to the radio speaker and shouted at it, I could get it to sing or provide some weather forecast upon request.

I left the chicken in my room and wandered through town, along alleys flanked by stalls that were piled high with buckets and broom heads, screwdrivers and cigarette lighters, ranks of cabbages and neatly stacked pyramids of carrots, and olives swimming briny in blue plastic bowls. A forlorn brigade of condemned chickens and turkeys was being marched into town. The legs of the birds had been tied so that they slithered across the dirty ice, looking to charm their way on to a passing shopping list that their fearful lives might be terminated. What jealousy the condition of my own chicken, in a warm hotel room and dead, would doubtless have occasioned amongst this miserable brood. Was it just me and the local poultry, or rather a general condition of the place that made everybody feel uncomfortable on the road to Kastamonu?

Atatürk, evidently, was another who had not enjoyed his approach to Kastamonu, although the comparison ends there. For while the poultry hobbled into town leg-tied and I turned up on public transport dying for the potty, Atatürk had arrived by cavalcade trailing clouds of glory. Still, for all that he had been just as uncomfortable. 'Approached the tour with unusual nervousness,' wrote Atatürk's British biographer, Lord Kinross, who also made mention of the Gazi's trembling hands.

It was August 30 1925. The Turks had long since routed the invading armies of the Greeks, and the new Turkish Republic with boundaries almost exactly as they stand today had been universally recognized in a series of treaties during the early 1920s.

Unprecedented change had been quick to follow. Atatürk abolished the Sultanate – the old Ottoman monarchy – in 1922, and moved Turkey's capital to Ankara where he proclaimed the founding of the Turkish Republic the following year. The Caliphate, the four-hundred-year-old embodiment of the Empire's leadership of the Islamic world, was swept away in 1924 along with the Ministry of Religious Affairs and the religious schools and courts that had perpetuated and underpinned Islamic influence in Turkey for centuries. The Western calendar and the twenty-four-hour clock were introduced in 1925. In the following year, a new Western-style civil code would ban polygamy and much else besides. The Latin alphabet would be introduced in 1928. Constantinople would be renamed Istanbul in 1930, women would get the vote in 1934, and the introduction of surnames along with the replacement of the Islamic Friday holiday by the Christian Sunday would follow in 1935. Fifteen years of Turkish history from which was supposed to emerge bare headed, at the other end of the century, the country through which I was now travelling. August 30 1925 was the day that Atatürk would first signal a ban on fezzes.

Throughout the spring of that year, fezzes had bedevilled the Gazi's dreams. As a military attaché and overseas delegate in the early years of his career, Atatürk had been subjected to undisguised ridicule for his fez. 'Why do you wear that ridiculous thing?' a blunt French officer had once asked him.

Atatürk's vanity was no doubt wounded, but his primary objections to the fez were ideological by nature. Just like Mahmud's intolerance of the turban a century earlier, he regarded the fez' continued use as symptomatic of a stubborn adherence among his people to discredited, obselete, and reactionary values.

Thomas Allom has recounted how the fez was reviled as a foreign and Christian innovation on its introduction in the 1820s. But in the hundred-odd years that had since elapsed, it had been appropriated by traditionalist Turkey and had come to be associated with a deeply felt conservatism, particularly in rural Turkey, that held Islamic orthodoxy dear and gazed askance on the new reforms. The fez largely assumed the ideological identity of the turban. The abolition of caliphates and sultanates had provoked widespread reaction, but Atatürk appreciated that the abolition of the fez was bound to cause an altogether more intimate sense of offence. Male Turks would be required to discard an article of headgear which was not only engrained in daily habit, but which also stood for their cultural, religious, and personal identity. 'The despotism which would exert a sway over individual tastes and feelings is most difficult of endurance,' Thomas Allom had remarked in the previous century. He was referring to Mahmud's introduction of the fez at the expense of the turban, but such are the convoluted processes of history that he might equally have been referring to its abolition.

In the early 1900s, even for the educated young things of Constantinople, the advances of European vogue were halted at the neck. 'I was seized with the ambition,' wrote the writer Halil Halid in 1903, 'of appearing up to date, and of dressing in the more modern manner; that is to say, European costume in all but the fez.' Perhaps a childish prank which he had played at high school in the last years of the nineteenth century had served as a reminder. During prayers, when everybody including his teacher was prostrate, the young man quietly gathered up his colleagues' fezzes and stacked them on top of each other in the middle of the room. As a punishment, he was bastinadoed (the favoured punishment of beating the soles of the victim's feet), which made him lame for several days.

Irfan Orga was a young army officer in Constantinople when the military were issued with modest peaks on their uniform fezzes in 1924 as a temperature-testing prelude to Atatürk's wider campaign against the fez the following year. But the sight of the peaks caused such invective from passers-by that most of the officers, Orga among them, wore them back to front to deflect the verbal flak.

Orga was too young to have fought in the Great War which loomed large in the summer of 1913. They were collecting precious lira on the streets of Constantinople throughout that summer to pay the British Vickers yard for two commissioned battleships, the *Sultan Selim the Grim* and the *Mytilene*, which were to become the pride of the Ottoman Navy and of a people chronically shamed by the sorry decline of their Empire. In August 1914, however, fearful of the Ottomans' developing *entente* with Germany and Austria, Britain reneged at the last moment on its commitment to deliver. Churchill justified the seizure by declaring it vital to British naval interests. Insult was added to injury when the British government temporarily confiscated from Vickers the £5 million downpayment that the Turks had already made, a payment originating not in some faceless treasury department but in a million Ottoman pockets, every one of them a heartfelt contribution towards the restoration of Ottoman pride.

Germany, recognizing a unique opportunity to engender pro-German sympathies among the Ottomans, immediately made available the *Goeben* and the *Breslau*, two warships of her own, complete with German crews. They appeared in the Bosphorus one late summer morning, sleek machines of war on which the sun shone warm and made them glitter so that for some time the crews that lined the decks could not properly be made out. Then, as the crowds looked out over the waters, a cry went up: 'Fezzes, they are wearing fezzes!' The German crews were decked out in the red hats of the Empire. Ottoman pride was not only restored; it came irresistibly gift wrapped courtesy of the Germans. That morning was perhaps the point at which Turkish entry into the war on the side of the Germans finally became inevitable.

The British meanwhile salted the wound by announcing that the retained battleships were now to be called the *Agincourt* and the *Erin*. The Turkish response was to rename the two German warships. They would have their *Sultan Selim the Grim* and their *Mytilene* despite the dastardly British. Furthermore, they now proceeded to delay on the crucial commitment they had made to replace the experienced German crews with less seamanlike crews of their own. The British then delayed in returning the £5 million. By the time the Turks had responded in kind by confiscating British property in Constantinople to an equivalent amount, Turkey's official entry in the war on the side of Germany and Austria had become a mere formality. And the symbolic payload of a shrewdly deployed consignment of fezzes was doubtless mentioned in German dispatches.

Memories are notoriously short, but in preparing for Kastamonu, Atatürk knew that they were rarely eleven years short. So little time had elapsed since 1914, and his file on the fez would have informed him of the hat's considerable significance in the Vickers incident. It will also have told him that Turks had died for the fez in defence of the Turkish ideal as little as six, five, even four years earlier. Between 1919 and 1922 the Greek army of occupation in Smyrna took to shooting indiscriminately at fez wearers, including even those Greek citizens who had become Ottomanized over the years. The greater number of Greeks, however, formed mobs and knocked the fezzes from the heads of surrendering Turkish troops. 'Numerous cases are reported,' wrote the city's British High Commissioner, 'in which Mussulmans, both men and women, have been mishandled, insulted, or threatened in the streets of the town, the fezzes of the former and the veils of the latter being torn off their heads and trodden on.' A Turkish colonel who refused to take off his fez and stamp on it was shot in the head. In Constantinople, the Greeks slung their own flags between the first-floor windows of the houses so that passing Turks were forced to brush against them. The fez was knocked violently from the heads of those that ducked out of the way. In the file marked fez, Atatürk would have found every reason to be nervous on the road to Kastamonu.

Furthermore, the popularity of the fez ensured the contempt in which its cultural counterpart, the Western hat, was held. A British traveller called Marmaduke Pickthall had rapidly learned to arm himself with a fez after he was stoned in the Muslim quarter of Ottoman Beirut in 1895. 'My only crime,' he wrote, 'had been to wear an ugly English hat.'

By the time of Atatürk's visit to Kastamonu, tentative moves had already been made against the fez. The radical head-dress of the army, introduced earlier that summer for young officers like Irfan Orga, was dismissed by its detractors as a folding cap akin to that used by skiing instructors in Switzerland. In July, policemen in Constantinople were surreptitiously passed orders to 'reprobate and, if necessary, arrest those conservatives who venture to mock at Turks who appear in the streets wearing hats'. But these comparatively clandestine measures had in no way prepared the population for the wholesale abolition of the fez.

I passed Ottoman houses, beautiful but dilapidated to the point of sliding downhill, and probably not the original hill whence they had started out. Catering-size olive oil tins, hammered flat to cover gaping holes in the woodwork, had rusted to a fine brown filigree through which the wind blew. Hunched men staggering under the weight of huge bails emerged from an old *bedestan*, a covered courtyard proudly announcing itself as the Kastamonu Hemp and Ropemakers' Market. Inside, men were loading the bails on to each other's backs while a few pigeons huddled on ledges around the domed and pillared ceiling and a man pissed in the shadows.

There had been a law passed against this, the hiring of porters to carry heavy loads, in 1937. It had been claimed that to work as a pack animal offended the dignity of the modern Turk, a nice theory but evidently one which didn't change the fact that there was work to be done.

'You want a bail?' a burly man shouted at me.

I couldn't think of anything I wanted less. 'I actually want the museum,' I replied.

'It's crap,' he told me. 'Have a bail instead.'

I eventually found the museum on the main street. It crouched in a garden full of Roman tombs and broken amphorae, and it was indeed crap. At twenty yards, it was one of those places you knew by instinct alone to be crap. It conveyed no sense of excitement, interest, or civic pride. It was just another function of government, a place where paperwork flourished as exhibits paled and died, arms fell off mannequins, and moths indulged themselves. A sign on the door, hung more out of habit than expectation, declared the place open even though the door itself was most definitely locked. When I knocked loudly, a face appeared at the window whose startled expression exclaimed: 'Visitor!'

A sceptical key turned in the lock and I was ushered into a place of gloomy corridors and uncertain doors. A young woman took my admission money. In return, she removed four and a half tickets from a docket with exaggerated care and handed them to me.

'Inflation,' she explained to my puzzled expression. 'You used to get just one ticket before the admission price started going up. Now that we have to charge you more, we give you tickets to the same value.'

'So if I come back next week, will I get four and three-quarters?'

But she was already leading off down the corridor, turning on lights and unlocking doors as we went.

'You don't get too many visitors,' I observed shrewdly.

'We had some school children last Tuesday,' she returned defensively, and stopped at a pair of old ornate double doors with a pattern picked out in faded gold leaf.

'This,' she whispered, turning the lock, 'is the Atatürk room,' And her hushed reverence echoed away down the empty corridors.

This was what I had come for, the building's moment of glory sixty-eight years earlier when it still served as the town hall. Inside, old sepia photographs recording Atatürk's visit to the town crowded the walls. The Gazi walked amongst befezzed crowds in a range of exotic costumes. Here he was dressed in a linen suit and panama; here, he had slipped into full military uniform with peaked cap. Later, he had found his way into a grey suit and homburg. He struck various poses, removing the hat of the moment to hold it by his side, or lifting it in acknowledgement of the crowds around him. Prior to the visit, his aides must have wondered why Atatürk had ordered what amounted to the fancy dress box for a tour of what was no more than a minor hinterland town. And why had he tabled so many separate walkabouts? There were only so many route permutations in a town the size of Kastamonu before the steppe, which crouched around the town's limits like wolves salivating beyond the light thrown by the camp-fire, swallowed you up in its endless expanses.

For a few hours, as the photographs demonstrated, Kasta-monu had served as Atatürk's catwalk where he previewed a radical show called the twentieth century. Both designer and one and only model, he rushed back to the town hall to change every few minutes before sashaying back down Kastamonu's main street in yet another of the designs that ushered in something rich, strange, and – to the people of Kastamonu – thoroughly offensive called radical social change. On that day in Kastamonu, jaws gaped open that have not closed since. For the fez was the national hat and here was their leader brazenly decked out in the reviled uniform of the infidel.

Earlier that year, Atatürk had done what he could to

prepare the ground for his campaign against the fez by wringing from a religious judge a ruling that justified the wearing of infidel hats. 'If a Muslim buys a cow from a Christian,' the judge had conceded, 'and the cow refuses to give milk unless the Muslim milks her while wearing a Christian hat, then the Muslim may wear such a hat.'

Milk-starved cow owners aside, the ruling was never destined to transform Turkish attitudes towards Western hats. For 'Putting on a Western Hat' meant something in 1925, something not the least bit flattering. An expression in common currency at the time, it meant betrayal or apostasy from Islam, or entering the pay of a foreign power, and probably meant it most fiercely in Kastamonu, a country town renowned for its entrenched conservatism. Donning a Western hat in Kastamonu wasn't just inappropriate. It was like wearing furs to the zoo, or pink to a funeral; it was inexcusable and outrageous.

Nevertheless, Atatürk brazenly carried the fight to the citizens of Kastamonu. 'I see a man in front of me,' he declared to the gathered masses, 'wearing a fez on his head and a green turban wrapped round the fez . . . would a civilized man put on this preposterous garb and go out to hold himself up to universal ridicule?' The people of Kastamonu were speechless. What they did know was that the fez and green turban, which their Gazi now declared ridiculous, had sufficed for as long as the oldest of them could remember as a revered badge honouring those who had made the *haj* to Mecca.

In 1873, a man called Hamdy Bey had prepared a book for the Vienna Exhibition called *Les Costumes Populaires de la Turquie*. In it, he photographed men and women modelling typical contemporary costumes, Muslim and Christian, across the Empire from Constantinople to Beirut, from Sofia to Baghdad. Its general historical significance apart, the book uniquely demonstrates the ubiquity of the fez in the nineteenth-century Ottoman Empire. There was the Constantinople boatman in his fez, the Muslim lady from Baghdad wearing a small fez bordered with black veloutine, the peasant from Jerusalem in a tasselled fez with turban wrapped low against the sun, and the Christian Beiruti wearing his fez turbanless – *à la mode Smyrniote*, or in the classic Smyrna fashion as it was known. There were city gentlemen wearing maroon fezzes only the slightest bit conical and so tall as to require regular pressing; there were the scarlet, tapering fezzes worn by merchants, and working men's fezzes, often of unstarched felt, knocked in and with a knob of felt where the tassle might otherwise have been.

And then there was the Turkish worker from Kastamonu.

Of all Hamdy Bey's many photographed creations, no costume was so uninspiringly shabby, shapeless, and plain sad as that worn by the Turkish worker from Kastamonu. All Hamdy Bey could think to declare in his caption to the costume, a brown felt smock, heavy leggings, and a fez flattened under indistinguishable layers of covering, was that it presumably kept the wearer warm. 'This rather fundamental outfit does not attempt to stress the qualities of the outer man,' Hamdy Bey excused it, with all the broad-minded understanding at his disposal. He then went further in mitigation to remind his readers that there was no such thing as perfection anywhere in the world, merely vanity; in Kastamonu, it seemed, there was neither.

In choosing Kastamonu, Atatürk was deliberately confronting Turkey at its most reactionary. Mahmud II had employed a similar tactic in causing his then radically modern fezzes to be manufactured in the shadow of Constantinople's most holy Islamic shrine. But there was subtle strategy behind Atatürk's confrontational stance. He figured that any Kastamonu hostility to his dress could be dismissively attributed to fossilized reactionary sentiments – and the rest of Turkey was not in the least above laughing at the funny old ways of Kastamonu folk. Conversely, any marked lack of reaction would allow him to declare that even Kastamonu had welcomed his sartorial revolution. No other Turkish town, the argument went, would dare to object where Kastamonu had acquiesced. If the argument held, then Atatürk could not lose.

'Oh no, not at all,' the woman at the museum replied to my musings. 'We in Kastamonu are well known for our sympathy to revolutionary and modern ideas. That's why Atatürk chose Kastamonu.' Her lies were not wilful, but they were lies nevertheless. Just as boring Germans are convinced they are amusing, and conventional Brits need to believe they are eccentric, so even the most reactionary Turks like to think themselves modern.

By suggesting that Kastamonu was old fashioned, I had offended the woman at the museum. I decided not to press my case by calling witnesses such as the brimless woollen caps that a great many of Kastamonu's men wore. I even decided against telling her what a hemp dealer had called her museum, and made my excuses just as she was about to subject me to the amphorae collection. As I left, I heard the door lock behind me.

I was returning to my hotel when an old man walked across the road in front of me wearing a purple, brimless hat, causing me to jump. More domed than conical and without a tassle, it was not the classic fez, but I suspected it to be a very close relation. It reminded me of Hamdy Bey's working man's fez. I began to track it, my heart beating rapidly, stopping to feign interest in a particular lamppost whenever the fez wearer greeted friends, or examining an apple at close quarters whenever he shot the breeze with stall holders further down the market. He crossed another road with me in surreptitious pursuit and started to describe a large circle until we passed the apple stall again. Gradually, it became clear to me that the old man was going nowhere in particular.

When we passed the apples for the third time, I fell back to talk to the stallholder.

'Why does that old man keep going round in circles?'

'He's bonkers. He does this every day. And why do you keep looking at my apples?'

I decided I had better buy some.

'I thought it was illegal to wear a fez these days,' I said, pointing at the old man as he disappeared between a pair of donkeys.

'He's not wearing a fez,' said the stallholder. But he seemed to say it instinctively, even before he had looked up. 'It is illegal. But, as I said, he's mad, probably doesn't know what he's wearing on his head. It's actually more like a beret. You owe me for the apples.'

I handed over a couple of notes and wandered away. It hadn't looked like a beret to me. Perhaps I was reckoning on too much historical aptness, finding a fez wearer in this nondescript, reactionary town whose inhabitants Atatürk had considered the hardest fez-wearing nut to crack. Perhaps all I had in fact found was a circular lunatic in a meaningless red hat. 'Stop!' a man's voice shouted at my back and I turned expecting to be confronted by an Islamic mullah outraged by the infidel in his midst. But there was only a young man sashaying across the street continuing his poor English pop rendition. 'In the name of lovv, before you break my heart.' Perhaps I was wrong; perhaps it had only been a beret.

That night, I sat among ranks of Turkish men in the lobby of my hotel, watching the coverage of demonstrations throughout Turkey against the murder of Uğur Mumcu on the television. There were protests in Istanbul and Izmir, in the Mediterranean cities of Mersin and Adana, and in Ankara, the city where Mumcu had worked and died. Some ten thousand people attended the march in Istanbul. As they passed the Iranian Consulate, they shouted: 'Here is the *sheriat*. Here are the murderers. Islamic fundamentalists back to Iran.' In Ankara, more than fifteen thousand people marched from the place of Mumcu's death outside his house where they laid flowers, to the city centre offices of his newspaper, *Cumhuriyet*. Candlelit vigils were held outside his house. Footage showed the journalist's desk at *Cumhuriyet* spilling over with red carnations.

Cumhuriyet (*the Republic*) is a left-leaning and highly respected newspaper which supports the basic principles of secular republicanism on which Atatürk's state was founded. Like the editors-in-chief of two other Turkish dailies, *The State* and *Freedom*, who were assassinated in 1979 and 1990 respectively, Mumcu and his newspaper represented an emerging democratic consensus. For the first time, the potential influence of voices such as Mumcu's within the framework of an increasingly free press was being recognized by elements accustomed to a blinkered and unadventurous media, one which had traditionally turned a blind eye to their malevolent and marginalized activities, or at worst churned out unsubstantiated and unconvincing propaganda in a vain effort to discredit them. Mumcu was widely read and respected, and in the struggle for the soul of modern Turkey his voice was perhaps too persuasive for his opponents to permit.

It was hard to imagine a journalist dying in similar circumstances in Europe, and harder still to envisage a comparable popular reaction. An upwelling of outrage had greeted Mumcu's murder. In Şile, near Istanbul, a mob armed with staves and stones attacked the local Refah party offices. But then I thought of Ali Bey in Soapmakers, and millions of convinced Refah men like him, and wondered what they would have made of Mumcu's murder. There had been no demonstration on Mumcu's behalf in Kastamonu.

I went up to bed. And as I dozed, I thought of Atatürk tearing through his wardrobe one hot summer's day sixty-eight years ago in this small town where he had come to unveil his vision of the modern Turk. I thought of those ranks of gaping mouths as the people of Kastamonu tried to absorb the deviant future tabled for their country. But after Mumcu's assassination in Ankara, the very heart of the secular republic, that future did not seem so certain.

And nor did my own when the radio burst into life and, despite repeated thumps and bellows, kept going all night.

chapter five

THE NEXT MORNING, even before opening my eyes, I knew
it was snowing heavily. The distinctive muffling which is the
effect of snowfall gave it away, bluntening the edge of every
street noise so that passing lorries seemed distant and unearthly
at my window. Besides, the radio that would not be silenced
had reported it on weather bulletins every half-hour throughout the night.

There was no time to lose. To reach the coast, I had to
cross the mountains to the north before the snow boxed me
into Kastamonu. I found myself tip-toeing out of the door,
abandoning the chicken to chance and the radio to talk on
through the morning. I experienced a strange kind of guilt,
like slipping away from the bedside of a stricken but impossibly garrulous old relative.

The bus wound through snowscape into white-shrouded
pine forests. As we passed through villages, the smell of coal
smoke invaded the bus. Slabs of snow had slid from the stove-
warmed roofs to disintegrate in heaps of white powder on
brown-trudged and pot-holed pavements. Hunched figures
were shovelling it on to the road only for the snow plough to
redeposit it on their doorsteps minutes later. Where others
might have considered this irksome in the extreme, the villagers seemed genuinely grateful for the diversion. Even the
sallow visages of the men could be seen to gather with what
for them passed as definite eagerness at the smoky windows of
the *kiraathanesis* or gaming halls to observe the passing of the
snow plough before returning to their backgammon boards

with a finality which suggested that nothing but an obscure memory of home would now disturb them till spring.

Personally, I could not wait that long. And as we began to descend the mountain, and the wheels which had previously slalomed free-style across patches of ice now found grip on the first brown patches of purest tread, I was thankful to be reminded that winter was not in fact a permanence. The first licks of grass and occasional apple trees, gnarled, knobby, but finally uncloaked of snow, lifted my spirits and, by the time we were corkscrewing towards sea level, only the faintest ridges of white still clung to the landscape's chill contours or dusted the tree trunks of the orchards. We followed a brown river past dilapidated buildings into the town of Inebolu.

A wind was blowing bitter off the Black Sea. Seagulls huddled like frozen vagrants above the spill of waves where the river met the sea, its bunched energy diffused among the long swells. Tractors were parked around the petrol station on the seafront, a long strip of concrete where the spray flew and a shoal of salt drops, icy cold, smattered my face. But they made me feel alive and the sunlight, however weak, turned the breakers jade and brilliant white and filled the sky. Modern buildings, grey and functional, dominated the seafront but I saw instead the few relics of Ottoman architecture among them, once exquisite houses fronted with salt-crumbled yellow plaster, dark wooden window frames, and filigree iron balconies below scrolled beams and high, sloping roofs.

The hotel was housed, of course, in one of the modern buildings but although the sunchairs outside were stacked now, they redeemed the place, lending it a welcome connection with summer. I stepped into a lobby which was bathed in sunlight and filled with recuperating pot plants. An elderly, owlish man rose to shake my hand and gestured me to a seat while he finished a conversation on the telephone. He was planning a trip to Batum in Georgia, eight hundred miles away at the eastern end of the Black Sea. The door to the lobby was patterned with stickers advertising tour operators in Hamburg and Munich, Amsterdam and Vienna. Under the glass-topped desk, holiday snaps showed the man in affectionate clasps with blond Europeans; young, summer-pink people who had found themselves a friendly Turkish hotelier.

Erdoğan Karagöz put the phone down and regarded me over his glasses. 'Well, well,' he said in the helpfully distinct Turkish of a man clearly accustomed to foreigners. 'Where did you spring from?'

'From Kastamonu,' I replied. 'Looking for hats.'

'Hats, eh? Well, we in Inebolu don't wear many hats any more. We're modern here.' And for once I was not tempted to dismiss the Turkish refrain out of hand.

'There is very little work left for the eight thousand people who live here now,' explained Erdoğan Bey. 'Many of us have been forced to seek work in Istanbul, and have spent long periods of time there. Our mentality is big-city.'

'Unlike Kastamonu?'

'Exactly,' he replied. 'There is enough work in Kastamonu to prevent people ever leaving. So they rarely do. The mentality is closed to the outside world.'

So the inward-looking people of Kastamonu worked shops in the shadows of their mosques and small acreages on the Anatolian plateau while the population of Inebolu remembered a past when sailors from Russia and Europe had come ashore here, maritime itinerants leaving the stamp of the wider world long after the freighters had slipped from their moorings and borne them away. In 1880, there had been a large Greek population, steamboat agencies, a customs house, and even a number of consulates in Inebolu. Inebolu had grown up facing the sea and despite the fact that the steamboats and the consulates were long gone the town seemed to keep a weather eye on the horizon. For the horizon was where the travel agencies of Hamburg and Batum's business proposals came from. The horizon was the future, and over the horizon, the sail of opportunity might one day reappear.

When Erdoğan Bey was a child, five boats a day used to call at Inebolu. The town flourished on the export to Istanbul and Europe of Black Sea coastal produce such as eggs, apples, and chestnuts. The arduous mountains of northern Turkey's interior had long safeguarded the ancient trade route by water through the Black Sea and the Bosphorus, and guaranteed Inebolu's continued significance. And so it was until they built what the Turks call the 'black way', or the tarmac road. It skirted the mountains well to the south of Inebolu to link Istanbul and Ankara with Samsun a hundred miles further east. Most of the freight was transported overland and Inebolu suddenly became redundant. The agencies closed and the consuls were recalled, and thirty years ago the boats finally ceased calling. Now the summer ferry service carrying tourists and freight between Istanbul, Samsun, and Trabzon did not even heave into view as it passed Inebolu miles out to sea.

Erdoğan Bey stubbed out a cigarette. 'Barring Natashas, I do not think the hotel will attract another guest this January day,' he said, winking mysteriously. 'Let me show you around.' He put on his coat and ushered me to the door.

'Look at this,' he said as we passed the tourist information office.

Through the broken, cobwebbed window, I could see a cracked windsurfer and a punctured paddling pool awash in slimy green water.

'Not much, eh? Not much. And yet' – his voice rose like an epiphany as we walked along the seafront – 'there was a time.' We were now standing by an old wooden longboat, painted red and yellow, in which lay the constituent parts of an old ox-cart. 'You know what happened in May 1919?' Erdoğan Bey asked me.

I nodded. 'I celebrated it once in Pomegranate,' I replied. And Erdoğan Bey reminded me how the Allies had proposed the post-war dismemberment of the Ottoman Empire. How they were sympathetic to various claims to large sections of Asia Minor since, chiefly speaking, the claims were their own.

And how that would have meant Turkey reduced to a swath of northern Asia Minor, including Inebolu.

Meanwhile, the Greeks tried to impose their own Pan-Hellenic version of the settlement upon the beleaguered Turks by landing at Smyrna and pushing deep into the Anatolian hinterland, taking out fezzes as they went. It was at this nadir in Turkish fortunes that a minor Anatolian sideshow redirected the course of history.

Rising tensions between the Greek and Turkish populations around Samsun and Inebolu had led the compliant government of the Sultan in Constantinople to propose that an inspectorate be dispatched to restore order and to suppress Turkish nationalists active in the area. Mustafa Kemal, who had kept his nationalist inclinations firmly under his fez – he still wore it when *realpolitik* deemed it necessary – and whose war record was beyond reproach, was chosen with the connivance of well-placed nationalist elements in Constantinople to lead the inspectorate. Mustafa Kemal, needless to say, had an unpublicized Anatolian agenda of his own.

The *Bandirma*, the steamer that was to carry Mustafa Kemal to his new post on the Black Sea coast, left Constantinople on the night of May 16 1919 and moored off Samsun on May 19, ensuring an annual public holiday in perpetuity.

'But what is interesting,' said Erdoğan Bey, 'is that Atatürk landed at Inebolu *en route*.'

'Not in the history books, he didn't,' I told him.

'History books!' he exclaimed. 'We're outside history books now. Nobody knew about it. Atatürk was supposed to be headed straight to Samsun to deal with Turkish attacks on the Greeks. Instead, I tell you, he stopped at Inebolu. There are old men in town who even think they saw him.'

Interestingly enough, Erdoğan Bey pointed out, it should not take a steamer much more than twenty-four hours to reach Samsun from Istanbul. It had taken Mustafa Kemal sixty. What had kept him?

In the months that followed, the fledgeling nationalist

forces would rally to Mustafa Kemal, who quickly proved himself a better resistance leader than inspector. Clandestinely armed and equipped by sympathetic elements in Constantinople and later by the Soviet Bolsheviks, the Nationalists would gradually grow strong enough to discourage Italian and French claims on Southern Anatolia, to rout the invading Greeks, to dissuade the British out of Constantinople, and to build an irresistible case for the Turkish nation. Their munitions mostly came ashore at Inebolu.

The port was perfect for the purpose; beyond the reach of the enemy, inaccessible by land, and small enough for illicit landings to go unnoticed. It is unlikely that Mustafa Kemal, a campaign veteran of Gallipoli, would not have been thinking ahead during those hours in May 1919, hours that have never been accounted for. He would have been quick to appreciate that they might land weapons at Inebolu unnoticed, and so stepped ashore to sound out reaction to his yet vague idea that this port might become the engine-room of the Independence struggle.

'And the result was this,' said Erdoğan Bey, patting the red and yellow boat which had once brought the munitions ashore before the oxen carted them up the mountain road I had come down only that morning.

A bust of Atatürk stood in the town square above a pair of bas-reliefs. One depicted the night-time unloading of armaments, the other Atatürk resplendent in a panama hat.

'You mentioned hats,' exclaimed Erdoğan Bey. 'This other visit of Atatürk to Inebolu you will certainly find in the history books.' And he took me to visit Mustafa Bey, with whom he had been at school in the days when five boats called.

Mustafa Bey was Inebolu's Director of Higher Education. He worked in one of the beautiful seafront buildings near the hotel. He presided over a neat desk, his few strands of hair pomaded back from his forehead above a precise pinstripe suit.

'I have some Georgian business to look after,' said Erdoğan Bey, excusing himself. 'Mustafa Bey will look after you.'

'Let me show you our little museum,' said Mustafa Bey.

'And then we will drink tea and smoke cigarettes, and talk a little.'

We descended several flights of stairs and entered a large room overlooking the sea. On the panelled walls were fading photographs of Atatürk, and strips of dirty wallpaper that flapped languidly like underwater seaweed when Mustafa Bey opened the window to the breeze. At one end of the room stood a makeshift stage. The wooden steps that approached it were festooned with old crêpe paper, yellow and sagging.

'We had a silly fashion show here some months ago,' Mustafa Bey explained. 'One day,' he sighed, 'I would like this to be a proper museum, with new carpets and without silly fashion shows.'

We were standing in the room where Atatürk had come, after the rigours of reactionary Kastamonu, to administer the *coup de grâce* to the fez. He had chosen with care this place where only six years earlier the men, women, and children had shouldered his munitions for him, had carried across the mountains shells half their own body weight. The people of Inebolu, who had given so much, would continue to buoy him with their support. As he approached Inebolu, the towns-folk showered him with late summer flowers, and he turned towards the sea light, the space, and the infinite horizon, remembering an unsung visit only six springs earlier, when all this had been a dream barely imagined.

The people of Inebolu sacrificed sheep, offered up the fruit of the harvest, and kissed their Gazi's outstretched hand as he passed. The boatmen displayed their skills of seamanship among the breakers and children sang Republican songs. Finally, he made his way to the room where Mustafa Bey had brought me, turned to the packed throng in front of him, and began to speak. 'The people of the Turkish Republic, who claim to be civilized,' he told them, 'must prove that they are civilized by the way they appear.' And that, he explained, meant boots and shoes, trousers, shirt and tie, jacket and waistcoat. 'And to complete these, a cover with a brim on our heads. I want to make this clear. This headcovering is called "hat".'

The men of Inebolu went on to the streets and discarded their fezzes. The women, the first outside the big cities reported to have done so, went further still by throwing back their veils and presenting their wan, unsunned faces to Atatürk in the street. A photograph in the room caught my eye. The Gazi is walking an Inebolu street amongst a throng of people. He is wearing a linen suit and a panama. He is also wearing a victorious smile, as if he knows he is amongst friends loyal to the point of excusing his extraordinary clothes. But he has just passed two local soldiers. Since the modern military headgear has not yet been issued in this remote part of the country, they are dressed in fezzes. In the photograph, they remain at attention but the Gazi has passed them and behind his back, their eyes at least are at ease to express astonishment. For the moment of the photograph, the soldiers are wide-eyed witnesses to a radically transformed world.

'And so,' Mustafa Bey murmured, looking at his watch as he led me upstairs for a glass of tea, 'the Turkish nation entered the modern world.'

By the time we reached his office, I wondered whether it had been irony I'd heard in his tone. For the first lesson of the day in the classroom next door comprised rows of young women hunched over antique sewing machines. Their heads were mostly shawled. An apprentice clatter filled the air as trial stitches patterned old cloth, and heads remained studiously bowed as we passed. For we were men, and for a moment it was as if Atatürk had never come here in 1925, and that all the monumental changes had only led back to this room by the Black Sea where a class of girls were learning the old skills as their mothers and grandmothers had done.

Mustafa Bey ladled sugar cubes into a slender-waisted glass of tea and smiled. 'I know what you are thinking. If I had known you were coming, I might have put these girls in a back room and organized an English lesson to impress the foreigner. But what would these girls do with their English? We are poor, and there is little work enough for the men let alone the women. Nobody pays any taxes. So we have learned to enjoy talk and tea. We have learned to entertain our visitors. Since there are some fifty gaming houses in Inebolu to support an adult male population of under three thousand, it goes without saying that we have also learned to entertain ourselves.' Like the men of the mountain villages whiling away an odd six months with chat and backgammon, cigarettes and tea, I thought, and wondered whether all this was in some way connected to the fact that 'Ottoman' had come to mean a comfortable couch in English, and whether it was also a coincidence that divan, another kind of couch, was also the Turkish word for the Ottoman ruling council – on which, incidentally, women had never sat.

In the classroom, the shawl-wearing women were learning not only sewing but their place. Atatürk's exhortations to the women of Inebolu in the autumn of 1925 were followed a year later in Trabzon, at the eastern end of the Black Sea, by a proclamation from the governor which forbade women to wear the veil. 'The veil,' it announced, 'deprives women of the possibility of earning their livelihood, the custom is well known to be insanitary, and it tends to hinder the work of the police by enabling criminals to conceal their identity. After ten days any women wearing a veil will be arrested.' But not even the possibility that they were aiding and abetting the local criminal fraternity, nor allegations that they were prevented from keeping themselves clean, persuaded the majority of Trabzon's women to unveil.

Besides, the police had quite enough of their own problems without wondering whether a veiled woman was in fact a concealed criminal, and whether to arrest the subject on either count. For a 1925 order had forbidden the country's policemen to wear the beard, in spite of the fact that only three years earlier the young caliph, Abdul Mejid, was attracting censure for not growing a beard, long regarded as an essential Islamic accoutrement.

Into these confusions sallied the Constantinople correspondent for the London *Times*, who set out along the Black Sea coast in 1926 to take the country's social and cultural temperature. He took a ferry of the Lloyd Triestino line, stopping at Inebolu as one did in those days before continuing on to Samsun, Giresun, and Trabzon. In Giresun, the correspondent happened across the performance of a group of strolling players sponsored by the regime to propagate the idea that women should be encouraged to work. A strongly worded proclamation ensured a healthy turn-out of local women. But such was their outrage on discovering that they were expected to sit alongside the men, and at the unabashedly radical content of the performance, that the women left in an incensed body at the end of the first act. 'The forces of reaction,' commented the correspondent, 'cannot be ignored.'

In 1935, the ruling party congress discussed nationwide legislation banning the use of the veil in Turkey, but eventually deemed it to be unnecessary since the rising generation were apparently discarding it of their own free will. Later, legislation was passed to outlaw the use of veils, shawls, or headscarfs in educational institutions but otherwise the female headcovering was left to gravitate towards its own demise.

Its demise, however, has proved a protracted one. In 1968, a female student of Ankara University's theology department queried the ban. Why should women not dress as they wished in educational establishments? By November 1988, sympathetic Islamic elements in Parliament had become sufficiently influential to cause the headscarf to be unbanned. But the President, true to his Kemalist beliefs, immediately lodged a veto (which Parliament ignored), and applied to the Constitutional Court for clarification. In March 1989, the ban was reimposed. There were protests that week all over Turkey. The secular President was accused by chanting crowds of being hand-in-hand with Salman Rushdie. Outside the mosques in Ankara, crowds chanted: 'Break the hands that wish to remove headscarves.' Crowds of women walked through Istanbul in silent protest. Eventually, the final decision on headscarf wearing was left to individual universities. But since the legislation was no longer enshrined in the constitution, this was regarded as a victory for the traditionalists. In early 1990, a Kemalist professor and lawyer called Muammer Aksoy was drafting an appeal to reverse the legislation when he was gunned down one January evening at the entrance to his Ankara home by an unknown group calling itself Islamic Revenge. Headgear in Turkey had claimed another life. 'Nobody knows what will happen next in Turkey. It's a shadowy situation,' as the *Financial Times* in London quoted a respected Turkish columnist. His name was Uğur Mumcu.

And so it was in Inebolu, the town where they had first discarded the veil, that ranks of shawled heads were bent over sewing machines, and in the sound of stitches in their thousands could be heard the enduring seams that bound Turkey to the past. It all made Mustafa Bey pensive. For him, change had only served to highlight what he regarded as Turkey's enduring backwardness. I cheered him a little by offering him an expensive Marlboro and reminding him of the improvements they were making in Inebolu. There was the upgraded road along the coast to Samsun, and the new port terminal at Doğanyurt twenty miles west, as well as the plans to improve Inebolu's own port facilities that summer. There was the fact that, true to their republican tradition, the majority of Inebolu's electorate had recently voted for True Path, the centrist, secular party. And then there were the town's beautiful wooden Ottoman houses, three hundred and fifty of which were now protected by law, to take pride in.

'I suppose you're right,' said Mustafa Bey. 'And there's always people like Erdoğan doing business with Georgia, which can only help the town.' I asked Mustafa Bey what his friend's business in Georgia was, and he told me it was snails.

'There is only one thing,' Erdoğan Bey told me later in his car, 'that snails like better than the lush mountain pastures above the Black Sea coast of Turkey. And that's the mountain pastures above the Black Sea coast of Georgia. You will see the shells of Turkish snails at the factory; imagine something a little bit bigger and you have a Georgian snail. A Georgian snail is hard to beat. Georgian currency, however, is easy to beat. In Georgia, God help them, they think of the Turkish lira as we think of the dollar.' The Turkish lira had struck me as the currency equivalent of skydiving, but to the poor Georgians that was stability beyond their dreams.

The villagers collected the snails in the spring among long grass and around the feet of trees and brought them down to sell at the factory in Inebolu where they were removed from their shells, packed in ice, and dispatched by truck to Paris where they would be defrosted, allotted temporary housing of their own, doused in garlic, and served.

There were no snails now, only trays of last spring's abandoned shells littering the building. In that it consisted of a table where the shells were removed and the snails bagged, a very large fridge, and a wall chart featuring different snail types, it was a very Turkish kind of factory, one that elsewhere might have been called a packing shed. The proud owner showed me round in three minutes. I timed it. Then he shrugged and said, 'That's all there is to it, really,' and I left them to talk, a group of men huddled round a gas stove waiting for the long, long grass of spring.

As I wandered through the town in the gloaming, I heard from somewhere the oddest sound. It reminded me of a distinctive brand of 1960s film soundtrack, a refrain plangent, mournful and French, Pigalle lamplit and in the rain – but played on a glockenspiel so that it actually sounded more than anything like a lovesick ice-cream van. When the origins of the sound hove into view, I saw that it was indeed a van but one whose song was advertising not ice-creams but gas canisters brand-named *Aygaz*. In the cold, they were selling fast.

In time, the *Aygaz* refrain would be imprinted upon my memory, the signature tune of the Turkish winter. But for now, my attention was attracted to a plume of smoke rising purple above the town. Word had spread and people forgot their *Aygaz* canisters as they spilled on to the streets and moved to spectate at an unfolding tragedy.

High on a hill stood one of Inebolu's three hundred and fifty beautiful houses. It was clapboard, painted a terracotta red, exquisitely scrolled and carved, topped by ancient wooden tiles, standing in a beautiful winter orchard, and it was on fire.

The fire brigade had arrived. A single hose threw up a lazy jet of water that in its indolence indicated it knew its efforts to be futile. The flames were sating their ravenous hunger from within and could not be reached. A gathering crowd stood transfixed, for there was much to see. You could watch sections of clapboard gradually glow, change colour, and incandesce, or notice the lazy way that sections of wall and roof seemed to soften seconds before collapsing. You could listen to window-panes explode or watch the next-door neighbour, fearful of sparks, play his well-rehearsed hose across the equally beautiful yellow exterior of his own wooden home. You could add your throwing arm to the hopeless gesture of others and fling snowballs at the inferno, but there was nothing you could really do, only watch the family standing close to the heat and try to guess how they must feel. It was a stove, somebody told me. Stoves were always going wrong and the old houses were constantly burning down until, today, only three hundred and forty-nine were left. Only the men at *Aygaz*, witnessing this impressive demonstration of the dangers inherent in competing fuel systems, may perhaps not have been moved to tears.

Inebolu had burnt before. On March 19 1881, the year of Mustafa Kemal's birth, three hundred and fifteen houses were destroyed by fire. At that time there had been a British Consul in town to telegraph for assistance. Today it felt, in spite of Atatürk and a venerable history, as if no Consul would ever return.

'Did they like the snail project?' I asked Erdoğan Bey on my return to the hotel.

'They loved it,' he exclaimed, slapping me across the back. 'Georgia, here I come.'

Night fell and Inebolu's electricity supply died with it so that the last embers of the burnt-out house could be seen fluttering against the dark of the mountains behind us. Erdoğan Bey reckoned that heavy snowfalls in the mountains had brought down the power lines. Moonlight filtered through the clouds and rose from the waves in a pale wash that touched at the windows of the hotel. Erdoğan Bey brought me a plate of red mullet and salad, and a glass of milky-white raki. From beyond a candle he watched me eat, and smoked pensively. He was thinking not only of Georgia's snails but of a possible ferry link between Inebolu and Yalta on the Crimean coast to the north. For it was his dream that one day ships might once more call at Inebolu. Five thousand dollars, he said, was all he needed.

But then just a few notes was all anyone ever needed, including the two Natashas Erdoğan Bey told me had turned up at the hotel that morning looking to exchange precious lira for routine favours.

'Ah, Natashas,' I murmured, understanding now.

'I told them the hotel was fully booked,' Erdoğan Bey explained. 'It's a big problem keeping Russian girls and Turkish men apart. They represent an irresistible trading opportunity. The Russian girls like Turkish lira,' he tutted, 'and the Turkish men like Russian *seks*.'

The Turkish language is littered with imported words, often exact phonetic transliterations, to describe objects or concepts originally foreign to Turkish. From the French, highly influential in the last century, comes *şöför* (*chauffeur*); *gişe* (*guichet*, ticket office); *gar* (*gare*, station); *bisiklet* (*bicyclette*, bicycle); *camyon* (*camion*, truck); and even, on the subject of couches, *şezlong* (*chaise longue*). From the English comes *şampiyon* (champion), *feribot* (ferryboat), *miting* (meeting), and even *aysberk* (iceberg). And from either language comes *seks*.

'I love your country,' I told Erdoğan Bey after a few more glasses of raki. 'But I am suspicious of any language that does not have its own word for sex.'

'Oh, we have a word,' he replied. 'But it's like your word . . . you know.'

'Which word?'

Anxious that none of the hotel's skeleton staff might hear him, he leaned forward. 'Fogging,' he whispered.

Sex had never been a subject for discussion in traditional Turkey. Not that it had ever been the only topic in, say Victorian England, but at least the English had never had to import a foreign word to fill the gap when the luvvie-feelie twentieth century came along. In Turkey, it seemed, there had been a samizdat sexual vocabulary to provide basic artillery for desire or insult – and no more. If the Turkish language was anything to go by, Erdoğan Bey could expect calls from a few more Natashas, for demand is as sure as water to find its own level.

The power returned and with it the television serving its traditionally long hours in homes and hotels throughout Turkey. Typical of the Turkish winter, a weather report told of several thousand villages cut off by snow. Further east, an entire village had been wiped out by an avalanche ten days earlier, taking the lives of fifty people. At the window, large flakes of snow were sticking.

'You should take tomorrow's bus,' Erdoğan Bey told me. 'Otherwise, you may be here for some time. Go east; it will be cold but if you find fezzes anywhere, you'll find them in the east.'

A television report told of another assassination attempt. This time, a gang in a car had trailed a prominent businessman through Istanbul. Only the jamming of their rocket launcher's firing mechanism had foiled them. But there had also been successes for the security forces in Diyarbakır, the capital city of Turkey's predominantly Kurdish south-east, where fifteen suspected terrorists had been captured. They had been made to stand in the corner of the room, faces to the wall like classroom delinquents, while the camera tracked across the table in front of them. A haul of machine-guns, pistols, grenades, and high explosives had been neatly arranged there. The centrepiece consisted of bullets standing on end which spelt out the words of the apprehending agency: 'TC Polis Diyarbakır': Turkish Republic Police, Diyarbakır; the spoils of war arranged as birthday cake decorations.

It felt like another version of the old story. For the Diyarbakır fifteen would choose to call themselves nationalists just as Mustafa Kemal's followers had done, only Kurdish ones in this instance. And the munitions that once came ashore in Inebolu were now smuggled in from Syria and Iran. Rocket launchers had replaced howitzer shells, but the patterns of resistance were always recurring.

That night, as I lay in bed, I heard the sound of breakers at the window and was reminded of another traveller who had come this way in 1935. Her ferry had anchored off the port, and she watched the pretty houses along the shore. Skiffs crewed by eight men and loaded with provisions were oared towards the ferry, and the traveller found herself marvelling at their skill among the breakers so that a fellow passenger turned to her and told her that the men of Inebolu were famed for their seamanship.

It was seamanship which had been honed during the secretive landings of munitions through the long war years between 1919 and 1922. I imagined red and yellow longboats beaching below my window under cover of darkness. I saw rifles, crates of bullets, and howitzer shells being unloaded and carried up the beach. I saw men, women, and children loading the carts. And when the carts were full, the people shouldering the boxes and the bullet belts and setting off up the long track on foot, over the mountains to the Nationalist armies at Ankara and to the east. The families surrendered their linen for bandages, their spare socks and shoes for the soldiers, and gave up their riding animals and their horsecarts. But more was asked of them, and they gave sons and daughters, husbands and wives to fall in battle or from the effects of cold and exhaustion along the way I had come that morning.

This, then, was the little port which had made modern Turkey possible. Rather than the inspiring example of Gallipoli in 1915, the great victories of the Independence War, the conferences where the Turkish ideal cohered, or the three towns whose names were assigned honorary prefixes – Warrior, Hero, and Glorious – in recognition of the Independence War bravery of their citizens, it had all begun in this unassuming place where the guns had come ashore.

The town was the packhorse of emerging Turkey, and in the high-profile glories of the Independence War its role was easily forgotten. But unsung heroism of the packhorse variety is often the best kind and packhorses do not mind being forgotten. All that had offended Inebolu was the attempted ban in 1937 on what was described as undignified portering. The Turkish people had roundly ignored the new law. I had seen them in Kastamonu, would see them all over Turkey, and in their refusal to countenance the portering ban was perhaps the grateful understanding that the country's very existence depended upon what the government had once chosen to call the indignity of heavy loads down by the sea at Inebolu.

※

chapter six

ON SEPTEMBER 2 1925, the day that Atatürk left Inebolu, Turkish civil servants were first compelled to wear Western hats, and lift the brims when saluting. Failure to do so could mean a year's imprisonment. It was announced that the fez would become illegal for all citizens, barring some branches of the clergy, on November 25, and would be punishable by three months' imprisonment.

That summer, Sir Telford Waugh had been on leave in England. He would go on to complete forty-four years of distinguished service in the dragomanate or interpreter's office, accompanying the Ambassador and other senior British diplomats on official visits in Constantinople, Ankara, and elsewhere in the Republic. It had been a beautiful summer in England but Sir Telford always looked forward to his return to Constantinople, the cool breezes among the plane trees as autumn blew its gentle way up the Bosphorus. Sir Telford thought he knew Constantinople as well as anybody, but as the time for his return drew near, a chance scrap of information led him to suppose that something momentous had happened in his absence; a hat manufacturer in London mentioned in passing that he had recently received an unprecedented enquiry from Constantinople. They apparently wanted hats, thirty thousand of them, and Constantinople did not often order hats.

In fact, hat demand in Constantinople was reaching fever pitch by late October, when the pressure on fezzes was stepped up. Although not yet officially illegal, nightwatchmen were given orders to go from house to house and seek out all surviving fezzes. On October 29, the anniversary of the founding of the Republic, the authorities exploited the nationalist fervour on the streets to openly admonish persistent fez wearers. That morning, hawkers did a roaring trade in what passed as hats. Fez wearers soon suffered Republicans knocking the fezzes from their heads just as they had habitually done to the homburgs of passing infidels.

The morning of November 25 broke strangely silent. In the heart of Constantinople near the Dolmabahce Palace, home of the last Ottoman Sultans, the muezzin trudged up the steps to appear on the balcony of his minaret, with a 1900 model bowler pulled down hard over his ears. With an apocalyptic sense of foreboding, he started to sing, wondering how long his incensed God would allow him to continue. After a few uneasy notes, he discovered to his surprise that he was still alive but in a world that had become unrecognizable.

In the weeks that followed, Western hats were imported into Turkey by the million. They came by ship and by train, bowlers and homburgs, panamas and flat caps, but they did not come in sufficient numbers to meet the demand. In Ankara, the hat stores were continually sold out. In Constantinople, even the countless new shops that sprang up overnight could not keep pace. Such was the shortage that the prefect of the city, Emin Bey, set restrictions on the profit that could legally be made on hats, 15% on the standard ones and 25% on more fancy models. On his return, Sir Telford discovered that several of his old bowlers and homburgs had been requisitioned by desperate Turkish staff members at the dragomanate. In fact, securing a hat in hat-starved Constantinople was only half the battle. It had always been a dandy's city where even the boatmen and the porters made a point of wearing their fezzes at just the right angle. How to wear the thing, this new-fangled hat, was just as taxing a problem. Not content with upsetting their world, the new order was now theatening them with sartorial humiliation.

'How to Wear the Hat' articles that appeared in the press

were voraciously consumed. Illiterate stokers, hawkers, and fishermen pressed passing teachers and lawyers into service to read to them from the relevant articles. But the problem was as much with the hats themselves as with the wearing of them; there was no correct way of wearing many of the irredeemable styles that were being unloaded on the unsuspecting Turkish population. The Borsalino Brothers, Italian milliners with an eye for the main chance, had been anchored in the Bosphorus waiting for official endorsement of the Hat Laws before landing at Constantinople a shipful of Western hats which, in the ephemeral fashions of 1920s Europe, were now laughably outmoded. Not that the local population was to know. The menfolk from a village near Izmir ended up proudly arrayed in a selection of pink feathered hats complete with ribbons as they went about their business as cobblers, blacksmiths, and farmers. 'Woollen bonnets on bearded porters, woollen Balaclavas on smart lounge suits,' read a contemporary account. Old stocks of fez felt were dyed a less conspicuous colour and fashioned into shapes intended to resemble hats. The *Times* correspondent in Constantinople reported creations made from 'materials more appropriate for a Christmas cracker or a seaside comedian . . . Duty before Dignity, as the bosun said; Progress before Dignity, says Turkey.'

By 1993, the passing of time had claimed many of Turkey's fez wearers. Those who survived had lived through such pulses of history that the abolition of a hat sixty-eight years ago had been largely erased from their elderly memories.

There was seventy-eight-year-old Faik Kurtar, who had been a baby when his family came to Turkey from Albania. Faik Bey remembered that he was a fez-wearing primary school pupil when the hat laws were introduced. 'We knew all about cowboy hats in American culture,' he told me in his Istanbul flat. 'Homburgs were so similar that we imagined ourselves as cowboys. And you can imagine how that made us feel as kids.'

Sara was an eighty-eight-year-old lady living on the Asian

side of the Bosphorus, in the grounds of what remained of the family's Ottoman estate. She sat surrounded by cats and by portraits of befezzed relatives including those of her grandfathers, who had come from Poland and Germany to settle in Turkey during the last century, and of her brother, who had been killed in action in the Dardanelles in 1915. I asked her what she remembered of the revolution.

'Which particular one?' she asked with the formidable panache of a seasoned witness of revolutions.

'The Atatürk one,' I replied meekly.

Sara's eyes brightened. 'Such fun it was,' she replied.

'And the abolition of the fez?'

Sara waved her arm, scattering a number of cats. 'It was time for it to go,' she replied. 'For most of us, the fez was quite out of date. There's a saying in Turkey: "If you don't know Paris, you're a donkey," and they never wore fezzes in Paris. Personally, I prefer Pakistan but there you are.'

Ziyad Bey, an eighty-two-year-old academic and journalist, was recovering from a stroke when I met him. He was attending the *lycée* in Galatasaray, Istanbul, on November 25 1925 and only harboured memories of a transitional chaos of Western caps, fezzes, and bare heads in a classroom that only the day before had harboured a sea of fezzes.

'In the east, the authorities knew that the conversion to hats would not be so easy,' Ziyad Bey told me. 'So the authorities chose a *bayram* – a festival day – to persuade everybody in one particularly reactionary area to wear a *shapka*, as we called the Western hat, if only for that day. The local people looked at the decree, scratched their heads, and wondered, knowing nothing of hat wearing, what sort of *shapka* they should wear. A dissident politician from western Turkey, who had been exiled to the area for his reactionary views, recommended to the locals a particular kind of hat. On the *bayram* hundreds of men appeared accordingly, wearing heavenly creations made from cerise taffeta. Heaven knows where they got them from. Apparently, Atatürk was furious . . .'

Ziyad Bey showed me a 1924 photograph of himself among the Galatasaray Lycée's alumni. The photograph was sixty-nine years old, the man it portrayed young and proud, and the fez that he wore served to place him in a different world. I had never seen such a thing, a photograph of a fez on the head of a Turk who was still alive.

The memories of young people going about their lives are not so long. Time has unravelled, and the red hat has receded. Dust has settled, all those old enough to understand what their fezzes meant to them are long dead, and the file has been closed.

Was this – the fading photograph of a man dressed in a fez, young and strong then but now stroke ridden and frail – as close as I would ever get? Was the rest just fezzes discarded by the million, as those Turks with a more theatrical sense of history had taken themselves down to the water and, after perhaps casting a last fond glance at the hat which had served them so well, tossed their fezzes into the Bosphorus in such numbers that the waters ran red with their drowning reflections? Or left them to be collected by the Red Crescent (the Turkish equivalent of the Red Cross) so that they might be turned into slippers for the infirm and the destitute? Doubtless, nobody will have smiled quite like the Gazi as converted fezzes were trod underfoot until the soles eventually broke up, and the detested badge of ignorance became dust that was lost on the winter wind, and Turkey was believed free of the past.

It was time to head east where, as Ziyad Bey had put it, the conversion to hats had not been so easy. I had been in Inebolu for as long as Atatürk, who had had civic occasions galore, revelled in the love of staunch Republican countrymen, and drunk plenty of raki. I'd left the love of his countrymen to the Natashas and settled for the raki, and fried anchovies fresh from the Black Sea in the little fish restaurant on the seafront.

Fresh snow, which had been menacing the town for days now, finally laid itself down in the vacuum hours of the night, falling along the promenade and the breakwater, ringing the steering-wheels of the tractors and piling silently against the gunwales of the fishing boats while the waves rolled along the shore, slurping at the shingle.

Amongst snowflakes and rogue ashes from the burnt-out house littering the wind, I left Inebolu early the next morning, but only just. Erdoğan Bey had made a few fixerly phone calls for me; the bus didn't normally stop for anybody but with his help, his expression suggested, it might just stop for me. It didn't; the only bus flew blithely past the hotel in a flurry of flakes. I liked Inebolu, but not sufficiently to stay until the spring. Erdoğan Bey swore richly, bundled me into his car, gunned it out of a snowdrift, and set off in frantic pursuit. We slalomed past the port on the outskirts of town, horn hooting and lights flashing. We attracted the attention of two men huddled on a fishing boat that swung at anchor in the bay. While they waved bemusedly and a stray dog watched us out of sight, the bus continued through the early morning unheeding.

It did not help that the wiper on Erdoğan Bey's side of the windscreen had frozen solid. In his attempts to free it, the wiper came off in his hands. He was left to brandish it through the open side-window while guessing at our direction largely by instinct.

'Right,' I said with the tentativeness of the passenger who has to balance a dislike of passenger drivers with the indubitable benefit of a functioning wiper as we approached a hairpin corner on two wheels. 'Left,' I croaked as the road swung violently the other way.

'Fogging bus—' Erdoğan Bey broke momentarily into English. He was a shy man but not shy enough to recognize that our best chance of catching the errant bus lay in lying across me, propping himself on an elbow that rested heavily in my crotch, and driving with one hand while he watched the road from the unimpeded view on my side of the car. I watched the back of his neck, where grey hairs sprawled from their pores.

'Fogg, fogg, fogg,' muttered Erdoğan Bey. But we were gaining. One hundred yards, fifty yards, twenty yards until, with a combination of flashing lights, honking horn, and flailing arms that must finally have struck the bus driver as unusual even by Turkish driving standards, we succeeded in bringing him to a halt. Erdoğan Bey bore down on the driver with his broken wiper.

'You were supposed to pick him up at the hotel, you idiot!' he shouted, jabbing at him. 'And you've broken my wiper.'

The driver looked apologetic. 'Nobody told me,' he replied. 'I saw you through my rear-view mirror. You were hooting your horn. You were in his lap. I thought you were getting married.' He looked at me curiously. 'Is he a tourist? What on earth is he doing here at this time of year?'

'He's looking for fezzes,' replied Erdoğan Bey, as if this were explanation enough.

The bemused driver waved me on board in a flurry of apologies and set off. We left Erdoğan Bey tending to his broken wiper as the snow threatened to engulf him, and headed east, deep into Turkey. An unbroken stand of pine trees, heavy with precarious ledges of snowfall, shepherded the road to our right, and the sea broke beyond the foreshore to our left. We passed isolated mosques and the skeletons of old fishing boats, and the remains of an old jetty, a few stumps black against the sea.

In a place called Türkeli, I waited for the next bus in a small waiting room where a gas fire hummed, alone except for a listless boy in charge of bus tickets. I could not see anything beyond the window except for a whiteness of snow and the suggestion of buildings. The place made me think that perhaps, due to an unfortunate convergence of low season, low temperatures, and sheer geographical remoteness, I had slipped quite by chance into a dimension not yet discovered by the outside world. My guidebooks revealed a chilling lack of reference to any place called Türkeli.

'English?' the boy asked me.

'English,' I replied without enthusiasm.

He pondered this for a moment. 'Glass?' he said, pointing at the tea in front of him. I thought for a moment that he was offering a traveller some fortifying kindness, but he was actually just practising his English.

'Glass,' I nodded wearily.

'Window?'

'Window.'

I took refuge in the fact that given the sheer lack of visuals, the English lesson could not last. As if to scotch that presumption right away, the boy said 'cat, dog' before settling into an unbroken stare at the television screen where mouths hung slack in American drawls long after each item of Turkish dubbing had passed. A team of karate experts were invading the grounds of a large house heavily guarded by men in ridiculous suits and irredeemable haircuts which unmistakably indicated the 1970s. Even the Americans, I reflected, had had their sartorial dark ages; it just seemed curious that the current Turkish one had continued so long.

I palmed away the condensation at the window and busied myself watching hats pass in the street. In Türkeli, it seemed, the homburg and the panama were not favourite. Here were grey flat caps tugged tight on to the head, crying out for an attendant whippet and pint of Tetley's above tattered grey jackets that had been stained and stitched a thousand times. Then there was a more colourful and flamboyant style where the cap extended beyond the head on all sides, a style Scottish in origin reminding me at once of that country's golfers, its football fans, and even of its rock bands, such as the Bay City Rollers, which had permanently scarred the vulnerable psyches of everybody unfortunate enough to have been young, impressionable and with access to radio or television in the early seventies. But even listening to the Rollers was as nothing compared to the sufferings of these people, who actually dressed like them. As I watched them meandering through the slushy town, I knew that whatever the wider social effect of Atatürk's dress reforms, they had condemned these people to a sartorial winter from which they might never recover.

Invariably, there was the same grey jacket with at least second-generation stitching (detectable by the alien thread colours) unravelling along the seam between the shoulders, and trousers that had come from quite another suit. The history of the trousers' previous owners was revealed – like the rings in a tree trunk – by the old stitch lines that encircled the material above a frayed and dirt-spattered conclusion – it could hardly be described as a hem – to the trouser leg.

Suffice it to say, I was thankful when the next bus eventually came and spirited me away, content to watch from my window as we wound up a cliff road above the sea, the rear wheels girded with chains to stop them sliding across the icy snow. When the chains alone proved insufficient, the passengers gravitated to the back of the bus to improve the grip there. For one alarming moment, when the driver's best efforts came to nothing, we slid backwards down a slope a few brief yards from a precipice but survived to pass a police car in a ditch, which caused much glee and prompted everybody to get out as if to help – but primarily to indulge in a few disparaging comments. The policeman's dependence on our assistance seemed to make my fellow passengers reckless. 'Yes,' said one, shaking his head as he leant heavily against the bonnet and started to push. 'You've got to know how to drive in these conditions.'

'Not the problem,' another corrected him. 'It's these cars, you know. Crap.'

Otherwise, I remember very little of that day, withdrawing into my own thoughts as the views at the window were obscured by white-out. Around me, the sound of sunflower seeds being cracked between teeth – and the slight whistle as the shells were spat out – induced a rhythm of indolent introspection. I fell to thinking of all the foreigners who had preceded me to Turkey to mourn one hat's passing and to resent the coming of a new one.

In the 1830s and '40s, no foreign traveller to Turkey had been the least bit enthusiastic about the new-fangled fez. Mockingly, they compared the appearance of its wearer, in combination with the standard black frock coat, as akin to a red-topped bottle of claret. 'A miserable substitute for the splendid turban,' one Reverend Walsh condemned it. 'The magical effects of a turban are well known,' wrote a regretful Sir Adolphus Slade in the 1830s. 'It gives depth to light eyes, expression to dark eyes; it softens harsh features, relieves delicate ones.'

Julia Pardoe, writing in 1834, was the most unforgiving of all. 'I cannot forbear to record my regret as I beheld in every direction the hideous and unmeaning fez. The costly turban, that bound the brow like a diadem, and relieved by the richness of its tints the dark hue of the other garments, has now almost entirely disappeared from the streets.'

Writing in the same period, Stratford Canning at the British Embassy in Constantinople wistfully observed that 'every person who has been absent and has returned notices the change, which has been most extraordinary. Very few years more and not a turban will exist . . . employees of every description now wear the red cap . . . no gold embroidery, no jewels, no pelisses.'

But just as the 'hideous and unmeaning fez' of the 1830s had become a cherished symbol of Turkish orthodox and Islamic identity by the 1920s, so a later generation of foreigners would bemoan the abolition of a hat which had become, in the words of Sir Harry Luke writing in the 1950s, 'part of the picturesque variety of becoming and aesthetically pleasing clothes'. Harry A. Franck, an American writer and journalist, wrote in 1928: 'To one coming from still colourful Syria and the lands south of it, the arrival in a defezzed Turkey was almost painful . . . the crowd was as drab as a bunch of Italian subway muckers . . . the average gathering of Turkish men suggests a tramp convention.' Like the Turks themselves, foreign travellers had adapted to the fez until they too felt it worth defending.

Unlike the Turks, however, these travellers did not seem to regard the prohibition of turbans and fezzes as a moral issue, and made no suggestion that personal preference rather than the law should dictate one's dress. Rather, the tone of their observations was aesthetic outrage, as if the Turks served merely to bring colour and decoration to the landscapes through which these travellers passed. It was hard to imagine that the Turks shared their view. 'We can't possibly wear fezzes,' will they have exclaimed in the 1830s? 'Think of Julia Pardoe's new book.' 'Surely not flat caps,' will they have agonized in the 1920s? 'Harry A. Franck won't forgive us.' 'I don't know what Sir Harry will say,' will they have shaken their heads ominously in the 1950s, 'what with all these aesthetically unpleasing clothes.'

But Sir Harry was more sympathetic when he made the following observation in 1955, not on the visual effect of the ensemble but on the Turks themselves. 'I have seen bald old white beards,' he wrote, 'look shamefaced in their cast-off *shapkas*, obviously and uncomfortably aware that with their fezzes has gone something of their human dignity.'

After an absence of five years, a war damage assessor called Harold Armstrong landed on Turkey's southern coast one summer's day in 1928. The impact of the hat laws struck Armstrong the moment he set foot on the shore. He saw bashed-in bowlers on barefoot porters, a villager in a decrepit straw boater selling curdled cream, and an old man in a battered tweed coat and what Armstrong described as a home-made dunce's cap. In Armstrong's description was a poignancy which did not bemoan the dowdy sights he himself was obliged to endure but rather regretted what he perceived among these people as an engrained sense of affront, as if their identities had been stolen from them. In these new hats was their rebirth, against the wishes of many of them, into a new world where God and tradition, and the order of things which had governed their lives for so long, had a vastly diminished place.

Afternoon became evening as we passed through groves of hazel and oak silvered by snow. At Sinop, I thought of the obedient old man of that town by the sea who had bought himself a brimmed hat at the market to satisfy Atatürk's new law in 1925. He was unaware that it was anything more than a *giaour*'s hat until his friends laughed at him and told him his choice of hat made him more *giaour* than the *giaour*; he had chosen a broad-rimmed, Catholic bishop's hat. When they told him so, the obedient old man lost his temper. He replaced his fez and took the *giaour*'s hat before the governor of the town, flung it on the ground, trampled on it, and gave himself up to arrest, prepared to hang rather than wear the hat of a world that was not of his choosing. In Inebolu, there had been times when I had sympathized with the banning of the fez. Now I was far enough away to think again.

We reached Samsun, easterly bastion of republicanism, in time for supper. I waited for the last bus inland in a canteen by the station. A football match was showing on the television which sat on an ornate metal sweet trolley suspended three feet below the ceiling. I watched, transfixed not only by the trolley but also by the fact that one of the teams hailed from Gaziantep, which translates as Warrior – or even destroyer of Christians – Pistachio. Atatürk had decided to assign the town an honorific prefix on account of its proud record during the War of Independence in the 1920s, evidently judging that Pistachio alone was by no means silly enough a name.

I ate stuffed peppers, watched Destroyer of Christians Pistachio get a creditable away draw, and took my seat on the bus. Outside, light fell on one of Samsun's many busts of Atatürk. The snow had perched upon his bare head. Perhaps it was the late hour, or thinking too much about Turkish clothes, but whichever way I looked at the bust it seemed to me that the snowfall had arranged itself to furnish the Gazi, the

Warrior, with one of those Türkeli flat caps. No doubt he would approve. Inland, where I was headed, the snowfall was much heavier. So I wondered whether meteorological revenge was just now being wreaked on all the unwelcome busts of the infidel Atatürk that dotted those high, reactionary steppelands as the snow topped them silently out in fezzes.

chapter seven

'There's a great stirring in Islam, something moving
on the face of the waters. They make no secret of it.
Those religious revivals come in cycles, and one was
about due now.'

John Buchan, *Greenmantle*, 1916

'Among the lower classes and the peasants, no matter
what headgear they wear, after a time it takes on a
shape similar to that of the fez.'

Report from Istanbul, *New York Times*, October 5 1930

'THE TURKS about here,' declared an exasperated Sivas missionary in the late 1800s, 'are just about the inside-outsidest
and the outside-insidest, the bottomside-upwardest and top-
side-downwardest, the backside-forwardest and the forward-
side-backwardest people I have even seen.' With weather like
this, who could blame them?

Not long before our arrival, I'd woken to the burr of the
engine as the bus climbed in low gear through the night, and
found my head stuck fast to the ice that had formed on the
inside of the window. When I pulled gently away, I left three
of my favourite hairs buried in permafrost.

Anyone who has seen films of the late 1950s when everybody travelled BOAC and always stopped, presidential-style,
at the top of the steps when disembarking to appear thoroughly
staggered by the heat will know what it felt like, but at the
other end of the thermometer, arriving in Sivas, even if it was
only by bus. 'Jesus Christ,' I remembered mumbling – the
wrong divinity but the right expletive – as I disembarked at
four thousand feet beneath a blue-black sky sequined with stars

and a crescent moon honed razor sharp as if by the carving action of frozen floes of air. Desiccated ice and snow, light as moon dust, flurried at my feet and swirled around my ankles, and for a brief moment I might have been a rock legend, but one that would die young if he did not find shelter.

It was -21° celsius, a meat-freezer city relieved only by the stipple of street lights and the warm yellow glow still showing at the last few windows of its insomniac residents. Around me, the steppe extended into an indistinct distance on all sides but beyond it the moonlit jags of white peaks rose clear into the sky.

The jaw of the slumbering hotel receptionist had come to rest on the counter, where a thin thread of saliva was gradually working its way earthwards from a slack mouth. He came to on my approach, wiped away the dribble with the back of his hand, transferred it to the seat of his trousers, and steered the hotel register towards me. The scrawl of visitor entries spidered across the pages. I dreamt of turning the pages of Sivas hotel registers that the moths had long since eaten, to find the entries for the closing months of 1925, of military judges and hangmen.

In November, 1925, *The Times* in London imagined 'the friends of the old order wearing the fez as a night cap, taking it reverently out of a secret drawer, and dropping upon it tears of forbidden affection'. But the people of Sivas, as they were soon to prove, would not stop at tears.

In December of that year, when no one could have blamed them for staying home and keeping warm, the people of Sivas took to the streets, the mayor and several town councillors at their head, railing at the iniquitous hat laws. Protest posters were plastered upon the buildings and the green flag of Islam was unfurled. Rioting broke out in Erzerum to the east where demonstrators closed down the bazaar and gathered in front of the pro-Atatürk governor's house, chanting that they would never recognize the authority of infidel officials. In Maraş to the south, the town which Atatürk had named Hero Maraş after its record during the Independence War, they gathered at the main mosque to denounce the laws. In Trabzon, defiant crowds wore their fezzes and accused the wicked government of irreligion.

A state of emergency had been imposed earlier that year to deal with a revolt in the Kurdish provinces in the south-east. Since these extraordinary powers had not yet been withdrawn, they could now quite constitutionally be deployed against fez wearers. The military tribunals which had recently dealt with armed, often fanatical Kurdish rebels were now directed to deal equally ruthlessly with people wearing the wrong kind of hats. The Navy dispatched a warship to move east along the Black Sea coast. The warship anchored off the town of Rize where rioters had threatened to kill panama wearers, her presence indication if any were needed that the government would go to whatever lengths were necessary to contain the riots – even to the point of deploying irony. For as her brooding grey shadow hung over Rize harbour, did it once register that the menacing battlecruiser, now in the service of the infidels, was named the *Hamidiyeh* in honour of Abdul Hamid II, one of the great fez-wearing Sultans? Or that Hamidiyeh was also the very name given to the particular type of fez favoured by Abdul Hamid II, a boxy model with only the slightest of tapers between rim and crown? Or was the appreciation of irony those days in Rize perhaps diminished by the prospect of long prison sentences or even the gallows?

For under martial law, few fez wearers would receive anything as innocuous as the three-month sentences specified by the hat legislation. Many of them would be faced with the ultimate test of their faith; of the earthbound pull of gravity against the noose on the one hand, and the ascension to paradise supposedly guaranteed by the fez wearer's tassle, which would prevail? The first sentences were passed in Erzerum on November 28. Most of the hundred and fourteen found guilty on charges varying between incitement to riot and violation of the Hat Laws received sentences of between two and ten years. Three were condemned to death. On December 21, two men were sentenced to hang in Giresun for refusing to abandon their fezzes; several others received long prison terms with hard labour for the same offence. Later in December, eight people were hung in Rize. On January 18 1926, twenty-two people were sentenced in Hero Maraş, six of them to death. Hassib Bey, the ex-deputy for the town, received ten years in spite of his ostensibly reasonable defence that he had not worn a hat since he had not been able to find one in the town. The six were executed the next day, on a cold January morning; among them were a local preacher, a pilgrim, the mayor of a nearby village, and a local muezzin. On February 10, six men in the central Turkish city of Kayseri received jail sentences of up to fifteen years for making anti-hat propaganda. And the author of an attack on infidel hats which was placarded on the walls of a Sivas village was hanged by the sentence of a local tribunal.

Even on the European side of the Bosphorus, Constantinople people were arrested for fez wearing and for publishing samizdat tracts with titles like 'Hats and Imitating the Frank'. A deputy in the Turkish Parliament who publically objected to the Hat Laws and had voted against the legislation was spotted wearing his unrimmed kalpak in Ankara. He was eventually charged with incitement and stripped of his rank.

If the authorities presumed that such draconian measures would do for the fez, then they were mistaken. By 1929, mass arrests of fez wearers were still commonplace across the country. Then, in October 1930, they found the fez packages in Bursa.

One hundred and fourteen packages of forbidden fezzes were uncovered by the security forces in this western city. The packets contained enough fezzes to dress a majority of the town's male population. The authorities claimed the discovery as a major security success but it might as well have been taken as indication of just how widespread the illegal fez trade had become. A warning was issued that anyone found engaging in the fez trade would be subject to the ultimate sanction.

Two months later, a revolt broke out in the town of Menemen, or Omelette, near Izmir. A local dervish called Mehmet, who regarded it as his divine mission to wage a holy war against the Kemalist regime, masterminded a plot that envisaged co-ordinated uprisings in Omelette and the nearby towns of Manisa and Balikesir combining to culminate in the sack of Izmir and the fall of the Kemalists, the restitution of the Caliphate and the triumphant return of the fez.

Dervish Mehmet embarked with eight of his religious lieutenants on a forty-day fast, an advanced course in outrage designed to ready them for insurrection. On the first day, they carried a stock of dates and a large jar of water into a room at Mehmet's house and, after locking themselves in, they each ate forty dates and drank plenty of water. On the days that followed, they each ate one date less and drank proportionately less water, a countdown to the fortieth day when, half-starved, mostly crazed, and wholly out of dates, they sallied forth in the name of God and fezzes.

Unfortunately, they quite forgot about Manisa and Balikesir. They could eat dates, but clearly could not keep to them. But for this, the revolt's impact might have been far reaching. As it was, when Dervish Mehmet and his incensed retinue set out to raise the ire of the people of Omelette, their fellow conspirators in Manisa and Balikesir were still at home, their date-eating far from concluded.

A large and animated crowd gathered. Amidst the calls for the restoration of Islamic law, the overthrow of the godless regime, the restoration of the Arabic script and of the fez, a young soldier was shot. Dervish Mehmet hacked the head from the corpse and paraded it round the town. A further nine lives – a nightwatchman, a young teacher, four local residents, and three rioters – were lost in the ensuing fracas.

Martial law was immediately imposed on the area and

some two hundred offenders, largely sheikhs and religious teachers but also policemen and officers of the state sympathetic to the uprising, were tried in January 1931. On February 3, twenty-eight people were hanged, among them a Jewish shopkeeper named Joseph who was accused of applauding the death of the young soldier. Even so, as he tied his own rope and kicked away the stool, Joseph shouted: 'Long live the Turkish Republic.'

But it was the dramatic escape from the gallows of a young man called Ismail Hussein that dominated the headlines. His captors mistakenly assumed from the way Ismail held his hands behind his back that the young man was already secured. But at the last moment he threw off his noose, leapt from the gallows, broke through the cordon of troops, and disappeared into the crowd.

For two weeks, the twenty-five-year-old ran the gauntlet of the authorities. He was rumoured to have been spirited away to the Greek islands but in fact had taken to the winter hills behind the town. From there, he might have migrated into Turkish lore as a fez-wearing bandit, like the writer Yaşar Kemal's Mehmet in his masterpiece novel, *Mehmet My Hawk*. The Turkish Robin Hood, Mehmet denies the authority of the state and is sheltered by sympathetic villagers. He strikes fear and awe into those who hunt him, at one with the mountain, its escape routes, and the hidden valleys in which he may find sanctuary.

But Ismail Hussein did not find his bandits and thence his escape into folklore. Instead, he succumbed to hunger and cold, and on his bedraggled arrival at a village was promptly handed over to the authorities in return for the thousand lira reward that they had posted. Ismail Hussein was successfully hanged on February 18 1930.

Such, however, was the continued resistance to the Hat Laws that rumours of their imminent repeal began to circulate. A cargo ship containing tens of thousands of fezzes bound for Bulgaria and its ethnic Turkish community was delayed for several weeks off the city which had recently been renamed Istanbul. The delay was the work of a prominent merchant who, inclined to believe in the rumours and looking to turn a quick profit, turned to understanding friends high up in the port authorities. Clearly, however, what friends the merchant had in the ministry responsible for hats were not so influential, for the rumours rapidly dispersed. The merchant was eventually obliged to allow the ship to proceed and to pay considerable demurrage charges.

In fact, as late as 1947, some six hundred people were being arrested annually for infringement of the Hat Laws. Those who had reluctantly succumbed to the ways of the infidel rarely did so unconditionally, and wore handkerchiefs on their heads beneath the hat to stop it defiling them. Police were detailed to pull the hats from suspects' heads, remove any handkerchiefs they found there, and jam the hats hard on to the crowns. And in 1950, in anticipation of the new religious freedoms promised by the popular opposition party, a wave of fez wearing occurred across the East.

It was in a village near Sivas in the late 1930s that the writer Lilo Linke met 'an old man with a white beard and a brown woollen cap – the nearest thing to a fez that he was allowed to wear'. The old man, resentful as ever at the Hat Laws, invited Linke to his house to hear his story. In spite of the laws, the old man had continued to wear his fez until the head of the village, that 'bastard pig of a man', had eventually fined him. His response was simply to stay indoors, befezzed, for as long as he could bear it. After two weeks, however, his resistance broke and he sent his son to the market in Sivas with instructions to buy him a hat, resigned to the fact that most of the other villagers had long since fallen in with the new laws and figuring that his God could hardly blame him for the irreligious impositions of the state. So the old man waited. 'And one day,' he told Linke, '*inshallah*, the wicked government would be swept away; until then, he kept his fez carefully hidden.'

Governments were indeed swept away, most of them on the whim of disenchanted army officers, but the fez policy of those that replaced them has remained almost invariably unchanged, and Turkey's old men are still waiting. As late as 1980, during another period of martial law in Turkey, Philip Glazebrook was travelling through eastern Turkey on a journey that would eventually become the basis for his classic account *Journey to Kars*. On the road east of Erzurum, Glazebrook found himself sitting on a bus next to an 'old fellow in a kind of turban' when they were stopped at an army road block. The old man's reaction was to remove the turban and replace it with 'a cap drawn from the bosom of his shirt'. Once they were clear of the road block, the old man replaced the cap with his turban, flouting a law which seems ridiculous rather than sinister only because it was circumvented in so dismissively perfunctory a fashion.

I remembered the turban I'd seen in Soapmakers two weeks earlier, and several similar ones I'd glimpsed since, dun head-wraps, Mrs Mop-style, with none of the neatness of the Indian equivalent. The turban was definitely about. How had it endured as part of the Turkish dress in spite of a hundred-and-sixty-year ban whereas the fez appeared to have been all but eradicated in sixty-five years?

Glazebrook's old man supplied the clue. Whereas the turban could be whipped off at the first sign of danger and buried in a pocket, as the old man so neatly demonstrated, the inflexible structure of the fez was not suited to such pragmatic resistance. Nor indeed was its colour. For while the turbans I'd seen in Turkey tended to be greys, beiges and faded yellows, unlikely to attract the censorious attention of officious policemen and soldiers, the fez was a defiant, unabashed, and conspicuous maroon that knew not a jot about camouflage. And there was dashing gallantry in that. It was the headgear equivalent of the Charge of the Light Brigade.

Ever since my arrival in Turkey weeks earlier, my own fez had languished at the bottom of my bag. No gallant, I was fearful of wearing it. Besides, it seemed unseemly to wear as a writerly experiment a hat for which people had once been hanged. In Sivas, it struck me, the impoverished tourist's hat I had bought in Pomegranate almost a year before might be restored to something of its true former danger, the badge of overt, uncompromised resistance that its history, shape, and colour had made it. Again, I was reminded of Yaşar Kemal's glamorous fictional brigand, Mehmet, who is handed the uniform by which he is initiated when he first flees to the mountains: 'Each brigand was wearing a red fez, as is the custom in the mountains, where the red fez is the badge of brigandage. A brigand wearing a cap or hat, as men now do in the villages and cities, has never yet been seen.' Mehmet is arguably the most popular character in modern Turkish literature. But in the eyes of the Turkish authorities, he has long been a subversive, wearing a subversive's hat. And like the hat, the book, first published in 1958, was outlawed itself for a period by the Turkish authorities.

In my mind, I figured, something of Mehmet's fictional heroics, resisting the wrongs perpetrated or at least condoned by the state, had rubbed off on all of Turkey's fez wearers. Fez wearing, fez trading, defiance of the Hat Laws, were brave if bizarre defences of a cherished way of life. In their defence of the fez was a refusal to accept the affront inherent in the Hat Laws; that by changing the hats of the people, the government could instantly reinvent them as citizens in the required Western image, as if they were ciphers, *tabulae rasae*, empty heads curiously immune to the centuries that had formed them.

'Your occupation, please,' the receptionist interrupted my musings as I stared at the register in the Sivas hotel. 'Write down your occupation.' Like other travellers who had passed through Ledgerland, that vast tract of Asia and the Middle East ridden by bureaucracy, I might have observed the old tradition and described my occupation as Time Lord, microlite pilot, or some other such nonsense for the simple pleasure of the receptionist's subsequent nod, satisfied in spite of his total lack of English that all was in order. But tonight, daring to hope I might be near my quarry, I instead wrote 'fez researcher'. No act of resistance, no gesture of solidarity was ever so covert, so compromised. The receptionist yawned and handed me a key. He evidently spoke English.

'You won't find fezzes here,' he said dismissively. 'We don't wear them. Good night.'

'Ah, a modern Turk,' I muttered to myself, and took myself off to bed.

I was back on the case again the next morning even as I awoke, and palmed away the condensation at the window. I had developed an obsessive's habit – of examining crowds from the neck up, my gaze skimming along at about five feet like a low-flying reconnaissance plane in the hope of glimpsing that maroon flash of resistance. But Sivas' main street was the same, a slouching sea of flat caps and bobble hats. Julia Pardoe, the nineteenth-century writer, had disparaged the befezzed Turkish crowd by comparing it to a sea of poppies. Was it in some way indicative of the twentieth century that I saw from my window nothing so colourful as poppies, just fragmented greys, a sunless hatscape as if of drear ploughed fields?

An accumulation of concrete façades reared above glass-fronted banks and kebab houses. Smoke poured from flues in the walls inches above the heads of crouched shoeshine boys and combined with the gouts of frozen air intermingled with cigarette smoke that streamed from their mouths; they looked irredeemably ablaze.

The ice that covered the street and pavements was worn and pockmarked. Old and unlovely, it had encased in the first winter freeze many months earlier scraps of litter and discarded bottle tops, and had imprisoned swirls of dark, muddy rain water. On the corners of buildings, crystal icicles thick as a man's arm plugged the exits of downpipes. Sivas was birdless, a place, in spite of its two hundred thousand inhabitants and the knot of buildings at its heart, that felt as arid and lonely as the steppes on every side. Desolation breezed through like spinifex tumbling down a New Mexico main street, mocking man's attempts to make it his own.

But man was here, and had been so for centuries. And in Sivas, he had built monuments between the eleventh and thirteenth centuries of such beauty that it was almost as if the civilizing power of that beauty alone had halted the desiccating march of the steppe. Now, however, those centuries were long gone, and Sivas was once more huddled down in her concrete redoubt, cowering at the expanses that surrounded it. The birds that returned here every summer from Syria and Tunisia – old outposts of the Ottoman Empire – found last year's nesting sites lost among fresh winter falls of broken masonry.

Ever since the decline of the Selcuks, in fact, the masonry of Anatolia had been breaking up. Like a neglected inner city, the geographical core of the Ottoman Empire fell into dereliction, and nobody cared. During the five hundred years of their pre-eminence, the Ottomans lavished their pride on Constantinople and other far-flung jewels in their possession, Aleppo and Cairo, Damascus and Baghdad. Perhaps it was of no consequence to them that the Imperial heartlands were fast becoming wasteland when vast expanses of Empire lay beyond. Indeed, to have fostered the Anatolian and Turkish core would have undermined the Empire's wider territorial legitimacy – predicated on quite another instinct, the commonality of Islam. Consequently, as the Anatolian hinterland was neglected, so its cultural heritage was buried amongst the forgotten ruins of the peoples who had once settled it.

The time came, of course, that the declining Ottoman Empire so mislaid or surrendered those distant territorial jewels that it was reduced once more to its Anatolian beginnings. The birds that returned for the summer now came from lands governed by others. When Atatürk and his beleaguered aides inherited Anatolia, the sparse local population needed convincing that such a place even existed. 'We fight for

Turkey, for Anatolia,' Atatürk's battle cry may have sounded. 'You what?' will have been the bemused reply; it was hard to devote oneself to a national ideal when one did not even recognize the nation in question. Upon the reclamation of so submerged a consciousness, then, the very survival of Turkey depended.

Atatürk set out to restore the Anatolian ideal in Sivas, ancient capital of the Selcuks. These nomads from the east had settled here in the eleventh century. Turkish nationalist thinking, which had succeeded the cosmopolitan empire-building ideas of the Ottomans, energetically promoted the forgotten Selcuks as the original Turks, the forefathers of twentieth-century Anatolians. With the Selcuks reinstalled, the seeds of a venerable Turkish genealogy were sown. The rallying standard of Turkish resistance might now be raised.

As it was, the Selcuks were perfect for Atatürk's purposes. Early Turks they might have been, but they were also the blueprint for modern Turks as Atatürk envisaged them. Seven hundred years earlier, their civilization had been founded on many of the same beliefs that would inform Atatürk's own version of twentieth-century Turkey. They encouraged commerce, education, and the arts. Their centres of learning specialized in sciences such as mathematics, geometry, astronomy, and medicine. Theirs was a society that emphasized rational progress.

Furthermore, Sivas itself had excellent Republican credentials. Unlike Constantinople, Sivas was not tarred by the brush of Ottoman sloth and conniving. Like Ankara, destined to become the young country's new capital, it was an untainted city of the steppe. The Gazi convened a conference at Sivas in late 1919 where the ideal of Turkish unity and nationhood was expressed and fleshed out. By so doing, Atatürk singled out the steppe people of Sivas and central Anatolia as the true representatives of the Turkish national birthright. During the War of Independence, they were among his most staunch supporters. A mere six years later, when he hanged them for wearing fezzes, the people of Sivas rejected him. I wondered whether he had ever got them back.

That January morning the *Şifahiye medrese*, a Selcuk medical school, surrounded by largely unconvincing attempts at civic parkland, rang to the sound of workers as they chipped away at the icepack with the bluntened edges of their shovels. One of the outstanding buildings of the Selcuk period, the *medrese* comprised an enclosed, arcaded courtyard whose engraved and patterned stonework was of considerable complexity and beauty – walls and arches of interlacing designs where vines, stylized scallops, and a host of other motifs formed a multi-dimensional brocaded illusion. I looked at the *medrese*, found myself following the logic of a single pattern, and was drawn irresistibly to those with which it was interlinked so that I soon lost my way and my beginnings in the sculpted, exotic brilliance of it all.

The art of the *medrese* led me to imagine a nomadic people coming at last to rest, settling down. The building struck me as a declaration of residence, a distillation of all the Selcuks had absorbed on their progress through the civilizations of the east, the jackdaw education of a people moving, moving, leaving few traces until they arrived and built as if – now that they had shed their nomadic skin for the very last time – they and their kind might last for ever. On the example of their reclaimed ancestors, Atatürk had hoped, the Anatolians might build themselves a twentieth-century nation.

Within the *medrese*, vaulted chambers led off the arcade on all sides. They had become the haunts of carpet dealers and of trinketeers, frequented by scrawny cats, where copper bowls, mohair socks, postcards, and keyrings were displayed. There were even fezzes stacked on shelves, but they were evidently for the few summer tourists; tamed and anodyne as they were, I doubted that anybody would be inspired to hang for this tawdry batch.

A tiny man with bright black eyes and curly hair under a

tight skull cap was watching me from the doorway of his carpet shop.

'Come,' he said, kissing me on both cheeks and leading me into his shop. 'You're looking for carpets?'

'I'm a writer,' I replied.

'Ah,' he murmured. 'Looking for ideas. Ideas are more difficult.' And he laughed heartily and hugged me. Semih would prove to be the most tactile carpet seller I had ever encountered.

He too was a writer. When not selling carpets or hugging people, Semih was in Iran studying Islamic society, and had written several books on the subject.

'You have read the Koran?' he asked me.

'No,' I admitted.

'I have,' he replied. 'I have also read Marx, Mao, Lenin, the Bible, Foucault, Sartre, and Bentham. The Koran is the best. You will drink tea?'

I nodded. 'You think an Iranian-style Islamic society is the answer for Turkey?' I asked him.

Semih's laugh was explosive and I was almost knocked from my pile of carpets by the accompanying hug.

'You people are scared of such things! But you know there are churches and synagogues in Iran. There are Christians and Jews. There's religious freedom. There's nothing to be afraid of.'

As he spoke, I found myself composing a sceptic's collage of images including the veil, an alcohol ban, hostages taken in the name of Allah, and Salman Rushdie and Uğur Mumcu.

'And will it happen here, Semih?'

He didn't hug me this time. He looked at me instead with an absolute conviction. 'Islam is rising,' he said, his hands separating as if to describe an increasingly exaggerated fish. 'Islam is rising here in Sivas, and in cities like Konya, Erzurum, Diyarbakır, and Tokat. It will come,' he pronounced. 'Maybe it will take ten years. But it will come.'

'And it will come with an alcohol ban? With Koranic law? With fezzes?'

'With what?' he exclaimed, and the ensuing hug actually threw me clear of the carpets and rolled us across the floor. Bodyguards generally do this in the instant before a pattern of bullet-holes is stitched across one's front. By contrast Semih was merely being expressive. He helped me to my feet and dusted me down.

'An alcohol ban, yes. Koranic law, yes. Fezzes, no. No no no. The Koran is clear on alcohol. The Koran is clear on Koranic law. The Koran says nothing about fezzes. I interpret the Koran to discourage brimmed hats but you see that around you already in skull caps like mine. And you'll see turbans.'

'But why not the fez?' I insisted. 'Good Muslims died for the fez, were imprisoned for the fez in Sivas just sixty-five years ago. Don't you owe it something?'

'Good Muslims they may have been but they were also reactionary old fools. The fez, you see, stands for so many things. Islam, yes, but it also means the time of empire and it's for this reason that good liberals like me don't want it back. When Atatürk banned the fez, he was certainly attempting to undermine Islam but he was also distancing his new republic from the vestiges of empire.'

'Do you therefore approve of Atatürk?'

'I admire him for his republicanism. I object to his attempts to undermine Islam. But we shall put that right. We have been putting that right since the man died.'

The man had died in 1938. Until then, the rising tide of democracy had lapped at Turkey but had been held in abeyance by Atatürk's iron grasp on the country. Democracy would come, but meanwhile Atatürk had demonstrated to those who might otherwise have opposed him that largely benign dictatorship of the kind he practised was best suited to Turkey, a country in radical transition. One way or another, the opposition was soon enough convinced of this.

In the aftermath of Atatürk's death, however, the democratic tendency rapidly gained strength. Suddenly, politicians found themselves responding to two contradictory stimuli. On the one hand was the recent memory of Atatürk and his ideological legacy – chiefly secularism; on the other was democracy. In the fast-track learning process (multi-party democracy was adopted in Turkey in 1945) politicians quickly came to understand that promising to extend religious freedoms meant votes and led to power in Turkey. Nodding regularly at the memory of Atatürk was important too, but nodding was sufficient.

Such is democracy. Upholding the honoured secular principles of the republic confounded the democratic process since the people, without even thinking to criticize their beloved Atatürk, voted for re-Islamicization whenever it was proposed. Islam quickly emerged as the outstanding electoral carrot. Gradually, vote-seeking politicians picked at the secular edifice. In 1947, a law restricting religious teaching in schools was lifted. A foreign exchange law was passed giving priority to those who needed it for the express purpose of making the *haj* to Mecca. In 1950, the call to prayer was once more permitted to be made in Arabic, the traditional language of Islam, rather than Turkish. Over the years the secular education system was gradually eroded until a period in the 1980s when Islamic education was made compulsory for all students in Turkey, even the non-Muslims among them. Now, vocational religious schools turn out some fifty thousand young Islamic priests a year, guaranteeing a massive oversupply that even the extensive mosque-building programme in Turkey cannot absorb, and so resurgent religious sentiment spills over and on to the streets.

In the city of Konya there were attempts in the late eighties to introduce segrated bus services for men and women. In 1991, the Byzantine basilica of Aya Sofya – originally Christian, then converted into a mosque by the Ottomans, and then deconsecrated as a museum by Atatürk in 1935 – was once again granted the right to hold religious services, and the call to prayer could once more be heard from its minarets.

In Urfa, the town in south-eastern Turkey which Atatürk had prefixed as Glorious after the Independence War, the Refah party mayor spent much of 1989 converting churches into mosques, banning alcohol in public places, and closing down fourteen of the town's fifteen cinemas.

In the same year, the country's devout Muslim President, Turgut Özal, ordered that Turkish flags be dipped in deference to the Iranian Ayatollah on the occasion of his death. It was reported that the Turkish flag flew at half mast outside NATO's headquarters in Brussels where embarrassed Turkish officials were simultaneously encamped, lobbying to join the EC. A cinema in Ankara stopped screening the harmless nonsense movie *Naked Gun* after threats were received from Islamic elements objecting to the depiction of the Ayatollah sporting a punk haircut.

The Islamic resurgence in Turkey is spearheaded by Refah. Bankrolled by Saudi Arabia, the party can actually deliver on its promises to construct not only mosques but also hospitals and schools. The disaffected suburbs and forgotten backwaters where Atatürk's promises of progress, education, and acceptance by Europe sound increasingly hollow are a fertile breeding ground for Islamic revivalism.

Nobody was surprised when Refah took Sivas province in the general elections of 1991 with some 35% of the vote. At the local elections a year later, Refah's average vote right across the country rose to an unprecedented 25%. When Semih had said ten years, he was not exaggerating the size of the Islamic fish.

Just as Semih was leaving to see some business acquaintances who, I imagined, were already bracing themselves in anticipation of his arrival, two young men wandered into his shop. They were dressed in that Turkish sartorial no-man's-land, fatally stranded by an attempt to convey two conflicting impressions at once. Their jeans and T-shirts suggested the strutting young blade, while their aged pinstripe jackets aimed at the impression of worldly businessmen. Needless to say, the girls would laugh at the jackets, the business associates at the T-shirts.

One of them shook my hand, offered me a cigarette, introduced himself as Irfan, and sat down. Guardedly, his friend held back.

'You're a Christian?' Irfan asked me, and I nodded.

'You're happy?'

I nodded again.

'Islam,' he declared without preamble, 'is better than Christianity because it came five hundred years later. It's an improvement on your religion.'

'You mean it's better because it's newer?'

He nodded. I frowned. Just because his T-shirt was brand new didn't change the fact that a cryptic English message 'Luxury Travel Kit – Rowing Club' was emblazoned upon it, and it was hideous. But I knew enough about Turks to know that I should not offend Irfan's T-shirt. Instead, I declared that just because Jim Jones had set up shop in Guyana some fifteen hundred years after the Prophet was no guarantee, as the Paraquat amply proved, of a quality spiritual product.

'You are not being serious,' Irfan replied with a slight smile, but with a smile nevertheless, which compared favourably with the stony countenance of his friend.

'Our book, the Koran, never changes,' the friend pronounced. 'The rules are the rules and we stick to them.'

I took the silence that followed as a cue to respond in kind.

'Our book never changes,' I said, 'but we interpret it differently as time passes.'

'To suit yourselves?'

'To suit the times,' I replied. 'Do you drink?'

He looked shocked; drinking was forbidden. Irfan smiled. 'Sometimes I am a bad Muslim and drink raki,' he conceded graciously.

Thank God, I thought, and turned to his friend. 'You smoke.'

'Of course,' he said. 'It is not forbidden.'

'But it is as bad for you as drink.'

'But you smoke too.'

'But not because my God allows me to. Because I am a fool.'

'Everybody is a fool without Allah,' he replied, running his bracelet of prayer beads between his fingers.

I was beginning to sympathize with the missionary's opinion of these upside-downest people. I persevered, intent only on convincing the friend that his arguments, and not his religion, were blather.

'Why does the Koran forbid drinking?' I asked him.

'It makes you feel bad. It is not good for you.'

'And if there had been cigarettes, especially Turkish cigarettes, at the time of the Koran, do you not think your book would have banned them? So, you have a problem which you solve by updating the book, which is not to say you change it. You don't offend Allah by adapting to new problems that He cannot have foreseen.'

'Allah foresees everything,' the friend pronounced.

'All right,' I said. 'Pork.'

'*Haram*,' the friend fired back: forbidden.

'And why?'

'Bad microbes,' he replied cautiously.

'At that time, microbes, yes. It was hot; there were no fridges but now you have fridges . . .'

'Of course we have fridges. We are very modern in Sivas.'

'So eat pork!'

'It is forbidden.'

We were into a serious tailspin towards mutual resentment. I reminded myself how much they had to resent. Since Atatürk's reforms, the Turks have been obliged to observe the Christian weekend and to live their lives by an alien calendar predicated on a principally Christian birth, whose miraculous nature they seem to find inherently offensive. They also resent the fact that the infidels dare to use the name of their country to describe the traditional mainstay of the feast that celebrates that birth, which just so happens to be an extremely ugly bird. The French steer clear of insult – if only in Turkey – by looking further east to name the turkey after India, a practice copied, not surprisingly, by the Turks. Perhaps, I mused, I should have been French, but soon thought better of it.

As it was, I was in for the full works.

'Kaptan Koostow,' said the zealot, punching out the syllables as if to pronounce the death sentence on Christianity. 'Kat Stevens, Anthony Quinn, Kristopher Kolumbus.' This was missionary Islam's role of honour; those famous names who, along with a number of servicemen and women in the course of the Gulf War, had turned to Allah.

I wished them well, I replied, tried to think of celebrated converts to Christianity, could only come up with Salman Rushdie, and wisely decided against enlisting him in my defence. Along with a guidebook in which the existence of Kurds in the country had been controversially noted, secular Turkey had banned *The Satanic Verses* in 1989.

'But people in Turkey are free in principle to convert to Christianity if they so wish?' I put to the zealot.

A stab of outrage passed across his face. 'No, no,' he replied, wagging his finger. 'No, no, no.' We had arrived at the non-negotiable point where Islam finally rejects the West, certain of its superiority.

Irfan had been closely examining the weave of a carpet. I assumed by so doing he was abstaining from the argument. But he soon put me right.

'Muslims cannot come to Christianity, with its tolerance of abortion and contraception,' he said. 'Christianity is full of wrongs.'

I tried one more time, suggesting that population control, even one as radical as abortion, was to the good of mankind if the option was massive overpopulation and the famines and conflicts that invariably attended it. 'All we know,' said Irfan with finality, 'is that it is not for us to give and take life, but for Allah. Very few babies are being born in the West, I believe. Here, we are always having babies. This makes us the future, this makes us powerful.'

From sweet Irfan, this was intimidating indeed, religious dogma co-opted to feed the notion of a weak, infertile and unpeopled West submitting to the irresistible virility of Islam.

The friend administered the *coup de grâce*. 'You say you are happy. No, you think you are happy. You would be happier with us.'

Not in your T-shirt, I mused, abandoning myself to frustrated insult. 'You are trying to convert me,' I told him; turning me Turk.

'No,' he smiled unctuously. 'Nothing of the sort. You will come of your own free will.'

A shiver ran through me. 'You are cold,' he replied in a marked change of mood that signalled a welcome return to Turkish courtesies. 'Let me bring you some tea.'

And after the shiver, the echo that had caused it; I was reminded of the words I had read only that morning. With considerable difficulty, I had scaled the ice-bound steps of the Sivas Museum, housed in the building where Atatürk's Conference of 1919 had taken place. Words of his appeared on a plaque. 'In my opinion,' they read, 'a dictator is one whose will dominates the people. As for me, it is my wish to rule not through breaking hearts but by winning them.' In his words and those of the young zealot was the common belief that their will was the general will. The truth, they each seemed to believe, only needed explaining. But apparently there were two truths, and like Turkey itself they were faced in opposite directions. And in the ice of the long Sivas winter, they had set hard.

The Sivas Museum was not up to much. In fact, most interesting was the unintended glimpse into an office where a man was sitting behind a desk. He was holding the pennant of an Istanbul football club called Fenerbahce in one hand while his other brandished a comb which he ran lovingly through the pennant's tassles.

The tiniest gesture can trigger a range of memories and associations, and in this case that single combing action carried me to the streets of nineteenth-century Turkey, streets filled not with today's shoeshine boys, but with tassle-combers kept constantly busy. For fez tassles, traditionally made of unspun silk, were constantly entangled by the effects of wind, rain, and dust. Was this a fossilized gesture from the past, turning up in a fezless world to ensure that the man behind the desk might one day rise effortlessly to Paradise, he and the entire squad of the Fenerbahce football team?

I considered this for a while before deciding it was more likely couch indolence, the filling of time. For the museum man's desk had been immaculate. Work drifted in as rarely as winter sunlight, lingered briefly and moved on after a cursory phone call, a dictated memo. Similarly, the table tops in the foyer of my hotel, had been covered by pieces of bubbly transparent plastic packaging cut precisely to size. When I fingered them in my own spare time, I noticed that not a bubble was intact. There was time in Sivas to run prayer beads endlessly between fingers and to track down every plastic packaging bubble, and pop them one by one to ease the slow passing of the hours.

Five months later, on July 2 1993, my hotel register in Sivas would be marked by the entries of a group of Turkish intellectuals and poets who had booked in while taking part in a summer arts festival. But the presence of the group, clearly identified with the secular left wing, irritated the city's Islamic community. When it was revealed that among the visitors was a well-known author, who had published inflammatory sections of *The Satanic Verses* to demonstrate his support for the principle of free speech, the city's Muslims were incensed. After Friday prayers, they marched on the cultural centre, recited from the Koran, burnt the statutory American flag, and then headed for the hotel. They torched cars outside and then set light to the hotel lobby. The register, and many of those who had scribbled their entries in it earlier that day, burnt with the hotel. Later, thirty-six corpses were found among the wreckage, some of them with bullet wounds. Among the protesters, it struck me, were doubtless the grandchildren of the fez wearers of 1925, responding to a similar provocation by the godless but this time leaving thirty-six charred and bullet-ridden corpses among the ruins of my hotel. The city's mayor had stood at their head then; now he was seen assaulting the Turkish publisher even as that man clambered terrified from the burning building.

History had repeated itself, perhaps so that its message might be heard; the Turks of Sivas were set in opposite directions.

chapter eight

'To remove the head-dress of whatever kind is, in the
East, an act of discourtesy; to strike it off is a deep
insult.'

– Encyclopaedia Britannica

IN EARLY January 1928, an apology headed 'Turkish Formal
Dress – does not comprise a fez' appeared in the *New York
Times*. A Washington dispatch describing the New Year
reception at the White House had included an inflammatory
reference to the 'long gold embroidered coats with bright
green fez' worn by the Turkish Embassy staff. The affronted
Turkish Ambassador had fired off a letter to the editor of the
newspaper in which he pointed out that the fez was not green
and, anyway, had been abolished in Turkey several years
earlier. 'Our only uniform,' he fumed, 'is the frock coat or
black morning coat. It was in this that we appeared at the
White House, I and the personnel of the Embassy.'

The *New York Times* stood corrected. The paper had
offended the Ambassador not only by associating modern
Turkey with the fez but by describing that hat as green, the
traditional colour of Islam and of the turbans that priests and
other Turks who had made the pilgrimage to Mecca customarily wore around their fezzes. It had dressed modern Turkey
in the wardrobe of religious reaction.

The apology, however, only served to mire the paper more
deeply by suggesting that the confusion arose from the fact that
members of the Egyptian Legation had worn the *tarboosh* at the
reception while the Persians had worn the *kullah*, which both
happened to resemble the fez. For the Ambassador, the representative of a country which regarded itself as modern, secular,

and above all nationalist, being confused with Arabs and Persians was hardly better than being presumed to wear a fez.

In fact, the resemblances were beyond dispute. The *tarboosh* was essentially no more than the Arabic version of the fez. But it was from the histories, of both the *tarboosh* and the Iranian *kullah*, that the most striking parallels with the fez emerged before these two hats followed its lead into the fancy-dress basket of history.

For centuries, neighbouring Persia was the Ottoman Empire's greatest rival. Sultan and Shah tended to view each other with profound mistrust, mainly because of their respective claims to pre-eminence within the Islamic hierarchy. Persia, which had never fallen under Ottoman control, was fez free. The national *kullah* was a fleece hat, which actually shared the most obvious similarities with the *kalpak*. Come the late 1920s, however, the Shah was quite ready to Westernize by hat, after the example of Atatürk's Turkey.

First, the Shah replaced the *kullah* with a peaked hat similar to the French kepi, and called it the Pahlavi after the dynasty that bore his name. In 1933 the army spearheaded sartorial reforms, just as it had in Turkey, by adopting a cap of more conspicuously Western design. In 1934, the Shah ordered road labourers in the government's employ to wear a full brim, a degree more Western than the peak. Besides, claimed the Shah, just as Mahmud II had done a century earlier, brims offered better protection from the sun.

In 1935, the Shah announced that all ministers, deputies, and officials discard the Pahlavi in place of European headgear and adopt the attendant custom of doffing the hat in salutation and upon entering a building.

But, just as in Turkey, it was the ordinary citizens who were subjected to the greatest humiliations. In his journey through Iran and Afghanistan in 1933 and 1934, the basis of the classic travel book *The Road to Oxiana*, the traveller and writer Robert Byron encountered Iranian men wearing home-made peaks fashioned from old cardboard boxes attached to their *kullahs*.

They perhaps had the worst of it, however, in Afghanistan where the fez was not introduced until the beginning of the twentieth century. But barely had his people got used to this belated innovation that Habibullah Khan was confusing them further by moving on to tweeds, and taking up golf. His son, Amanullah, who took over in 1919, continued with his father's fast-track policy. By 1928, he had kitted his wife out in cloche hats and short skirts. His introduction of the bowler hat was the last straw, and Amanullah was soon deposed. 'The local officials have learnt,' wrote Robert Byron in May 1934, 'thanks to Amanullah's bowler, that the people they seek to inspire with it are still prepared to fight before throwing away tradition for a mess of technical pottage.'

In Egypt, the *tarboosh* had originally been adopted several decades before Turkey, but its use was reinvigorated there and throughout the Middle East by the imperial endorsement of Mahmud II. When Atatürk banned it in Turkey, the *tarboosh* experienced a surge of popularity in Egypt on the back of Islamic and anti-republican reaction. Egyptian college students who had formerly persisted with turbans finally forsook them for the *tarboosh*.

But the *tarboosh*'s high standing in Egypt could not protect it on overseas duty in Turkey, as an Egyptian minister called Hamsa Bey discovered to his cost. At an official government banquet in Ankara on October 29 1932, the ninth anniversary of the founding of the republic, Atatürk espied the befezzed minister among the crystal and the cigarette smoke. From this moment in the proceedings, accounts differ. According to one, the Gazi took exception and dispatched a message to Hamsa Bey on a silver salver which read, 'Tell your king I do not like his uniform.' Hamsa Bey promptly left the reception.

The Turkish government, fearful of a diplomatic furore, countered with its own version of the incident. It claimed that as all the guests were in official uniform, Hamsa Bey had observed protocol to the letter in wearing his fez. 'In the course of the evening,' the release explained, 'the Gazi, seeing that the Egyptian Minister was feeling the heat, suggested from entirely friendly motives that he should remove his fez. The Minister gladly complied with the suggestion. No offence was intended and none was taken.' The Turkish explanation, however, for the Minister's sudden and undisputed departure – 'The fear that other members of the diplomatic corps might misinterpret the motive which had prompted the removal of his fez' – was hardly convincing.

Furthermore, this interpretation of the incident only seemed to spawn more sensational versions, such as that which alleged that when Hamsa Bey had bowed in front of Atatürk, the President had actually sent the man's fez flying with the back of his hand.

Whatever the truth, it is known that Hamsa Bey reported the incident to Cairo, which lodged a formal protest. For a slur upon the *tarboosh* was deemed a tilt against the old order and the monarchy at its head. Egyptian Kings Fouad and Farouk's championing of the *tarboosh* betrayed an intuitive awareness of the imminence of their own demise. Shortly after Farouk was finally overthrown on July 23 1952, Naguib, Nasser's forerunner, presented himself in front of the people without a *tarboosh*. No Egyptian leader had attempted such a thing for a hundred and fifty years.

Although Nasser never legislated against the *tarboosh* among the civilian population, he did what he could to discourage it. His Pan-Arab socialist regime branded the *tarboosh* as a vestige of the Ottoman Empire, an unwelcome reminder of Egypt's former vassal status. As in Turkey thirty years earlier, the religious authorities were put to work digging up ancient fatwas, or pronouncements, which deemed it to be perfectly acceptable for Muslims to wear hats or caps without offending either religion or country. The *tarboosh*, the newspapers claimed, symbolized reactionary fanaticism. In

September 1952, the Ministry of Finance ordered its employees to abandon the *tarboosh*. The police adopted a beret. A commission charged to examine national costume suggested replacing the *tarboosh* and *jellabaa* – the standard Egyptian cotton robe – with European hat and suit.

Iran, Egypt, and Afghanistan had gone the way of Turkey, introducing brims and throwing out fezzes or their equivalents in their frantic haste to Westernize. Now Iran was an Islamic republic, Egypt was under increasing threat from her Islamic fundamentalists, and Afghanistan was embroiled in a civil war in which the secularists and the Islamic fundamentalists were lined up against each other in the wake of the Soviet occupation. Tinkering with fezzes, it seemed, could only lead to trouble. Would Turkey go the way of such countries?

'What chance,' I would ask a British journalist specializing in Turkey several months later in Istanbul, 'an Islamic revolution in Turkey?' He thought a moment, 'Twenty years,' he replied. It was at least an improvement on Semih's ten.

※

chapter nine

I'D BEEN intending to head further east, for east was the pioneering point of the Turkish compass, the romantic's bearing. East was where one went as naturally as birds flew south. The difference of course was that birds did their flying in the autumn, and in travelling east at this time of year I was proposing a reverse migration towards temperatures that might conceivably kill me.

Semih shared my concerns. 'East?' he exclaimed. 'To Erzurum, twelve hours away by train, two thousand five hundred feet higher into the mountains than here? You don't want to go to Erzurum at this time of year,' he assured me. 'Fill a fridge with mud and stick your head in it for six months. That's Erzurum in the winter.' According to the weather reports, temperatures in Erzurum currently varied between −12° and −30° celsius. Which meant that Semih was not entirely right about fridges. The fridge, positively mild by comparison, was where you went to get warm in Erzurum. There had even been times in Sivas when the fridge had struck me as a pretty attractive kitchen appliance. In spite of the lack of wind, the temperatures were such that bank notes buried deep in my wallet would emerge crinkly with cold, tens of thousands of deep-frozen lira with their images of Atatürk chilled to the touch when I peeled them off to pay for cigarettes or lunch. I decided against heading east.

Once I'd revised my plans, I returned to Semih's shop to say goodbye. 'Yozgat,' I announced, 'I'm going to Yozgat.' He responded with an incredulous hug that seemed to expel, for ever, what little air remained in my ice-seared lungs and left me gasping among the carpets.

'Why?' he asked me once I had recovered.

Sensing I had chosen inadvisedly, I gave the practical reason; all the other roads were closed by snow.

Semih considered my predicament for a moment. 'You could always take the train to Erzurum, you know.'

So something was severely wrong with Yozgat. In fact, that had already become part of its perverse attraction; the sheer ugliness of that country town's name alone merited a visit. There was also the vaguely remembered quote from a nineteenth-century traveller's account which threw an intriguingly unlikely cast over Yozgat life: 'There was a great deal of immorality amidst the fair sex in Ankara *although nothing to what existed in Yozgat.*' (And this from an Italian doctor of the time, no slouch in the immorality stakes.)

But Semih dashed my expectations. 'Yozgat,' he told me, 'is known as the Castle of the Racists. It is the home of Mr Turkeş, the Turkish Hitler.' He observed me closely, with undisguised concern. 'You're not Armenian, are you?' Not so much short skirts, then, as brown shirts.

The bus left Sivas in a snatched hour of bright sunshine. Patches of bone-dry grass poked through the snow blanket and a thin hawk, reckless with hunger, swooped down for an improbable second look at us, the only movement on the dormant landscape below him. Evidently, his hunger had not yet driven him to Mercedes buses. I watched his wing patterns, striations of browns against the blue sky, before he turned away to pick at his own plastic bubbles until spring came.

From what Semih had told me, Yozgat was a farming community of about forty thousand souls deep in the Turkish steppe. Refah and Mr Turkeş' extreme right Nationalist Action Party, I had learned, had formed a coalition in the last election to unite Islam and Turkish nationalism under one effective vote-winning banner. They had done well nationwide, but best of all in Yozgat, where the coalition party had won the seat with about 40% of the vote. The Turkish Hitler was Yozgat's MP.

It may have been a racist's town but to call Yozgat a castle was generous in the extreme. A castle would have transformed Yozgat. Instead, there were cars buried deep in snow among a large number of unfinished tower blocks. Arriving at Yozgat bus station had the powerful effect of sending my imagination into panic-stricken overdrive so that the destinations brightly painted on the bus company windows there transmitted messages of hope and indescribable beauty. I almost cried at the thought of distant towns I had never seen but felt sure that they were all I could ever want, home and sanctuary for the rest of my life after what I had seen of Yozgat.

Only the polite enquiries of two young men prevented me from leaving Yozgat immediately and for ever. They attached themselves to me, accompanied me into town, and nursed me through my crisis. They were very attentive; perhaps, unknown to me, I had been triumphantly identified as the town's inaugural overseas tourist. Excepting those unfortunate enough to call it home, nobody had ever had cause to stop at Yozgat. When the young men told me they worked at the town's museum and would be pleased to show me round, I was tempted in the light of my museum experiences elsewhere to ask them exactly what did they think they were doing, being so uncharacteristically amenable.

Night was falling as we walked through the town's icy streets. Unearthly figures muffled against the cold disappeared down alleyways carrying translucent purple bags lumpy with fruit and vegetables. Hacking coughs sounded behind yellow-lit windowpanes. I, who had prepared myself for jackbooted Turkish supremacists wrapped in white star and crescent on red background, shorn heads, the cursory lynchings of passing outsiders, felt strangely let down. It was just an ordinary town clad in snow and concrete.

Ömer and Mehmet led me to the museum and showed me round the few pieces of Hittite masonry plundered from obscure sites near by, odd articles of early twentieth-century Anatolian clothing, the reconstruction of Yozgat life from an indeterminate period in the town's history. Then they offered me tea in an office so small that the three of us shared the only creaking desk and I was forced to dangle my legs in the wastepaper bin. Ömer emptied it for me before thoughtfully returning it upside-down so that I might rest my feet on it. They took up positions either side of me, small, studious men who reminded me vividly of barn owls.

Yozgat seemed so removed from the outside world that I half expected the young men to ask for an update on what had been going on out there beyond the outskirts of the town. What of this band called the Beatles? Americans on the moon? Just how is the twentieth century? Mehmet's actual question was far more direct. 'Bosnia,' he said. 'What do you think of Bosnia?' The question was simple, but laden with outrage.

And by turning on Turkish television at almost any time I would have understood the feeling, those countless images of a broken and burned-out Sarajevo that have left the Turks despairing and vengeful; the bombed-out mosques and teetering minarets that date from the times when Bosnia was an Ottoman province, serving to reinforce the links not only of religion but also of empire. Wisely, I allowed Mehmet to answer his own question. 'You Christians in the West do nothing,' he said bitterly. 'You let the Christian Serbs kill our people, murder and rape our women and children. Yet you allow the Muslims no weapons, people who would never think of killing or raping women and children.'

'Never ever consider such a thing,' Ömer emphasized Mehmet's words with a large gesture of the hand.

'I am not responsible for state decisions,' I replied. Sometimes you have to lie in situations like this.

They ignored my facetiousness. 'You bomb in Iraq, but you do nothing in Bosnia. And you know why?' Mehmet asked me.

'Oil,' Ömer replied for me, somehow finding a small section of available desk to thump in emphasis. 'For what do the West have to worry about in poor old Sarajevo?'

'Yes, you tell us what,' Mehmet challenged me. The way they worked was like a conversational co-operative.

I'll tell you what the West have to worry about in poor old Sarajevo, I told them. Over the years, the West has learned a few major history lessons in Sarajevo, most recently the one in 1914 which it is unlikely to forget. It knows that the Balkans are a tinderbox, I told them. It is doubtless aware of the dangers of Turkey coming to the aid of the Bosnian Muslims. It knows that Turkish involvement would be likely to provoke overt Russian support for the Serbs, not only because of the historical ties between Serbs and Russian Slavs but also because of the parallels with the situation on Turkey's eastern border where the war between Christian Armenia and Muslim Turkic Azerbaijan compels Russian and Turkish support respectively. Thinking I'd really told them, I leaned back, quite forgetting myself, and was only saved from falling off the desk backwards by the quick reflexes of two Yozgat museum assistants. The moment of persuasion was lost, my argument torpedoed by the ridiculous, and my saviours did not look impressed.

'Send in soldiers,' intoned Mehmet.

'To Bosnia,' Ömer confirmed.

'We will not stand for it much longer,' Mehmet announced.

'We have had enough,' Ömer confirmed.

'Furthermore, we will be at the rally at Taksim Square in Istanbul next week,' Mehmet said.

'Yes, we will,' added Ömer.

'Özal, our President, will be speaking although our Prime Minister disapproves.'

'Our President will speak.'

Four years earlier, it had been the same; just as now, the President had spoken, the Turks had staged rallies, and had pressed to send soldiers to another nearby country: Bulgaria. Since 1984, 'Turkish' enclaves in north-east and southern

Bulgaria, where some one and a half million Muslims lived, had been subjected to forced assimilation by the Bulgarians. Names were forcibly Bulgarianized, mosques and Turkish schools were closed, and the use of Turkish was punishable by a fine equivalent to three days' wages.

By the summer of 1989, three thousand refugees a day were arriving at the Kapikule border post between Bulgaria and Turkey. Their Lada cars were laden with bedsteads, furniture and mattresses. They came with stories of beatings, the desecration of village cemeteries, forced deportations whereby they had been issued with new red passports and told in no uncertain terms to make use of them. They had been forced to surrender wedding rings, valuables, and money on the Bulgarian side of the border. The Bulgarian authorities had found a Turkish book during a search of a young man's house. In spite of his appeals that the book had belonged to his grandfather and was only a keepsake, he was beaten heavily before being deported. By the end of July, over a hundred thousand refugees had arrived to swell the tent city populations established in western Turkey.

For his part, the Bulgarian Ambassador to Britain explained away the refugees as a hundred thousand happy tourists. 'According to the new Bulgarian legislation on foreign travel,' he declared, 'all Bulgarian citizens enjoy complete and unlimited freedom of movement.' If they don't like the way they are treated here, in loose translation from the Bulgarian, they can always bugger off.

Besides, the Bulgarian authorities argued, far from being the descendants of ethnic Turks who had migrated to Bulgaria during Ottoman times, these people were actually Bulgarian Slavs by origin who had been forcibly Islamicized under the Ottomans. All they were doing, they claimed, was returning the Ottoman compliment by restoring to people their proper Bulgarian roots.

But the Muslims of Bulgaria and of Bosnia, whatever the truth of their forgotten origins, had considered themselves

Turkish, by instinct if not by blood, for hundreds of years. They had been left behind when the Ottoman tide in Europe had steadily receded between the seventeeth and nineteenth centuries at the hands of European resurgence and the Empire's own military and diplomatic failings, rockpools of Turkishness above the shoreline of retreat. The writer Patrick Leigh Fermor had reached an island on the Danube situated at the convergence of Romania, Bulgaria, and fledgeling Yugoslavia in 1935. The island had a Turkish name which translated as Island Castle.

The flow of the Danube had insulated it against the Ottoman retreat so that Island Castle at that time remained an outpost of undiluted Ottomanism. There were worry beads, rose-petal jam, nargilye smoking pipes, raki, the emphatically Turkish truncated nod of the head to refuse Leigh Fermor's offer of payment, veils, and fezzes. Faded, plum-coloured fezzes, as Leigh Fermor described them, 'with ragged turbans loosely knotted around them'. The *hoja*'s fez was lower and less tapering, 'with snow-white folds' arranged around it. In this memorable, magical image it was self-evident that these people too were clear about their genealogies.

'We are all Turks,' said Mehmet.

'All Turks,' insisted Ömer vigorously. And yet, despite the distinctive community at Island Castle, the Ottomans would have laughed at such an idea. They were accustomed to referrring to themselves not by ethnic background but as subjects of a multiracial Empire, as Ottomans. Ethnic labels fell into disuse, and thence to abuse. For much of the Ottoman period, to describe somebody as a Turk was to invite a punch in the face. 'A thousand Turks for a radish,' as the saying went; 'poor radish!' Not since the Vandals had a single ethnic caste been so vilified. To inspire a wholesale reorientation of Anatolian thinking on Turks and radishes was no mean feat.

But Turkish stock was soon rising in value, and passing that of static radishes. As early as 1908, the mystically imbued idea of a Turkish homeland was being actively bandied about in intellectual circles. Although some queried whether the concept had ever existed, more vociferous voices wondered how it could have been neglected so long. Dusted down or simply invented, the Turkish homeland emerged peopled with irrestistible historical figures rendered thoroughly Turkish such as Attila, Genghis Khan, and Tamberlaine. 'These heroic figures,' wrote Ziya Gökalp, the leading Turkish nationalist thinker of the time, 'which stand for the proud fame of my race, appear on the dry pages of the history books as covered with shame and disgrace, while in reality they are no less than Alexander and Caesar.'

By the 1920s, Turkish nationalists were actively propagating notions of Turkishness. They worked to uncover Turkish equivalents for Arabic names which they then gave their children, enthusiastically adopted the name Özturk, or 'Pure Turk' when surname time came to Turkey, and turned to the *kalpak*, the hardy hat of the steppe wherein all Turks were supposed to have their origins.

The more extreme saw the Turkish race as launching the genealogies not only of all Turkic-speaking peoples, Kazakhs, Uzbeks, Azerbaijanis, but also of those races – Hungarians, Estonians, Finns, Bulgars, and Mongols – who are thought to have originated in the same area as themselves, between the Caspian Sea and Mongolia. School books current at the time of Atatürk claimed that the Turks came from a great inland sea in central Asia which dried up during a drought and so caused them to become nomads. Consequently, the version went, they established separate but distinct Turkish civilizations as far afield as China, India, the Levant, North Africa, and Spain. This conveniently put the Turks at the heart of most leading civilizations and also explained why they became nomads, insisting that they had never been nomadic – a bit primitive, nomadism – by instinct, but rather by climatic necessity.

Turkish myth-making did not stop at drought. The Turkish origins are traced to the aftermath of a great massacre; Turks are the fruit of a mystical union between the last Turk left alive – and a she-wolf. All that can be said is that stranger things may have happened on the Anatolian uplands.

To this day, the wolf remains a potent nationalist symbol for the Turks. When the journalist John Simpson interviewed the Azerbaijani Minister of the Interior in 1992, he was singularly disturbed by the presence in the corner of the room of a complete stuffed wolf which presided over the proceedings with a lupine malevolence, a bizarre but memorable means of stressing the ethnic ties purported to exist between Turkey and Azerbaijan. The two countries' respective flags, only nominally different versions of the white star and crescent on red background, only emphasize the point.

What the Minister's wolf served more specifically to do was align him with the Pan-Turkic extreme right and with the Grey Wolves, a nationalist terror group responsible for numerous killings in Turkey's anarchic seventies including the assassination attempt on the Pope in 1981. The former head of the Grey Wolves' political wing we have met before. His name is Mr Turkeş, now Yozgat's MP. His choice of surname now acquires a particular significance.

Wolves, pure Turkish surnames, and Genghis Khan were a far cry from the tradition of tolerance that the Ottomans practised upon the Empire's numerous religious and racial minorities. All were bound by fealty to an Empire which did not attempt to disguise its complex racial make-up. The Ottomans would have laughed at wolves, pure Turkish surnames, and Genghis Khan. And so too would the fez.

When Mahmud II introduced the fez in the 1820s, he declared the new headgear was intended for all Ottomans, regardless of race or creed. Under the fez, the people of the Empire were to be indistinguishable. 'Henceforth,' said Mahmud II, 'I recognize Muslims only in the mosque, Christians only in the church, Jews only in the synagogue. Outside those places of worship, I desire every individual to enjoy the same political rights and my fatherly protection.' The fez encapsulated the ideal of benign cosmopolitanism.

'Racial geography is nowhere very simple between Bagh-dad and Vienna,' wrote Arnold Toynbee in 1917. While no Ottoman would have thought to query such an obvious statement, the Turks in the aftermath of the Great War had no choice but to claim Anatolia as an exception. For their nation's very legitimacy rested upon the claim that Anatolia's racial geography was in fact inherently simple – in that it was Turkish. To have accepted Toynbee's dictum, to have pursued a policy of cosmopolitanism, would have been to entertain the claims of the Armenians and Kurds to most of eastern Anatolia, and of the Greeks to the west. And so the lie of Turkish nationalism was born, distilled from the pure instinct to survive. Like the cornered chess player who resorts to over-turning the board as the only way out, the appeal of such simplistic nationalism is often irresistible. Chess, interestingly, is not much played in Turkey. And Turkey, equally interest-ingly, is where the Gordian knot was cut.

One of Atatürk's most popular dictums refutes Toynbee with similar knot-cutting simplicity. 'Happy is He who can call Himself a Turk' is inscribed across countless Turkish mountainsides; in spite of which, there are in Turkey millions of Kurds and, for specific reasons, not so many Armenians, who do not count themselves happy – and neither they, nor the mountainsides, Turkish.

Mehmet threw up his hands so that one of his outstretched fingers buried itself in my left nostril, but not out of anger; it was simply a peril of desk-sharing.

'We are supplying aid to the Armenians in the east even though they are fighting our brothers in Azerbaijan,' he wailed. 'And yet we cannot help the Bosnians.'

'The Bosnians,' Ömer confirmed.

Mehmet's eyes narrowed. 'The Armenians and Jews are the richest people in Turkey. They own all the big businesses, they have all the opportunities. Why is it?'

Semih's castle was showing through the mist.

'Those of them that are left,' I replied unwisely. And not

for the first time, I was told that the alleged massacres of one million Armenians in eastern Turkey in 1915 was a lie, an American–Armenian plot, and a massive insult to Turkish honour.

'They were trying to move the civilian population out of the fighting area,' Ömer explained. 'It was war, you understand and, sure, some of them will have died. People die in war. But nobody was trying to wipe them out.'

'Why would we do that?' Mehmet asked. 'Weren't we the people who invited the Jews here in the late 1400s when they were expelled by Christian Spain?'

But you were Ottomans in the late 1400s, and you owned the world. You could afford to be munificent. But when you are fighting for a much reduced tract of land, when you are about to lose everything including the fragile sense of nationhood that is the only glue binding a new ideal, up goes the chess board and the pieces are scattered.

It was time for Ömer and Mehmet to leave for the mosque. Religion and race bound these young men to Bosnia and to Azerbaijan, and made them ill disposed to those people who were not their own. The fez's attempts to resolve those diferences had failed and late in the nineteenth century, as the Ottoman Empire showed signs of imminent collapse, the Christians and Jews of the Empire were required to sew identifying strips of black ribbon to their fezzes. It was a defining moment, a ghastly parody of what the fez had originally stood for, strips of black ribbon that were perhaps the harbingers of Armenian massacre and the identification tattoos of the Nazi death camps.

I thought to raise my spirits with a drink, but a restaurant waiter told me that they did not generally serve alcohol. They could probably make an exception and serve me a beer, but raki was out of the question. And I was not a hundred miles from Ankara, the city where Atatürk had all but killed himself with the stuff. I drank *ayran* instead, a salty yoghurt concoction, ordered a joyless kebab, and stared out of the window.

Everywhere I looked the sticker *Huzur Islam'da* – Happiness in Islam – was posted on walls and in car windows. *Allah'a Emanet* was painted in decorative yellows and blues across the tailgates of the local lorries. I knew *Emanet* to mean 'left luggage' and it took me a minute to understand that this apparent reference to Allah's left luggage actually translated as 'In Allah's safe keeping'. That cheered me up. For about two seconds.

At the back of the restaurant, two men were playing backgammon, the board perched on a low stool between them. I watched one of them, an unshaven man with a small rodent for a moustache who repeatedly raised his hand in fury at the increasingly unfavourable fall of the dice. Eventually, he caught the side of the board with his fist and catapulted the markers into the smoky air. He had opted for the simple solution.

The bill came to the equivalent of 70p, and was served up with a flourish on a plastic silver salver. As I headed for a despairingly early bed and slid wildly on the treacherous ice getting there, I saw the shadows of several veiled women moving with surprising ease and balance before the town statue of Atatürk. All I could think was that Yozgat might one day produce a very fine skater indeed.

✳

chapter ten

'The origins of the fez, you say? From the penis, of
course. Like your English top hat, it represents the
primal human instinct.'

> From a conversation with a Turkish
> anthropologist as recorded in my notebook

AT FRIDAY lunchtime, the muffled wailings of Yozgat's
muezzins floated across the wintry town and mingled among
the wind-tugged plumes of coal smoke. From the window of
my hotel room, I watched huddled figures streaming towards
the mosques, making fresh tracks through the snow or picking
up the spoor impressions of old ones to guide them safely in.

Every lunchtime, the deskbound hotel receptionist turned
his place of work into a place of prayer, his body into a vessel
of obeisance to the will of God, his mind into a pure conduit
of divine communication, his thoughts towards the Almighty,
all of which he did most assiduously on Fridays. In spite of
Atatürk's adoption of the Christian weekend, Friday's religious
significance has endured, and on that day thousands of faithful
foreheads were buffing up desk surfaces in country towns
throughout Turkey, leaving rounded patinas of shiny, rever-
ential sweat as testament to their devotions.

The receptionist's forehead lay between outstretched palms
upon the counter in front of him. Every so often he would lift
his head a few inches to offer up rhythmic mutterings. And
whenever he did so, I would lean forward with a raised finger
to signal my presence. I was beginning to worry about the
time, and increasingly hoped he was working up to a
devotional climax.

It was the old dilemma: he had a God to talk to; I had a bus to catch. I respected his God, but I also knew that the Turks respected their bus timetables. Perhaps I only imagined the signs in the gloom of the lobby that read *Do not disturb upon sentence of ritual emasculation by Yozgat's Islamic Tribunal*, but even imagining them convinced me that anything as earthbound as bill settling would have to wait.

I was running short of patience. I'd had my fill of supine receptionists, and of being trailed, cornered, and finished off by hunting pairs of angry young men peddling their confused Turkish mantras. If only for the weekend, I had decided, it was time to get Christian. And Yozgat being no place to get so, I was doing the Christian thing, and fleeing.

When the receptionist finally surfaced, I informed him a little briskly that I was leaving.

'You're leaving Yozgat?' he asked, eyes narrowing. *Didn't anybody tell you? You can't just come and go in Yozgat; you have to stay, for ever.* In fact, he asked me for my room key, and where I was going.

'Church,' I told him.

'Ah,' he said. 'Christian.'

'One of the very best,' I replied, handing over a few bank notes.

'Perhaps you should think about—'

'Don't,' I interrupted him, and left for Cappadocia.

Cappadocia was the obvious choice. I knew that much wine was drunk there, and that the Cappadocians played host to large numbers of wine-drinking tourists. Cappadocia had churches, four hundred of them. Besides, Christians had been evading the Turks in Cappadocia for hundred of years. History's example was enough to prompt this harried Christian to seek sanctuary there, if only for the weekend.

The long road took us past the country town of Kirşehir where, a passenger told me, Uğur Mumcu had been born. From the bus, I could see enough to know that it was exactly like Yozgat; doubtless, Mumcu had jumped at the first escape opportunity to present itself. And when we came to a road block yards from Kirşehir, I understood what it must feel like, that cloying web of small-town Turkish life threatening to foil one's dash for the easy-breathing open spaces of Cappadocia. *We won't keep you long,* went that sinister gentle reprise inside my head. *Just for eternity.*

Palming away the condensation on my window, I could see beyond the several rows of waiting traffic two shivering police officers venturing from the warmth of their car. It became clear, as I watched, that the foray was one of a series designed to deter the tide of impatient drivers salivating at the grid as an enticing gap opened up ahead whenever the wind nudged like minor demented daleks the two traffic cones from their position, across the icy road surface, and into the ditch. Repositioning them, the policemen would stare down the drivers and quieten for a moment the sound of gunning engines.

After half an hour, one bus driver had had enough. He climbed down and skated across to the police car. Reluctantly, a policeman wound him out three inches of window gap through which to speak.

'You can't leave us here,' the bus driver told them. 'The weather's only going to get worse – and then our retreat will be blocked too. Besides, the road's obviously passable.' By way of illustration, he pointed at the uninterrupted flow of traffic coming in the opposite direction.

'Listen,' a policeman told him, jabbing up at him through the window. 'We've been up that road, and we got stuck.'

'That's because you drive crap cars,' the bus driver replied, turning away in scorn. And the reaction of the four seated Anatolian policemen was a lurch of barely restrained intent at his words, and it was as if only the confining space of the car had halted their avenging reflexes.

A stronger gust of wind blew across the steppe, a snow-bound blast of pure Siberian cold, and the two cones skittered frantically from the road and disappeared for good into a snowdrift to an accompanying cheer from the stacked vehicles.

In that moment, the policemen's fragile baton of authority was snapped; the driver turned for his bus with unmistakable resolve, and engines on all sides growled an appreciative chorus of anticipation. When he gunned his engine and moved forward, ten rows of vehicles moved up in unison. The policemen knew that they had lost, but not that they had already lost face. As if to hijack credit for the road-opening decision, all four at once flung open their car doors and took up frantic waving positions to direct the oncoming traffic through the breach that the bus driver had made.

They were still waving as we passed and the bus passengers around me waved gleefully back at them, those forlorn figures decked out in a uniform of a nauseously rich green and learning to live with unpalatable concepts such as accountability. Like the Ottoman Janissaries, ultra-Orthodox guardians of the Empire, the Turkish police had long operated according to a code entirely of their own composition, but were now finding themselves publicly distanced from a disapproving state. When Süleyman Demirel was elected Prime Minister in 1991, one of his party's more memorable slogans was *Transparency – police station walls will all be made of glass*. People in glass houses, it might be said, could no longer throw stones, punches or electric switches with quite the same impunity.

The Turkish police force certainly have some bizarre arrests to their credit: a sixteen-year-old girl who spent seventy-five days in prison for hanging an anti-war poster in her school in 1991; a female German tourist who was dragged from her bed and subjected to a virginity test, which she quite reasonably failed (apparently, she had been mistaken for a Romanian prostitute after a tip-off from a rival hotel trying to close down the competition); and an elderly ex-mayor of Istanbul originally tried for possession of a weapon – an ornamental musket decorating his mother-in-law's sitting-room. It was a telling measure of change in Turkey that you could even insult a policeman's car these days and get away with it.

Cappadocia began at the town of Avanos where the first

landscape eccentricities could be seen. The evening light fell upon a distant skyline, a pinkish range of soft rock meringues. A red river ran through the town carrying swirls of clay north to the coast near İnebolu. Unimaginatively, it was called the Red River. More impressive, however, was the fact that they had already called one of their roads after Uğur Mumcu, and I knew then I had put a safe distance between me and Yozgat.

The bus dropped me at the village of Göreme. I found a hotel, refurbished in the remains of an old merchant's house. It had been carved from the soft rock in a town where soft rock, rough carved by the elements and then further customized by humans, was largely the town itself. There was the odd implanted construction such as the single minaret or an occasional whitewashed breeze-block wall. But the rest, as the last of the evening light performed across an impossible volcanic landscape, was geological fantasy, and endless cones perhaps one hundred feet high, the product of lava, wind, and time that had formed a decidedly priapic landscape. Tourist brochures have exhausted the lexicon – see under 'Moonscape', 'Haunting', and 'Sculpted' – in their valiant attempts to avoid the most glaringly obvious adjective. But finally they have submitted to the inevitable, and 'Phallic' has crept into even the most prudish of Cappadocian guidebooks.

Christians have never been particularly good with penises but they had taken to Cappadocia in spite of them, these great knobbed sandstone shafts on every side. To seventh-century Christians, it must have appeared a very rude landscape indeed. Could they really settle amongst this geological orgy? They could and would; the phallic aspect could not be allowed to dissuade them since, like rabbits, they could dig their way out of persecution here, and persecution was routine stuff for the Anatolian Christians of the seventh century. In the countless underground cities that have been found in the region they burrowed to secure themselves, complete with all the requisite facilities of the early Christians – grain stores, churches, assembly rooms, wine cellars, and stables – and thumbed their noses at the rampaging hordes above. It was presumably an added relief that the penises were safely out of sight. But there was more to it, I suspected, than security from marauding Turks and unseemly priapic totems. The look of the place distinguished it from the high, interminable steppeland which the Islamic Turks, hearing echoes there of their own distant Mongolia, had made their own.

The idea that the Turks remain mystically linked to the distant land of their origins has done good box office in the twentieth century as a natural extension of nationalist thinking. In truth, and despite their claims to the contrary, the Turks do not seem to like the Mongolian look of their landscape. They seem happiest in the confines of their towns. They shrink from the intimidating treeless sweep of the steppe, and the unvarying duns of its colour palette. They borrow instead the idealized rural landscapes of others as backdrops to their dreams. In Turkey's kebab houses, the same repeated images on large posters are papered to the walls.

Most commonly, there is a verdant mountain scene in which an eternal late spring has settled – judging by the lines of the ubiquitous wooden chalets – somewhere in southern Germany. I had seen something similar on the calendar two weeks earlier at Mehmet's house in Soapmakers. Then there is the little bay by the sea with a few yachts at anchor and a sprinkling of red-roofed houses, an image on the wall of bus company waiting-rooms hundreds of miles from the coast. 'The Turk and the Arab came out of big spaces, and they have the desire of them in their bones,' wrote John Buchan in *Greenmantle*. On the contrary, it seems to me that Turks are actually in awe of Anatolia. Far from the desolation of the steppe, they have the desire in their bones of a smoky crowd, a gathering after work in the warm, muggy gloom of a good friend's shop.

The Cappadocian Christians, however, had always loved their adopted landscape as if its alien geology endorsed and befitted their alien status. From the hotel terrace, I could see in the gloaming the neat lines of vines, vegetable patches, and apple orchards crowded amongst the towering cones. Despite a geology that was certifiable, Cappadocia's was a tended landscape. It looked benign, and I felt no qualms the next morning about leaving Göreme behind and setting off into the frozen dawn on foot.

It was cloudless. Soft splashes of sunshine fell among the apple orchards and the spidery-black vines. The earth was chocolate brown where it showed through the snow. Pink cones cast long shadows across the road. A silhouetted woman carrying firewood on her hunched back appeared in the distance, slipping below the horizon into the shadow of the road before rising up to pass me, silently habituated to the pattern of her life. Men, I might have muttered, catching her eye sympathetically, but she would not have understood my objection to a division of labour ingrained so deep into the expectations of her predecessors that the unfairness of it all had never touched her.

At my back, a horn sounded and I turned to see a man with a rifle waving at me from the back of an approaching pick-up. His frantic gestures indicated unmistakably that I move away. And then I saw the dog, large and black, a hundred yards away and closing. It was spinning along the road like a deranged top, sputum draped from its jowls and arcing from the centrifuge of its sweat-drenched body. Whining and snapping, it wolfed down great chunks of Cappadocian sky. I scrambled up the bank, my heels spinning like cartoon wheels in the fresh snow, clambered past a couple of apple trees, and raced for the nearest rock cone. The neat doorway which had once been carved in its base was now eroded on all sides. I took sanctuary in the gloom of the interior where my boots crunched on the charcoal remains of an old fire. I could smell musty stone.

My pulse was racing. I heard the sound of the creature spinning dementedly between the apple trees, and I gave myself up to the prospect of an arse punctured not only by an exercised set of canines but also by a subsequent course of rabies jabs. Only when I heard the shots, four loud reports amid squeals, whimpers, and silence, did I understand that what I had heard was the wind, only the wind ruffling the snow. From the road, I watched the pick-up disappear out of sight in the direction of Göreme.

Heaven protect me from fanatics and wild dogs, I mused, as I reached the building at the entrance to the rock churches. A man stood outside, stripped to the waist and washing in a bowl of water. He was not the cowled troglodytic guardian with chunky iron keys swinging from the waist cord that I had imagined. He towelled himself down, lit a cigarette, and ushered me inside. Beyond the desk where he issued tickets, the heap of blankets from which he had recently emerged lay upon the concrete floor. The whistle of a teapot upon the stove drowned out the early morning television.

'Eight clock open,' he told me in English, indicating in the direction of the churches. Since they had been doorless and open for some twelve hundred years, keeping me waiting until eight o'clock seemed strictly unnecessary. But I was grateful for the tea.

'Christian?' he asked me, straightening his moustache in a small, cracked mirror above the stove.

'Christian. Muslim?'

'Muslim. Country?'

'England.'

'Teacher?'

'No. Major.'

'Ah. Major. Ser-terling?'

'Sterling.'

'How many lira?'

'Fourteen thousand.'

He whistled. 'Rich man. Football?'

'Football.'

'Milano?'

'No. That's Italy. Manchester.'

'Ah. Manchester. Man-ches-ter-Un-it-ed.'

I told him that I spoke Turkish, and the attendant filled out as Metin, a good Muslim tending to the relics of Christianity. I wondered how he felt about that.

'They are beautiful churches,' he replied. 'Christians, Muslims, it makes no difference to me.' Admittedly, he did not approve of everything that Christians did. He remembered the people who had come here from Europe twenty years ago when he first came to Göreme.

'Heepies,' he called them. 'They came here in the seventies on the overland route to India and used to camp in the chimneys and make much love.'

'I can see where they got the idea from,' I replied.

Metin blushed an Islamic red and turned away. 'Only Christians think like that. We call them fairy chimneys,' he said coyly. 'Anyway, I do not believe good heepies ever needed prompting,' he continued, humouring me but changing the tack of the subject if not the subject itself. I marvelled that Metin could be so coy, working long days as he did in one of the most phallic of all valleys, about the penises which had surrounded him for twenty years.

Yellow sunlight crept in at the window. A single bird sang. A pat of snow shook itself free of an apple tree. 'OK,' he said, as the clock eventually struck eight, smiled and set me on my way. I found the churches secreted among the lips and rumps of the landscape. Beyond their dark entrances were pillars, altars, and arches carved from the rock. I rapidly worked my way through some seven of them; that many stood within two hundred yards of each other. It was as if the Cappadocian Christians had built an out-of-town prayer mall in which parishioners could choose differently frescoed settings for their worship. In fact, in the moderate size and the proximity of these churches was contained an inspired ideological resolution. Early Christianity in Cappadocia was much troubled in its approach to prayer and its wider implications for the nature of Christian society. Should it express itself as a community or as a collection of individuals? Should churches encourage assembly or personal reflection? Should the hermit or the congregation represent the primary Christian inclination?

In Cappadocia, the resultant compromise was expressed in the very design of these beautiful churches. They were of a size and number in which both communal and private expression might find voice. And although the plaster frescos were mostly recognizable images from the New Testament – the Nativity, the Marriage at Cana, the Feeding of the Five Thousand, the Raising of Lazarus, the Crucifixion – the feel of their execution was in no way textbook. Instead, they had a fine beauty that felt introspective; these were expressions of an uninstitutionalized spirituality. Often they were naïve, the iconography of an inchoate, dawning sense of faith drawn in faded colours simple and earth-bound. And in many cases, a monstrous intolerance, the frescos had been disfigured.

The faces of saints, Christs, and disciples had been obliterated with some sharp flint so that a neat oval of rough stone showed in their place. I felt anger rising inside me, a contempt for Islamic orthodoxy that doubtless was spurred by my recent experiences in Sivas and Yozgat. It was the meticulousness of the desecration that outraged me. I might less have minded an energetically chaotic violation born of fury, but this was a knowing perpetration hiding behind a zealot's knowledge of the rulebook. For does not Islam forbid the depiction of the human image? For can not God alone create man? Furthermore, the desecrations had most probably occurred long after the Christian community in Cappadocia had been dispersed. The rock churches had been attacked not as symbols active in their affront of Islam, but as unthreatening, inert relics of a religion that locally had had its time. Religious wrath I could understand, but this was pious pettifogging of a sort that filled me that morning with fury.

Metin had made his bed by the time I returned. How could they? I asked him. How could they scratch the plaster from the gentle fresco faces of two-thousand-year-old saints? It was a desecration. He smiled, took me by the arm and made me a cup of tea.

'You're feeling upset? People have been feeling like you for hundreds of years in Turkey,' he told me. For the first portraits of Mahmud II which had been hung in public buildings in the 1830s had so incensed people that a guard was posted below each and every portrait to protect them from attack. Even under the Young Turks, it was considered an offence to religion that the human form be represented in school textbooks. In 1914, when the Sultan's head first appeared on the country's stamps, public outrage was but partially mollified by the official explanation that He only appeared on the most expensive stamp. Even in 1922, there were serious doubts as to whether Prince Abdul Mejid was fit to become Caliph, the head of all Muslims, on the grounds that he had once painted portraits of his friends.

By October 1926, the Caliphate had been consigned to history. On October 4 the remnants of Koranic Law were replaced by a civil code based on the Swiss and German models. The day before, they had ceremoniously unveiled on the banks of the Bosphorus, in full view of the affronted ghosts of the past mouldering in the old Sultan's palace at Topkapi, Turkey's very first statue. It was of the Gazi. He was wearing a dinner jacket, his arms were folded, and he was bare headed.

'Think how that made good Muslims feel, a bare-headed statue?' asked Metin. 'That was a desecration every bit as bad as your defaced fresco.' The various Islamic brotherhoods that took to attacking the proliferation of busts and statues of Atatürk in towns and cities across Turkey leant support to his view.

Tradition and progress, East and West, traded punches with each other in Turkey. They had learned with the aid of sharp flints and statues respectively how best to insult each other. So far a resolution of the Cappadocian kind, churches for hermits and congregations alike, appeared to be beyond them.

There was a time, early that same evening when the sun had fallen low on the horizon, the snow was hard on the ground, and the light had turned the stone a ferocious purple, that the truncated cones did not remind me of the euphemistic fairy chimneys of the Muslims nor of Christian penises. Even in the landscape were now reminders of fezzes.

chapter eleven

KONYA, CITY OF mystic rituals and whirling, of floating turquoise domes and entombed dervishes, had bigger things on its mind the morning I arrived. For when the local football team is in trouble, hard fact tends to intrude; there's no refuge in the spirit world from the fearful threat of relegation. Whirling was one thing, the eternal footballing attributes like passing to feet quite another. Survival in football is an empirical business, the hard-graft accumulation of points that act as vital ballast against the drop. And in Konya, where they had won once in eighteen attempts, those points were just not accumulating fast enough.

Wistful, soon established as the nickname of the young man who had greeted me at Konya's bus station, agreed. Wistful by nature, his personality was currently in the grips of a football fan's profound disillusionment. 'If you want to watch football,' he said, 'don't watch Konyaspor.' And yet, like every addict, he had known all week that he would surrender to the compulsion when the time came.

We had met as I got off the bus. 'I am pleased to help you on your arrival in Konya?' an English-speaking voice had impressed me, and I turned to the sight of a young man with a football scarf wrapped around his neck. When, however, I replied in English, Wistful's eyes clouded over in articulate admission that this one sentence was the sum and tally of his English. Wistful had learned that these alien noises usually sufficed to kick-start a satisfactory series of nods, smiles, and scraps of mimicry that passed for communication – and at least got visitors back to the shop, which was the purpose of his vigil. Wistful was regularly dispatched by his boss to trawl the bus station for foreigners newly arrived and presumably wealthy. The idea was that suggesting budget hotels and helping tourists to gain their city bearings might encourage them to spend a few hundred thousand lira at the bric-à-brac shop where he worked. But Wistful ended up with me, who only wanted to accompany him to the football game.

We dropped my bags at the shop, lifted a couple of prayer mats on which to rest our bottoms (Wistful had a certain antique élan) and headed for the game. Inside the stadium, the grass was as yellow-brown and ice seared as the steppe outside; I had somehow imagined that Anatolia would not apply here, that the climatic and scenic rules would be waived for the few hundred square metres of earth inside the stadium. But I was wrong; it was a relatively flat piece of typical goat graze furnished with the standard Anatolian elements. Besides, there was the police presence, despite a home crowd so used to losing that only the unique experience of winning might stir them to trouble. The police were massed in huge numbers behind each goal complete with visors, batons, and riot shields. Oncoming forwards, springing the offside trap, must wonder whether they are destined for glory or a good thumping. Furthermore, the crowd was so much an extension of the exclusively male, smoking, and sunflower-shell-spitting hubbub found throughout Turkey that the whole stadium felt like the quintessence of Anatolia.

The opposition came from Bursa, city of history and a hundred and fourteen contraband fez packages. Venerable Konya could match Bursa stride for stride in the history stakes, but when it came to football it soon became clear that the visitors' abilities left the journeymen locals for dead. The ball fairly flowed between the yellow-shirted visitors. The every touch of one Ali Reza was greeted with a torrent of abuse, for he had been unwise enough to transfer from Konya to Bursa a few months earlier.

'He's only a professional footballer,' came the voice of reason from a teacher on my right.

'And may he fuck his mother,' returned the chant from the surrounding crowd.

When Konya hit the post on a rare breakaway, the crowd braced itself for a shock win. Although there were younger supporters among the crowd who needed reminding of the fact, such wins had happened before. Although it seemed like a lifetime ago, Konya had actually won as recently as the previous year. There were even those who remembered it. Despite all this, however, another win was considered highly unlikely, and nobody was surprised when Bursa broke the deadlock in the second half. The collective expression of prayer daring to call itself hope gave way on every side to the Turkish gesture of disgust, the single thrown arm that asks why, why did you do that so badly?

Even the reasonable teacher joined in. 'He's not a footballer,' he screamed at a Konya player's fumbled touch. 'He's a carpenter!' And the crowd around him roared their approval as the teacher abandoned reason as a bad job.

'If we don't win this one, we're down, we're down,' the cry went up. Hard-nosed realism rather than wit was the Konya crowd's discerning feature. 'If you don't win this one, you're down, you're down,' they then sang, cruelly withdrawing any emotional investment in the fate of the team. And then turning to each other, and further yet from the players, they taunted them with feigned indifference. 'If they don't win this one, they're down.'

The mass rejection seemed to spur the Konya players. With ten minutes to go, they grabbed an equalizer and the air was filled with flat caps and skull caps, pistachio nuts and dried apricots. They were pushing for the winner when the final whistle blew. Then the air was filled with the polystyrene mats which spectators without access to prayer mats had bought before the game, signalling the white flag of relegation in lopsided flight above the stands. That was it; a draw just would not do. No crowd in the entire history of the game had ever had to fall back on mathematical notions of survival so early in the season. Starved of results, the team had needed a high-protein diet of wins starting today to stand any real chance. Wistful was close to tears as we streamed out of the stadium. I offered to buy him a döner kebab.

'Cheer up,' I comforted him. 'Your city has other things to be proud of.'

'But all we want,' Wistful replied, 'is to stay in the first division.'

Whatever Wistful's feelings, however, Konya was not really a footballing city. The performance was hardly surprising in a place that has been the home of Turkish Sufism, a highly mysticized form of Islamic belief in which football plays no immediately obvious part, since the thirteenth century. It was a lot to ask of a dervish people who spent years perfecting a trancelike whirling dance called the *sema* that they adapt to the various footballing permutations of sweepers and flat back-fours.

Turkish Sufism was inspired by Mevlana, who was born in northern Afghanistan around AD 1200 and whirled his way across the Middle East as a young man with the rest of his father's family in flight from the invading Mongols. They reached Konya via Baghdad and Damascus. Baha Veled, Mevlana's father, was the kind of man who, when challenged as to his origins and destination by Baghdad's city guards, replied: 'We are coming from God, and we are going towards God. No one but God has the power and the energy to stop us. We are coming from beyond space and we are bound for a world beyond space.' 'Yeah yeah,' you can hear Baghdad's guards reply, 'but what do we put on the visa?'

Mevlana quickly proved himself to be every bit the son of his father and awoke in the people of Konya an enthusiastic devotion to his spiritual ideals. Every spare minute, he led them on a frenzied whirl in pursuit of the divine, ecstatic love that the *sema* induces. It is said to serve as the conduit through which man's spiritual journey to God is channelled. As I finished my kebab that afternoon, it struck me that the Turkish adjective used to describe the *sema* whirl is also ascribed to the movement of a kebab on its vertical spit. I briefly imagined strips of lamb departing the spit in centrifugal frenzy and plastering themselves to any passing custom.

At the Mevlana Museum, where dervishes whirled around the mausoleum of their spiritual leader before they were proscribed by Atatürk in the 1920s, a leaflet explained the *sema* thus: 'Contemporary science definitely confirms that the fundamental condition of our existence is to revolve . . . The shared similarity among beings is the revolution of the electrons, protons, and neutrons in the atoms . . . Everything revolves and man carries on his life by the revolution of his blood, by his coming from the earth and his return to it, which is also a kind of revolution, by his revolving with earth itself.'

Then, I thought, there was the endless revolution of worry beads between Turkish fingers, not to mention the döner kebab. Still, devoting one's life to *sema* whirling when so much whirling, planetary, biological, and culinary, was going on elsewhere struck me as excessive. Whenever I'd whirled as a child, I quickly felt dizzy and sick, and the one thing my mother did not seem to feel for me when I threw up down her front was divine love.

But this is to quibble with a magically off-beat manifestation of spirituality. Since Atatürk's proscription of the dervishes, they have only been permitted to dance in cultural festivals, a context that not only unshackles the *sema* from its religious anchor but presents it less as an extraordinary rite of personal faith than a commercial performance. The Mevlana festival takes place every December in Konya – in a large hall resembling nothing so much as a gymnasium. The setting only reinforces the sense that the *sema* has been terminally emasculated of its original spiritual potency. The dervishes also tour; I once saw them at the Royal Albert Hall. Men who once whirled for nobody but their God now perform for audiences at events brokered by international cigar-smoking impresarios.

Dervishes are perhaps too far gone to worry about mere human interference of the kind imposed upon them by Atatürk. But in their more conventionally conscious moments, it may have dawned upon them that there has actually been a counter-current running over the past few years, in the form of a tacit encouragement to return to the original spirit of the *sema*. President Özal attended the Mevlana Festival in 1989. The Festival was introduced by the Minister of Culture. Rather than appeal for a cultural appreciation of Mevlana – he was after all the Minister of Culture – the Minister called for a veneration of Mevlana and his religious beliefs.

If anything might substantiate the trend, I thought, hat sales would. So I went to see Mehmet Girgic, the only man in the world to make true dervish hats or *sikkes*. It was true; Mehmet was making more such hats than ever before. He had just sent a consignment of ten *sikkes* to America, where he reckoned there were some one hundred practising dervishes, but more tellingly had recently finished two for apprentice dervishes in the city of Elâziğ, some four hundred miles to the east. For if whirling was no more than the latest passing fad in an aerobicized America, then it was the real thing in remote and dusty Elâziğ.

Sikkes have often been described as fawn fezzes but the description is not entirely accurate. For it is not only their natural wool colour (mohair fawn or sheep's wool white) that is different; *sikkes* are twice the height of fezzes. But there are unmistakable similarities in that they too are truncated cones. And they are made of felt, like fezzes generally were until twenty years ago when it began to be recognized that tourists were quite inattentive to the material from which their souvenirs were made.

In the gloom of his back-street atelier, Mehmet told me his story. He came from a long line of *sikke* makers. His grandfather had specialized in *sikkes* until Atatürk's proscriptions when he diversified into other felt products such as shepherds' cloaks, called *kepeneks*, and tents, known as *yurts*. It was only fifteen years ago when Sufism first started to revive (the dervishes were first permitted to whirl once more, if only as cultural exhibits, in 1953) that the family firm received its first *sikke* commission for over forty years. And Mehmet set out to fulfil it.

'I never saw my grandfather make a *sikke*,' Mehmet told me, 'but I remembered him explaining the process.' The staff at the Mevlana Museum laughed at Mehmet when he visited to examine the exhibit *sikkes* there. Did he really expect to learn, with the aid of memory alone, a notoriously difficult art that had been passed down the generations by hand? For the teaching chain was surely broken, the links of knowledge were severed, and the art of *sikke* making was consequently lost for ever.

It took Mehmet a number of abortive attempts, but he finally succeeded, and has been honing his art ever since. He reckoned to have made around a thousand *sikkes* in his lifetime. One of the commissions which had given him the greatest pleasure was from the Mevlana Museum; to supply new exhibit *sikkes* as replacements for the moth-eaten objects topping the sarcophagi of Mevlana and his various acolytes. Not because he particularly revered Mevlana – he in fact thought it might be to the benefit of all if dervishes did a little more conventional work – but because the museum staff had mocked his original efforts. And so he called those same *sikke*-eating moths his little foot-soldiers. You could almost imagine him sprinkling surreptitious moth larvae around quiet corners of the museum.

We agreed a price for my own personal *sikke*. I asked Mehmet if it would succumb to the same mothy fate. 'Not so long as you whirl in it,' he replied. 'Moths don't like whirling although you wouldn't imagine it from the way they fly round this light in summer. Otherwise, seal it in a plastic bag with a couple of mothballs when you're not planning to whirl. 'Luckily,' he explained gleefully, 'that's not an option for museum exhibits.'

In spite of Mehmet's down to earth approach, Sufism and felt making were a potent combination as far as that gland of mine devoted to mystical theorizing was concerned. While Mehmet waxed lyrical on the excellence of mohair and fine winter sheep's wool or condemned the standard practice of chemical washes, I was digging up half-forgotten fleece references from mythology; Jason and his Golden Fleece, or Odysseus escaping the clutches of Cyclops by clinging to the fleecy underbelly of a giant ram.

'Ah, you want that kind of stuff,' replied Mehmet with an artisan's proper disdain for anything other than ability, a practised eye, and quality materials. 'You'd better have a cigarette. You want the story of the central Asian nomad who is broke and cold, and possesses nothing but a useless pile of sheep's wool. The guy's tears fall on to the wool, it felts and – hey presto! – he's Mr Felt-Patent.' I just managed to stop myself saying, 'But that's a wonderful story,' and looked knowingly cynical instead.

The story was apocryphal and Mehmet was dismissive of it but it contained an important truth. Felting, which occurs naturally on sheep, occurs equally naturally with a pair of hands, soap, and water. Mehmet was now working on my *sikke*. He took two flat pieces of mohair fleece and hemmed them together with his fingers working soapy water along the join, and then into the rest of the fleece until he was left with a hairy, sealed bladder. 'Look,' he said. 'Try and pull it apart,' and I couldn't. Mehmet was on practical ground, and he was happy there.

He then rolled and kneaded the bag with his hands, a process he described as 'cooking'. In English, this process of causing the hairs to knit closely together is called 'fulling' while the Scots, who used to tread felt to the same end, called it 'waulking'. Mehmet then stiffened the bag with a sugar solution before drawing it, double-thickness, over a wooden *sikke*-shaped mould called a *kalip*.

I was watching a version of what Julia Pardoe had seen at the Eyup Fez Factory in Constantinople a hundred and sixty years ago, the original fez-making process. Making some one hundred and eighty thousand fezzes a year, the workers at the factory had preferred the Scottish method. The fezzes, explained Pardoe, 'are flung into a marble trough . . . where they are trodden by a couple of men; and afterwards given to the blockers, who stretch them over earthen moulds to enable them to take a good shape'.

'I used to make fezzes for the more discerning tourists in exactly this way,' Mehmet told me. He rummaged amongst the chaos in a corner of the room and passed me two pieces of wood which, when placed together, formed a truncated cone. It was an old wooden fez *kalip* which he had not used for twenty years: 'It came from my father and my grandfather,' said Mehmet.

On this wooden block genuine Ottoman fezzes had once been made. It was like discovering a perfect fossil, all that remained of something long since considered extinct. It tantalized me. It also convinced me, as the fez *kalip* and my drying *sikke* stood alongside each other, that the two hats shared a common ancestry. That they came from the same place, however distant and uncertain.

And yet Atatürk had claimed that the fez originated with the hated Greeks. But then, I figured, no suggestion was better designed to dissuade Turks from wearing them. Atatürk was sure to have claimed the fez as such, just as the anthropologist would have been tempted to see it as a penis. The convincing similarities between the two hats, and the fact that the *sikke* had been established in Konya since the thirteenth century, suggested an older, more Turkish, and certainly less penile ancestry for the fez.

Legend has it that the soul of Mohammed had a previous existence in the spirit world, where Allah placed him in a vase of light shaped like a *sikke*. Mehmet had his own theory.

'You know,' he said, 'that the *sema* represents a form of rebirth, a spiritual journey to a new understanding of life; well, the white smock the dervishes wear is said to represent the death shroud and the *sikke* stands for the tombstone.' He was evidently sceptical, but that did not deter me from thinking of befezzed tombstones all across Turkey. Like yew trees, something drew these two hats towards death. It was another connection that bound them.

Mehmet, meanwhile, was measuring my head. 'Large,' he declared, 'very large,' and took a wedge of wood which he drove between the two halves of the *kalip* over which my *sikke* was now fitted until the size was right. My *sikke* would be as tight-fitting as all good *sikkes*, for in the centrifugal frenzy of the *sema* an ill-fitting *sikke* would not only bust trances but become a positively lethal weapon. Was the tapering shape of the *sikke*, even in the highly spiritualized atmosphere of the dervish world, primarily a design consideration, a safety feature? Was it primarily a hat which would stay on?

It did not surprise me that Mehmet, practical Mehmet, much preferred this theory to tombstones and vessels containing essence of Mohammed. So I told him about a man called Tommy Cooper, the much-loved British comedian who had been very fond of his fez ever since first encountering it in Egypt during the Second World War. When Cooper collapsed on stage in London in April 1984, it is said that in his fall his fez stayed on his head, and as he died he was still wearing it. It was a stubborn hat, a hat that would not willingly leave the head.

chapter twelve

'In England, at any rate, the hat is never free from the
touch of the comic . . . It is the plain truth that hats
generally, and any particular hat, even the word "hat",
are apt to raise a smile.'

— *The Times*, London, November 4 1925

ON THE OUTSKIRTS of Konya lies a suburb called Mehram
where the ugly tower blocks of the city give way to small
groups of stone houses that were once steppe villages. Mehram
has been swallowed by the encroachment of the city but
among the winter apple trees, the mud walls, and the snow-
dusted pathways, the trace elements of a rural past, you can
sense that Mehram has not yet been digested.

Like Mehmet Girgic, Mehram resident Fevzi Bircan was a
forty-year-old hat maker. But where Mehmet was fending off
orders for *sikkes*, Fevzi Bircan's fezzes were proving slower
than ever. Konya's only fez maker stooped as he directed me
to a cushion on the floor of his tiny front room while he tried
to make himself comfortable on one of his own. Fevzi had
been to hospital that morning for an examination of his
rheumatic back. 'It's all the fezzes,' he complained. 'That's
what does it.' Fevzi made between one and two thousand
back-hunching pieces a year. But increasingly it was patterned
hats that the retailers were demanding, bastard hybrid things
made from coloured curtain material with an ersatz oriental
feel. Fevzi shrugged. 'I'll make such things,' he said, 'but I'm
not proud of them.' He wanted to make fezzes. Fezzes did not
cost him any more pain than the other hats, and he enjoyed
making them. The trouble was nobody seemed to want them

any more. Rheumatic Fevzi was the last of a dying breed. He sighed deeply, the woes of the world upon his shoulders. 'And the football,' he said.

'I was there,' I said consolingly.

'Don't tell me how bad they were.'

I had hoped to watch Fevzi make a fez, but he did not want to work today. In the intense winter cold, he felt the pains in his back most acutely. So we talked instead about his trade and he told me that he had not made a fez in felt – the original manner – for twenty years. Since that time, Fevzi had made 'karton' fezzes from a cardboard shell across which red baize was stretched and secured before a tassle was sewn into the top. It was not perhaps the old way but Fevzi was nevertheless proud of his work. 'Bircan', I would soon hear people tell me, 'Bircan makes a fine fez.' He could make three such fezzes an hour, a speed skill which he reckoned had taken him fifteen years to perfect.

'And now,' he repeated, throwing open his arms and wincing at the pain as he did so, 'people do not seem to want them.' He patted the head of his fifteen-year-old son Aydin who had sat quietly next to his father since my arrival. The pat was reassurance for a son set, in spite of its decline, on the fez-making business.

'How many fezzes,' I asked Aydin, 'can you make in a day?'

'One.'

'One?' I could hardly look impressed.

'But he will get faster,' said Fevzi rapidly, patting his son again. I truly hoped so. For even at twenty-four times Aydin's current fez-making speed, his father was hardly wealthy.

'But since you say nobody is buying fezzes any more,' I asked, 'why doesn't he just learn the patterned ones?'

It was an insensitive remark. I might have suggested that an orchestral conductor spin the hits at the local social club disco, but I was surprised and humbled by the sheer dismissiveness of the shrug that greeted my suggestion. I had not known shoulders were capable of such seismic movement, especially not arthritic ones.

'We are fez makers,' proud Fevzi replied eventually. And that was that.

Mrs Bircan brought us coffee in cups as tiny as her fleeting appearance in a man's world. There were snow flurries at the window and shudders of sunshine that flickered across a portrait of Fevzi's grandfather dressed in a turban. Did Fevzi resent the abolition of the fez?

'It has certainly not helped business,' he said, smiling gravely. 'Besides, people should be able to wear what they like. And since we are allowed to make fezzes for tourists, maybe we should get some support or encouragement from the tourism ministry.'

'Especially since the fez means so much to Europeans, certainly to people in England,' I told him.

Interested, Fevzi asked me why. I told him that a comic magician called Tommy Cooper had always worn one; it was regarded as one of his best jokes. Fevzi looked disappointed.

'Maybe that is wrong,' he said. 'To make a joke of the fez is wrong.'

He might have been thinking of the revered livelihood of his family, of his God, or of those fez wearers who had been hanged. In fact, as I soon realized, Fevzi did not like such jokes chiefly because they reminded him that he too would soon be reduced to making them. Fevzi was set on going to the resort town of Bodrum on the Aegean for the summer. He would take Aydin, pack a bag of red baize and cardboard *kartons*, and set up a fez-making workshop for the tourists. He had a cousin there who had already promised to help arrange matters. 'Nobody knows how to make fezzes in Bodrum,' he explained. 'I'm sure the tourists will come.'

It was a very good idea. In Bodrum, Fevzi was sure to sell plenty of fezzes. But Fevzi would finally have to face up to the unpalatable truth that he was selling no revered article of headgear but a favourite joke of the Europeans. In Konya, Fevzi had long been able to sustain the dream, the dream that he was a simple milliner making respected fezzes like his forefathers to sell with an artisan's dignity into the unchanged mainstream of Turkish life. For in the view from his Konya house there was nothing to disturb the fantasy, nothing to remind him that the fezzes he made were actually destined for tourists in search of a laugh, nothing to suggest that his fezzes would actually frequent the bars, beaches, and discos of the infidels rather than mosques, tea houses, and Turkish homes as they had always done. Perhaps, a lifetime after the abolition of the fez, Fevzi knew that the dream was no longer sustainable.

Leaving Konya for Bodrum would mean leaving Turkey for the world I had witnessed in Pomegranate. Fevzi would court tourists face to face. He would enter that shadow world where he not only made hats but performed them out of the shop. He would reinvent himself as a jolly heritage figure, the fez maker forced to sing for his supper, develop a patter, and laugh at the joke that the fez had become. Could he enter into the joke? I asked him.

He nodded slowly. 'What else can I do?' he replied, his hands outstretched. 'Tourists are all that there's left. Besides,' he smiled, 'the Bodrum weather will be excellent for my back. And they say it's beautiful in the summer.' The modern world was busy digesting Fevzi Bircan.

By the time I came to leave, his mood had visibly lightened.

'That English magician man,' he said; 'can you write his name for me?' And I could already see it, the freshly painted sign saying 'Tommy Cooper Fez Factory' above the door of a back-street Bodrum workshop. I asked to take Fevzi's photograph but he pointed at his son and said, 'Take a photo of him; he's the story.' Aydin Bircan, fifteen and already a story, stood framed in the front door as the snow fell, fez on his head and looking straight at the camera, proud of his father's expectations.

It felt entirely typical of Turkey's many paradoxes that while Fevzi's forefathers had made hats for Turks in the country's most avowedly religious city, his son would improve his strike rate making hats for tourists in the tabloid town they jokingly referred to as 'Bedroom'.

I said goodbye, turned up my collar, and trudged through the fresh snow in a whirler's city that wanted nothing but to be known for its football. It was evening, and a maroon haze was cast above the city. Snowflakes buzzed frantically like night insects in the glare of the street lights and car headlamps. And out here, beyond Konya's heart of domes and minarets, monuments to beliefs and traditions so entirely of the spirit world, the wool markets, long arcades of gloomy concrete shops, stockyards, grain silos, industrial felt factories where they turned out rolls of the stuff for use in blackboard cleaners, and kebab houses with broken lightbulbs, all looked earthbound, just like the footballing heartland that Wistful dreamed of.

The light was yellow at the night-time windows, nurturing a profound sense of welcome that led me to Wistful's, where the day's haul of tourists were being entertained. It was a curious shop, for in the several visits that I had made there, I had not encountered so much as a single conventional customer. Admittedly, midwinter was not the best time for the sale to wealthy tourists of prayer mats, rugs, pieces of furniture, musical instruments, hats, jewellery, or wooden carvings. But it no longer felt so much like a shop as an ill-lit but rather cosy living-room. A convivial parlour atmosphere had crept up on antiques putting on the posh, mugged them, and restored them to use as amenable pieces of furniture. The chairs and the kilims were regularly sat on, prayer-mats were requisitioned to guard against the chill of the football stadium, the *nargilye* water-pipes were smoked, the copper ashtrays were filled with cigarette butts, and items of jewellery were examined, fiddled with, worn, and then left lying on a low table among a wreckage of resting feet. All in all, it was a profoundly comfortable place washed in that soft, buttermilk light. Wistful and his boss had originally embarked with brave ideas of a proper antique shop in which tidy pieces stood in exhibited isolation. But it had rapidly gone the way of other Turkish shops and become a home, a retreat that even now was hosting a party consisting of Wistful, two Australians, a Belgian, and several bottles of raki.

The Australian couple were recounting the story of their journey. From the window, I'd noticed Wistful shudder, as if nails were being singly removed from his toes. I entered with some concern only to discover it was the pronunciation as the Australians roamed Turkey like linguistic Mongols, condemning blameless towns and villages on their itinerary to such utter destruction of the pronunciation that nothing of the original remained.

Less expansive was the Belgian, who wore a beard. His suspicious mien suggested that even the disclosure of information about his journey might leave him feeling robbed. Despite the fact that he was drinking raki freely supplied by Wistful's boss, he continued to wear his money belt. He told me that he had recently come from Iran. 'Now there's a cheap country,' he said. Meanwhile, the Australians admitted to spending, even by my standards, a stupefyingly low sum of money in Turkey. Something had gone awry with Wistful's tourist-trapping system. Far from selecting the fat cats, he seemed to have developed an unerring eye for bus station strays.

But tonight it did not seem to matter. As the travelling foreigners described places he would never see, Wistful was discovering what amusing company the raki bottle could be. He was a young man and perhaps this very night was losing his alcoholic virginity. The abject failings of Konyaspor were forgotten as he picked up surrounding artefacts and gazed at them with an ardent concentration, as if some aspect of each particular object left him staggered by an electric storm of mystical recognition. And then he noticed the object to his right which eventually swam into focus as the Australian girl. While her boyfriend remained deep in conversation with the Belgian, Wistful took my dictionary and buried his face in it. He finally surfaced, patted the Australian girl on the shoulder, and pointed to a word among the pages.

'Fondle?' she asked.

'Hah!' Wistful could not know whether this was precisely the right word, but suspecting from his cross-referencing that it was from the right lexical family, he chanced his arm with it, and said 'fondle' too.

The Australian boyfriend was transfixed in the headlight intensity of the Belgian's relentless description of a seventeen-hour wait somewhere on a snowbound train. Not that the boyfriend's awareness would have moderated Wistful's behaviour, now whirling with the magical discovery of alcohol-induced indiscretion. But try as he might, his failings with my dictionary turned his intended indiscretions into nonsensities.

'Flounder?' asked the girl, drawn by Wistful's pointing finger to a second entry in the dictionary. Perhaps Wistful did not like the sound of the word, for he repeated 'flounder' with no more confidence than she. From the deep raki-inspired wells of feeling, poor Wistful was drawing flat fish.

Later, I discovered that he'd been trying to convey the floundering nature of his attempts to communicate with her. But it had not worked, a fish having got in the way of this apologetic prelude to a grander statement. So he dispensed with the prelude altogether and, the boyfriend still captive on a snowbound Iranian train, leaned across, kissed her on the mouth, and said, 'I lovv you.'

And so it was that Wistful actually delivered an English sentence whose meaning he properly understood. The first thing he learned in a language he did not know was how to express love. Or perhaps it was only inebriation. Vulnerable intimacy would probably be the guiding condition of his life.

Did he think that this leap of faith might move the girl to understand Turkish, or he English, or that their feelings for each other would far outreach any need of conventional language? As for her, would she slap him?

She did not slap him. Nor did she turn aggrieved to her boyfriend. All she said was that she lived in London, and that was the uselessness of it all. That cold winter evening, there was nothing more pitiful than Wistful's blank expression, which indicated that he had not understood a word of her careful reply. Mere language had defeated them. Into the pure futility of the moment a money-belted Belgian voice manoeuvred itself. 'I am thinking maybe we are here, in this snowdrift, until spring comes.'

Wistful looked up. 'Where's this man from?' he asked, with drunken contempt.

'Belgium,' I replied.

Wistful smiled and spoke a few words of Turkish. 'Oh, that small village in France?' After defeat in a language not his own, he could still triumph at home.

✳

chapter thirteen

WHEN YOU arrive at the bus station in Istanbul, the taxi drivers offer to take you to a hotel. In Ankara, they invariably assume you want to go to the airport. Most, when you direct them otherwise, will query your instruction. When I said that I wanted a look around the town, mine swerved in astonishment and almost took out one of the city's many statues of Atatürk. For the next few minutes, I was aware of his eyes scrutinizing me in the rear-view mirror as if my interest in the city made me exotic and unpredictable.

'Why?' he asked.

His surprise was typical, for not even Ankara's own people – and few of them would describe themselves as such – take much pride in the city. Convinced that they have somehow been tricked into staying, most of Ankara's citizens find it hard to believe that anyone would be here of his own free will. They wear the bemused expressions of those who, after a protracted pinch, have just discovered a distressing truth: *I actually live here. And since we have had children here and watched them turn into adults, I have evidently lived here for some time.*

Certainly, they never meant to. Their intention was to do the statutory time here, the rich to oil a few contacts and be seen around in the regime's favourite city, the poor to make some fast money before getting out. Ankara is an in-and-out-fast kind of place at Turkey's geographical hub, a place of planes, trains, and buses which bring people in only to dream of the day that they are finally taken out. But that day does not tend to come. Ankara is a transit lounge now containing three million people who have been about to go home for years.

In the early 1900s, this dusty steppe town was home to a mere thirty thousand souls. It boasted a modest reputation for cats and wool. With no port nor river of any significance, Ankara was just one of the towns on one of the ancient trading routes across Anatolia. In Hittite times, it had been a caravanserai for royalty, but that was long ago. And yet this town awoke on October 9 1923 to the news that it had just been crowned the new capital of Turkey.

The diplomatic community in Constantinople was aghast at the idea of being posted to a distant town where the communications and facilities were practically non-existent, and made their Turkish counterparts aware of these feelings in no uncertain terms. Since, by definition, diplomats were supposed to be diplomatic about their posting's choice of capital, they obviously felt strongly about it. One recently appointed foreign ambassador asked a visiting English writer, something of an old Turkey hand, what changes she had seen in Ankara since it became the capital.

'When I stayed in this hotel seven years ago,' she replied, 'the room next to mine was occupied by goats, sheep, and donkeys. Now it is occupied by Your Excellency.' The ambassador shuddered.

But as far as Atatürk was concerned, the foreigners could learn to live with lingering farmyard smells. Ankara was Anatolian, and that was the end of it. The town may have been nowhere, but nowhere rather than the shores of the Ottoman-tainted Bosphorus happened to be the geographical heart of the new nation. Nation and capital would share a fresh start and a new city European in style would rise from the unsullied expanses of the steppe.

On our approach that morning, however, the landscape was clueless, devoid of the merest suggestion that it was working up to some kind of metropolitan head. Beyond the

bus windows were bleak brown hills and poplar trees, telephone lines running a dance of sun slivers to the horizon, and
goats champing at the thin scrub. All was as it should be in
rural Turkey when segments of city suddenly appeared
between the folds of hills – brown roofs and towers and
factory chimneys – and it looked most improbable, like a
planner's mightiest howler. *Here?* asked the incredulous voice
in my head. They told you to build it *here?*

Evidently, a city tour had never before been requested of
my taxi-driver. While he shrugged his shoulders, throwing
confused turns left and right like an outmanoeuvred boxer, I
tried to concentrate on evidence of the young capital's republican idealism: the wide European thoroughfares with names
like Independence Street and Republic Boulevard, the opera
house, the Empire-style railway station, and the Youth Park.
There were the statues to Atatürk, who was also remembered
in a nearby state farm and a cultural centre as well as at least
two main roads, Atatürk Boulevard and Gazi Mustafa Kemal
Boulevard. We passed the ministries, the parliament buildings,
the museums, the official guest house, and the Central Bank.
These shiny levers of the young capital, which the new nation's
first bureaucrats, civil servants, bankers, businessmen, and
politicians had been posted here to operate seventy years ago,
seemed to confirm that Ankara had not been built on the
organic principle that position attracts trade attracts population, but as an extended monument to an abstracted ideal of
Anatolian national pride and rebirth.

Atatürk envisaged the development of his city as stylish
suburbs in stately encroachment on the steppelands, a harmo-
nious extension from the civic core. But he and his planners
had not taken into account the fact that the bankers and the
diplomats, the bureaucrats and the politicians, the editors and
the businessmen needed the help of more than their thrusting
young assistants. They needed tea-boys and secretaries. They
needed grocers and taxi drivers, tailors and policemen. They
needed waiters and plumbers, park attendants and road sweep-

ers. Their new-fangled typewriters needed repairing, their shoes cleaning, letters processing, telephones operating. The hotels needed doormen and bellboys, cleaners and cooks. The embassies needed drivers and gardeners, secretaries and maids. In short, they needed a population.

But fledgeling Ankara was foot-bound like a pretty Chinese girl. And so long as the city looked good, with the adminstrative and cultural functions gleaming, the pain and the deformity went unnoticed. Visible status symbols such as the opera house and the ministries were what mattered, with a few statutory minarets where absolutely unavoidable.

But it could not last. Ankara would break free of the bindings. To the anger of the authorities, new migrants started to build on the hilly outskirts of the city. Convinced that they could control what they considered their own creation, the authories forbade construction. But the new legislation was not watertight, and the migrants eventually traced the leak to the fact that the building restrictions could be interpreted to apply only to the hours of daylight. And so the *gecekondu*, the 'night-built' house, was born. Like vampires, the migrants went about their construction in the hours of darkness, the hammers falling silent at dawn, and the *gecekondu* spread and grew strong, drawing what little life remained from the anaemic vision of Atatürk's planners. In its place, a big-city pulse, weak at first but growing steadily stronger, rang out across the *gecekondus*. Toytown was starting to function, to hustle. It was as if this unreal creation had gradually adapted to the rigours of metropolitan rhythms until it finally sat up all on its own and breathed. By 1960, the population had reached half a million *en route* to the three million who now live there.

Soon, exuberant vistas of colourful shacks and houses mottled the hillsides of the suburbs, and Ankara was uncomfortably surrounded on all sides. It was as if the Anatolian village had come to call on the pretensions of the unreal city, and the city pretended not to recognize it. *But you must remember me*, persisted the village; *it was only a few decades back*. And the city blushed, turned away, and said: 'What an idea!' and everybody laughed politely.

But everybody knew. With the chaotic suburbs, Ankara was at once shorn of its grand European ideas. The showpiece for visiting overseas dignitaries had instead become Turkish, all buses, buildings, and coal dust, and the splendid reverb of Turkish life. In beds of cement that had once been fresh, the numerous imprinted paws of stray dogs and cats were evidence of what the city had become: alive.

We drove up Constitution Street in balmy sunshine. The mildest day for weeks reminded me of the coldest winter for years, nine winters ago when the air had been thick with lignite from the boilers and smuts decorated the washing hanging grimy from the windows of the apartments, when slabs of ice swept broken-backed from the roads lay piled along the pavements, and people trudged through the snow past the constructions at Kocatepe, due to become the biggest mosque in the Middle East, or made for the terracotta-painted opera house.

I had taught English here in 1984. The Kocatepe mosque, whose vast shadow had fallen across the windows of my apartment, was almost finished now. I walked down the hill to my old school building, but the school had moved premises. Beyond shutters that rattled in the wind, the classrooms were empty and a school table that had been abandoned on the patchy front lawn had collapsed at one end, as if to its knees.

On the television in the nearby café, an afternoon football match was beginning in Istanbul. Before the kick-off, the teams unfurled a long banner advertising Saturday's Bosnia rally, and the crowd roared its approval. I had often come here in the afternoon to treat myself to honeyed *baklava*, the syrupy walnut pastries that the Turks adore. In the years of my absence, the boy waiter had grown a moustache, a belly, and become a man. In the kebab house opposite, the man who operated the till had grown old and grizzled. His eyes were soft now, all enquiry gone. Neither of these old acquaintances volunteered any memory of me, and it all seemed too long ago to start again. The warm expectation of old familiarity soon shrivels at blank faces and empty buildings.

I stood above the ruined snow wainscottings that hung mud-caked where road and pavement met and hailed another taxi. I might have headed west to Atatürk's mausoleum, resembling an enormous classical temple manned by a guard of honour and decked out in marble high on a hill above the city where the man's remains lie in a great sarcophagus. But, temporarily, Atatürk's example had been eclipsed in the jarring sound of an explosion that had given secular Turkey its latest martyr. So I headed east across the city to the Modern Cemetery in the suburb of Cebeci, where the remains of Uğur Mumcu had been lying for a week.

For days, Turkish television had screened nothing but Mumcu's funeral. The service at the Maltepe Mosque in the middle of Ankara had brought two hundred thousand mourners on to the streets. Mumcu's coffin, draped in a Turkish flag, was carried to the mosque as the crowds showered it with flowers while a storm laden with rain and sleet swept across the city and left black ribbons of mud and broken rose petals draped among the feet that filled the crowded streets. After the ceremony, a crowd several miles in length set out towards Cebeci. The air was rent with utterings of grief and slogans of outrage. 'Damn Hezbollah', they screamed. 'Turkey will never be another Iran.' They also damned their overweight President, Turgut Özal, considered to have given official sanction to the Islamic revival in Turkey, screaming: 'The fat man, the enemy of secularism.' They also screamed at the police who were attempting to supervise them, for in the present police vigilance there was a reminder of unforgivable laxity. From the constantly manned look-out post just twenty-five yards from where Mumcu's car had been parked prior to the explosion, the police had somehow failed to notice a large bomb being planted.

Today, last week's rain was only a memory among the

damp road-wrack, the mixture of cigarette ends, litter, old twigs, and mud that lay as if abandoned on a high tide by the wayside. As I watched, the weak sun was desiccating the surface mud and a light wind was releasing into the air the first granular stirrings as an early reminder of the dust that would come with summer.

Within the walls of the cemetery, all was quiet. Scarce low evergreens cast brief chill bars across the earth. Magpies made slow-motion progress, laden, skittering flights between the headstones to perch above the Modern Cemetery's many modern deaths. None of the headstones was inscribed with dates from the old Islamic calendar, which had been abolished in 1925. There was little lichen and not a fez top in sight, only neat lines of graves with inscriptions that gave names, dates, and the towns from which the dead had originally come. 'From Diyarbakır', 'From Konya', 'From Balikesir', said the stones, marking the resting places of recent migrants to a city that during long lifetimes had evidently failed to become home. In these inscriptions was a denial of Ankara and the modern world it represented, as if death only confirmed the old ways and the avenues of the past.

As I looked for Mumcu's headstone, I wondered how it would read. I guessed that he who had died for the cause of secular democracy might at least tie himself to his adopted city, Atatürk's secular citadel, perhaps the first of all these migrants to look forward, to choose as his epitaph the words not 'From Kırşehir' but 'Of Ankara'.

As I searched for Mumcu's grave among the stones, glimpses of sunlit, snow-covered hills showed beyond the trees, and in the stillness I thought I could almost hear the relics of those bitter screams echoing through the cemetery long after his burial. And the noise of those television scenes returned to me. The wailing, the screaming and tears, the upwelling of emotion on a sea of human movement reminded me of Ayatollah Khomeini's funeral in Tehran four years earlier. Only nobody had blown the Ayatollah into one hundred pieces for his beliefs.

Like an Edwardian murder mystery where it soon transpires that every surviving guest possesses the motive to have slipped the cyanide into the champagne or bludgeoned the victim with the candlestick, it was unclear who had killed Mumcu. He represented the persuasive voice of the established version of Turkey, and his murder was a calculated strike against any number of modern Turkey's defining principles – secular, democratic, unitary, and Western-oriented – in the hope that it might not always prevail. The only certain conclusion that could be drawn from the possible suspects was that they made for a long list, and Mumcu's modern Turkey had made many enemies.

The list was initially headed by radical Islam. Three separate Islamic terror groups claimed responsibility for the assassination. Since Mumcu was a staunch secularist and had been repeatedly scathing of the Islamic movement in his journalism, an Islamic plot made eminent sense. Iran was soon implicated in the Turkish press and by Turkish politicians.

Another organization, however, was soon to claim the killing as its own. The PKK, the Marxist-inspired Kurdish Workers' Party, had been the subject of detailed investigations by Mumcu. He was categorical in his condemnation of the PKK cause, and in his support for the unitary Turkish state. The PKK had every reason to silence a voice which so persuasively opposed them.

Then there was Turkey's criminal fraternity which Mumcu had investigated, ruffling gangland feathers in so doing, while alleged links between the PKK and the Turkish Security Service suggested another possible suspect. Mumcu had apparently been investigating these links at the time of his death. Had the Security Service ordered Mumcu's death in a bid to protect itself from damaging revelations? Had the state itself murdered a journalist who had become fatally over informed?

The plot thickened when Refah suggested that the CIA was actually responsible. America, Refah argued, was anxious to prevent Turkey's emergence as a regional superpower and, as a destabilizing measure, had murdered one of its leading secularists. The subsequent heightening of tensions between Turkey and Iran, Refah explained, would serve America well by increasing Turkey's military and strategic reliance upon her.

Enter the 'document'. Produced by Refah, it purported to confirm the involvement of the West, specifically Mossad and CIA agents, in the murder of Mumcu. According to the document, six such agents had apparently infiltrated Turkey under cover of darkness and by boat. Under inspection, however, the document was instantly revealed as a blatant fake. But the question was: what kind of fake? A fake attempting to pass itself off as an original or a fake banking on being exposed as such? Was it a best effort to appear genuine, prepared by Refah so as to pin the blame on the West and divert it from the Islamic movement? Or was it the work of Western agents, deliberately strewn with errors so that it would appear after the most cursory of examinations as a fabrication, and lead to the elimination as murder suspects of the US and Israel?

Mumcu might have died at the hands of radical Islam, Kurdish nationalism, the Turkish Mafia, the Turkish Security Services, or the Americans and Israelis. A young couple standing quietly in the gloaming finally alerted me to the whereabouts of Mumcu's grave. I asked them who they thought had killed him.

'The EC,' the man replied.

'The EC?' I was not sure I had heard him right.

'Definitely. If they can point to the murder of a few journalists in unstable Turkey, they need not take our various attempts at membership so seriously.'

Resistance to the Turkish state, it seemed, was on every side. But on a wet day a week ago, two hundred thousand Turks had gathered to defend it.

His grave was a long bank of freshly turned earth piled high with fading red and yellow carnations, and sprigs of privet and bay whose stalks were wrapped in crinkles of silver foil. There was no headstone yet. As I left, the last rays of alchemical sunshine above the cemetery wall were turning a few black branches to gold.

I emerged on to the street beyond the wall. The day was drawing to an end. Young children were walking home from school. The girls were neat in skirts and tights but the boys wore their trousers in the inimitable Turkish style, an inch too long, so that mud had become a permanent caked feature around their hems. On the far side of the street, headstone makers were working from a long line of cramped ateliers amidst the wail of angle-grinders. Commerce hugged the cemetery with an unseemly closeness, as if drawing a lover's corpse to its chest. The masons were coated in a ghostly white marble dust which made me fear they might at any moment abandon their equipment and make for the cemetery gates for the night before the sun finally disappeared. After a moment, I beat off these morbid feelings and understood how appropriate it actually was that headstone making and cemeteries should coexist, a healthy recognition of life's eternal verities, until I noticed what was being manufactured in the lulls between headstone commissions. The masons were turning out kitchen unit tops.

On each was a draining-board scored with fine long grooves, while discs cut from the marble to make room for the sinks lay around like prototype wheels. It might have been an early Roman discount tyre centre.

Outside one atelier, two rooks were sitting on a stack of recently completed headstones. The top inscription remembered one Ibrahim Ersoy, 'Of Ankara'. The city was growing up. It was becoming home, and I no longer needed to know how Uğur Mumcu's stone would read when they finally installed it above his remains in the Modern Cemetery. For Ibrahim Ersoy was staying, without condition, in Ankara.

※

chapter fourteen

THAT NIGHT, I caught the Blue Train to Istanbul.

'You're leaving,' said the taxi-driver as we set off for the station in a night mist gathering above Ankara's boulevards, and he pulled on his cigarette. An errant foreign body common to Turkish brands, a length of barbecued treebark, supported an exceedingly long stub and glowed to illuminate the driver's face in the mirror like a Hallowe'en mask.

'I'm catching the Blue Train,' I told him.

'Give me a ticket for the Blue Train,' I told the man at the ticket office. The name of the nightly service between Turkey's two major cities withstood repetition. The sound of it promised mystery and intrigue. While Turkey's other trains, mostly known by their scheduled departure times, slipped colourless and unsung from the platforms, I imagined the excitements I must encounter on the night run between the young capital and the big city.

Still, I wondered why it should be blue.

'It just is,' shrugged the man at the ticket office without enthusiasm. '11.21 p.m. Platform one.'

And blue it evidently just was to the junior businessmen and civil servants, students and families ranged along the platform making routine, broken conversation or reading early editions of the next day's newspaper. *Milli Piyango* men, the state lottery-ticket sellers, dodged among the waiting passengers swivelling their round wooden boards to which bundles of tickets promising billions were attached. But these were billions of lira, in which sorry currency a mere £70, and £69.50 by tomorrow morning, made you a millionaire. '*Milli*

Piyango', they sang, but the lateness of the hour had wrung all enthusiasm from their dirge-hollow pitches. In their peaked white caps, they looked like dispossessed and slightly crazed U-boat captains, toothless sharks cruising the platform for titbits.

At the carriage window, I watched a flurry of torch signals, flag motions, and whistles clear the train for departure. As the Blue Train moved out with a lurch, the uniformed functionaries waves their goodbyes with a fanfare, frontier zeal as if they at least understood the romance of this particular train. Railyards, distant stadiums, and low concrete buildings passed, where pale yellow lights at the windows illuminated patches of thin scrubby grass outside and fell across stacks of sleepers. As I watched, we passed beyond the suburbs and the lights fell away, only gathering as occasional pinpoint thickets to indicate distant steppe villages in the darkness.

I was sitting next to a meticulous man, greying and moustachioed. After attending to the fastidious organization of his affairs, he turned to me and said: 'Perhaps you will drink some raki?'

I followed in the wake of this man-sized introduction to the buffet car.

We took the last seats in a crowded carriage where waiters in white were pirouetting among the throng with bottles of beer and glasses of raki, salads and savoury pastries, plates of white goat's cheese and baskets of bread. In spite of the cigarette burns and the meals that the moths had made of the damask tablecloths, what little remained had been heroically ironed and then draped with care across the tables. Water glasses served as vases for small sprays of pink flowers, and saucers supported white candle stubs. The evident effort had infected the passengers, who seemed temporarily released from the shackles of routine and were taking their enjoyment on a tube painted blue as it thundered through the Anatolian night. Amid the noise and the light catching on raised glasses, my host calmly caught the arm of a passing waiter.

'A bottle of raki. Seventy-five centilitres. And water. Now. Please.' He turned to me with a courteousness devoid of unnecessary expression. 'I assume,' he continued, 'that you have eaten.'

I hadn't. But there was something in the man's manner which suggested that I should pretend I had. Even his assumptions, I guessed, did not brook contradiction. As I went hungry, the bottles arrived. He poured measures, filled our glasses with water, gave a tiny, precise bow from the neck and demolished his glass. He looked up and with the merest gesture of the head suggested in no uncertain terms that I was to follow suit. I did so, then screwed my empty glass into the table top, gasped out loud, and looked up. But the man's eyes were elsewhere, flickering with amused interest around the carriage. The Blue Train was living up to its reputation.

He prepared himself another raki, administering the water to turn it cloudy. When I asked him what he did for a living, he threw back his head in silent laughter which I took for a moment to be the prelude to his answer until I realized it was the answer itself. He downed his raki with a wolfish smile and dabbed precisely at the corners of his mouth with a paper handkerchief. He lit a cigarette, sucked down a mouthful of smoke, and in so doing swallowed much of his first question.

'Tanbul?'

I nodded. 'And you to Istanbul?' I countered. And he smiled fulsomely, but that was all he did. It was a pleasant enough smile but once again it was no answer. He was drinking fast enough to do himself damage but I somehow imagined that his innate elegance would safeguard against any deterioration in his deportment. So when he first hiccupped, it surprised me much as a royal fart might have done.

The man held my gaze until one o'clock in the morning. Lifting every refilled glass to within an inch of his lips, he raised his eyebrows defiantly and threw the raki down his throat. Whenever I smoked, he leaned across to light me up. Whenever I asked a question, his attention was gone. Finally, in the ruins of the emptied carriage when the waiters sat among the drooping candles reflected in the sheeny pallor of their faces, the man closed his eyes. He sat still, his breathing light, and two large teardrops formed, one at the corner of each eye.

It was as if we had taken a late-night branch line into another story entirely. In the tradition that I had always associated with this train, that of the intrigue-filled thrillers of Eric Ambler, I had expected this mysterious man to slip me a scribbled address as he left, that of an Istanbul shipping agency or perhaps the commercial attaché's name at some shadowy Balkan Consulate. Or he might have recommended me a hotel, or addressed me by name on leaving so that later I might have disturbing cause to wonder, since we had never been introduced, how he could have known it. But I did not expect my Blue Train contact to turn to tears, fall asleep, and leave me to pay his bill.

'Every week the same,' said a sympathetic waiter, jerking his head at the sleeping form as I handed over a cripplingly large wad of notes. 'Manages to drink his way through a complete stranger's pocket.'

In the sleeping carriage, a few late-night cigarettes were being smoked. Elsewhere, sleepers lay childlike and crumpled. It was hypothermically cold; every rhythmic movement of the train ushered fresh draughts of steppe air through gaps in the windows. Now I understood why they called it the Blue Train. The wheels had settled into a long rhythm that broke at regular intervals with an echoing report; it carried me off into sleep.

Morning was a foul-mouthed, premature desecration. Light flooded the carriage through torn curtains and provoked a muttered tide of cringing affront as if the daylight had invaded a covey of sleeping vampires. Heads surfaced waxy and dishevelled. Sons disentangled themselves from elderly mothers, stretched in the aisle, and lit cigarettes. Istanbul, crumbly concrete and gnarled trees, gathered at the windows.

My tearful neighbour's luggage had disappeared during the night.

'You do this for fun?' a man mumbled, rubbing his eyes with his fists above a black-stubbled face. 'Try doing it twice a week.' My rucksack had given me away as a tourist, but his words although addressed to me were primarily intended for a nearby colleague. They served to make me realize what differences existed; just as one man's romance was another man's free drinking opportunity, so it was another's regular commuting nightmare. The Blue Train was no strange encounter on the periphery of experience, but getting to work on a grey winter's morning. The man felt every impact of the train's last few jolts low in his back as it slowed for the station and the beginning of another working day. And I saw the train winding down through Istanbul's shabby poetry of mosques, factories, and wintry gardens to draw up at Haydarpasha Station on the shores of the Bosphorus. Perhaps it was because I did not live here that I could still dream of a time when these waters leaped with fish, when people swam from the banks on summer evenings, lay among cypresses full of turtle doves below a canopy of stars and a crescent moon while a hundred minarets stood bright above the city. My Blue Train journey was drawing to a halt in this breathless spirit; I had come to the end of the line, the end of a continent. But for the commuter, it was merely time to disembark.

Steps led down to the quay and a ferry bound for the European side. A slumbrous swell lifted the bows, snatched at the oily warp lines, and slapped along the quayside. As we moved into open water, a woman was tugging at an old bread roll and tossing scraps to the waiting gulls. They arrived in squadrons, making measured approaches from astern to pluck the bread from the sky before winging away to circle and return. Occasionally they would collide in airshow nightmares, and the bread would tumble from their clasp to the jackal birds that attended them. Beyond the breakwaters, sudden wind ran a file across patches of water, turning them grainy and textured for a second before moving on.

As we approached the European side, I could make out a crowd which had gathered on the quay to join the ferry for its return voyage. Bags and heavy coats jostled for space, and I understood that I was seeing for the first time the city through their eyes. Heedless of Istanbul's fabled views, people were going to work across the city, to join the gulls in the ceaseless hunt for scraps. And so it was a grey February morning, and the mosques and palaces, minarets and cypress trees of the imperial city looked monochromed and without substance. Shreds of filthy cloud hung around the Galata Tower and fishing smacks cast off into an oily, fish-depleted sea. These were beleaguered commuters contemplating no postcard view of the city but poorly paid jobs and children to feed, high rents and medical prescriptions which they could ill afford. It was Istanbul without the evening lights glimpsed through sea drizzle, Istanbul infirm and shorn of illusion. Above me, I heard the seagulls and their cries on the wind as they dived for bread scraps. The wind was cold and it soon drove me inside.

A travelling salesman was pitching to the passengers in the cabin, with considerable success. He was selling what he described as magic torches, which worked without batteries. 'Ladies and gentlemen, a unique opportunity this morning to purchase a magic torch. Such a torch that lasts a lifetime. The perfect camping accessory . . .' It was the camping that sealed it, opened pockets and purses to make the salesman's morning. Camping caused crumpled lira notes to change hands as underpaid, urban people, who would never go camping in all their life, got kitted up just in case. Camping meant arriving for these people. Camping meant leaving the big city behind for a few well-earned days' rest in the country. The camping torch sustained their hopes for the future, as if planning for opulence staved off the realities of a low-wage present.

So they had not abandoned dreaming. No matter that the torches were not designed to last; some did not even survive the crossing. A young girl returned hers to the salesman two minutes after her mother had bought it, but clearly did not feel cheated by shoddy goods. All she wanted was a replacement. It was only expected that her camping dream might remain intact until they reached the other shore. Then it might be allowed to flicker and go out. In Istanbul, it was known that dreams did this.

As the passengers disembarked, the salesman stashed his lira and busily dug out another box of torches from his bag to pitch to dreamers on the return voyage.

'A good sale,' I remarked.

He chuckled. 'Lesson one, my friend. I used to tell them how useful a torch was in power cuts. I got nowhere. Nobody in Istanbul needs reminding about power cuts.' In this there was a perverse logic; such was the grinding poverty of these people that they had given up on fuel bills, repairs, new clothes, abandoned the purchase of practical essentials before dreams, as if dreams alone could help them now.

I sought lodgings at the Péra Palas Hotel, Istanbul's *belle époque* glory built to accommodate those wealthy Europeans from London and Paris who disembarked from the Orient Express. No such hotel had ever been built for Blue Train passengers, blue-collar, dust-covered arrivals from the Asian wastes. This gilt-edged box of a hotel stood on a high period island while concrete, traffic, and twentieth-century thoroughfares tore past on all sides as if development and growth had burst their banks and were threatening to sweep the old hotel away. Japanese tour parties were racing among the pot plants and the ottoman couches, admiring the ancient giltwork and the creaking lift, exploring their sleeping museum. A belly-dancing *soirée* complete with befezzed attendants was scheduled for that evening. Meanwhile, the hotel staff were preparing for a lunchtime fashion parade. But first I had a couple of museums to visit.

At the city's Naval Museum, I found befezzed mannequin sailors. Twenty-six of them manned Sultan Abdul Aziz's huge barque. There were another fourteen of them in the barque of Sultan Abdul Mejid's harem. I had been drawn to them in the hope that I might be able to examine up close the material and structure of an original Ottoman fez. But such things were typically hard to come by, and here the boats were high up, the fezzes' secrets out of reach. When I tried to explain my mission to a museum attendant, he merely wagged a finger at me. So I moved on to the museum's statutory Atatürk Room. There were pictures of the Gazi as a young officer when first he entered the War College in Constantinople aged eighteen and also when he passed out of Staff College as a Staff Captain in January 1905, aged twenty-three. In both pictures, he was wearing a fez.

But the most memorable photograph was dated November 22 1931, a winter day in the hinterland town of Amasya, a place not unlike, and not far from, Kastamonu. The photograph showed a bare-headed Atatürk staring deep into the eyes of a turbanned man, old and white bearded with a nut-creviced face. The two faces are close to each other, and Atatürk is holding the man by the shoulders, a natural posture for shaking sense into someone. There is affection there, but there is also exasperation. I am doing all I can to make you modern, says Atatürk's despairing expression while the old man stares back, stunned, into the face of his Gazi, two faces looking deep into the Turkish dilemma that the other represents.

I continued my search for period fezzes at the Military Museum north of Taksim Square. My ticket was numbered one, as was the tag I received at the left-luggage desk. Three receptionists stared aghast at my intrusion. As I moved into the first exhibit hall, a man in a suit (doubtless numbered one) appeared from nowhere and latched on to me ten yards back. I did not need to have experienced tailing to recognize the feeling for the first time. The man actually coughed nonchalantly as he fell in behind me.

At first, I enjoyed his attentions. He made me feel important. Perhaps I constituted a threat to Turkish national security. Incidental music played inside my head. I think I in fact surveyed him more effectively than he did me. I was aware that he lingered at every corner until my progress through the exhibits made space for him to advance the surveillance. His suit was ill fitting and his hair tufted on one side of his head. One hand spent much of its time patting the tuft flat. The other hovered above a pocket as if to threaten with a spank the walkie-talkie tucked there so that it might not crackle, and thus rumble him with quite such regularity. Whenever it did so, my tail would make an admirably heroic effort to ignore it and appear like any normal visitor to the museum even though, judging by the admission ticket numbers, no such thing existed.

Being soldiers, the mannequins here could hardly take refuge from the curious public in high-altitude boats. Instead, they inhabited glass cases at ground level and stood around as if in convivial conversation that made light of the fact that they came from different armies and different periods entirely. A sergeant in the service of Abdul Aziz (1861–1876) was chatting animatedly to an officer of Mahmud II (1808–1839) while a gunner from the reign of Abdul Hamid II (1876–1909) looked on. What they did have in common were their fezzes. I fished out my notebook and started to write.

Renewed crackling indicated the frantic relay of information on the nearby walkie-talkie. The tail had taken cover behind a late-ninteenth century artillery officer to report that the subject was at this very moment taking notes on Ottoman cavalry uniform, and would they please advise.

The exhibits broke the laws not only of conventional time and space but of social etiquette too. What was that private daring to suggest to that officer, aside from the fact that a century separated them? I had seen collections of stuffed birds which somehow resembled this, where the kittiwake has inadvertently ended up in a case originally inhabited by the golden eagle so that it is surrounded not by appropriate fish and seaweed but by mountain heather and by a freshly slaughtered lamb that much bigger than itself. So it was with the soldiers. Their medals and decorations did not seem to correspond to the descriptions that purported to accompany them. Generals and guardsmen seemed to have ended up in each others' uniforms, to have dressed in haste and without due care, as if a museum cleaner had surprised them late at night in a moment of unbridled mannequin passion where differences in rank had served only to arouse.

And then I saw it, my best and perhaps only chance of examining a period fez close up. In one corner of the hall, a single mannequin stood unprotected by glass. I set about losing my tail for the ten seconds I calculated I would need to remove and examine the fez.

So I led him down the far side of the longest case of exhibits I could find, slowing my pace considerably so that he was obliged to do likewise. I figured he would maintain the pace for some time after I had disappeared from view, allowing me the time for my investigations. As I disappeared out of his view around a corner, I beetled silently across the hall to the mannequin soldier, apologized for the humiliation, and rapidly removed his fez. But it had been glued to the mannequin's head so that everything above his neck came off ghoulishly in my hand. My valiant soldier stood to attention with a three-inch steel peg where his head should have been. In the seconds that remained, I tried to replace the head but in my rising panic was quite unable to locate the hole in which the peg lodged. Suddenly, no time was left to do anything but place the befezzed head at the feet of the victim and flee through the nearest door. Another stubborn Turk had just lost his head for refusing to remove his fez.

And then I forgot fezzes entirely as I realized that I had stumbled upon one of the museum's unsung glories. I was in the presence of what looked like the unedited, rough-cut collection of presidential, prime ministerial, royal, and sheikhly gifts to Kenan Evren, the general who had emerged from the military coup of 1980 to become the country's President for much of the decade that followed. There were plates and plaques, vases and trophies, ornaments and pistols from all over the world. Highlights included a huge bejewelled sword from the King of Saudi Arabia and another sword, the same in every detail, from his brother. Were such repetitions deliberately modish in Saudi Arabia? Or had heads rolled among the Saudi advisers responsible for official gifts? And specifically, would either brother mind if the hard-up Turks sold one?

There were gifts from the Kuwaitis, the Syrians, the Bangladeshis, the Malaysians, and the Chinese. There were machine-guns from Pakistan and revolvers from Albania. There were presentations from UNESCO, from Yasser Arafat, and from the Greek Orthodox Patriarch in Jerusalem. What gave the collection a personal relevance, it struck me, was the fact that I would have none of it in my house. I wondered how many people had wandered through this hall and also thought how strange it was that the stewardship of nations should so regularly be entrusted to people with taste of such grotesqueness. Since the highlight of the display (a diplomatic incident in itself), a green frosted-glass vase of hideous design, had been presented by Romania's Nicolae Ceaucescu in 1983, one could dismiss as irrelevant parallels between taste and fitness to govern at one's peril.

As I slipped from the room, I noticed that the mannequin had not yet been rescued from decapitation. I did not know how the Turks treated those who dealt thus with their military heroes, but did not mean to find out. A valedictory crackle from a walkie-talkie was the final sound I heard as I crossed the museum compound, gratefully reached the street, and headed immediately for the anonymity of the city's Covered Market.

After my experiences with the mannequin, the idea, I suppose, was to lose myself in the mercantile flow. But where-once I might have disappeared into the heavy smoke of the nargilye pipes, amongst piled brocades from Baghdad, shimmering silks from Bursa, muslins from Bengal, and cashmeres from Persia, I was reduced to secreting myself among cheap factory kilims from the Turkish town of Denizli, pirated Naf-Naf bags from Istanbul sweat shops, trainers and leather jackets, backgammon boards and leather pouffes, and to tussling with slogans emblazoned across T-shirts purporting to be English, such as *Quite War in the Sea*, or *Green Peas Eco-Team*.

On the walls largely obscured by the T-shirts the names of the market's many gates and alleyways indexed a range of largely forgotten trades. There were streets called Quilt-makers, Bagmakers, Polishers, Needlemakers, Glassmakers, Swordmakers, and Shawlmakers. There was Clothes Cleaners, Bookbinders, Spoonmakers, Goldsmiths, and Jewellers. There was even a Kalpakmakers' Alley, and a Fezmakers' Street where over a hundred fez makers, it is said, had worked as late as the 1920s. Now there was a bank on Fezmakers', and endless boutiques with credit-card stickers on the doors. There were serried ranks of jeans and subtle spot-lighting, sharp suits and the sound of calculations in four or five currencies. Fezmakers', true to the slavishly slick reinventions of the twentieth century, had become The Arcade of Those Who Willingly Take Mastercard.

Eventually I found fezzes on Shawlmakers' Street. A young man studying to be a lawyer was minding the family shop while his father recovered from illness.

'You want a fez?' he asked dubiously.

'I want a fez maker.'

He smiled. 'Try the nineteenth century.' He would make a good lawyer.

'Somebody somewhere must still be making fezzes,' I insisted.

'You could try Bircan in Konya,' he suggested. 'He makes a nice fez.'

'I already have. I was there earlier this week.'

He looked at me over his young lawyer's glasses. 'I see,' he said. 'You really do want a fez maker.' My persistence apparently inspired him to leaf through an old ledger. 'You may be in luck,' he told me. 'I think there is still one fez maker in Istanbul.' He wrote down an address and sent me on my way.

His directions led me out of the high-rent confines of the Covered Market; evidently, the artisans who once worked there could no longer afford to do so. Retailers had long since colonized the pricey square-footages of the former workshops. In modern Istanbul, the graft of those who made things with their hands could no longer compete with the earning power of premium salesman's patter. My steps traced the artisans' retreat into the low-rent labyrinth of obscure, tatty alleyways beyond the market walls.

I eventually found the fez maker on the second floor of a lonely building where furtive cats darted at my approach. There was a faint smell of mildew, and windows rattling in the draught which disturbed the dust hanging in the shafts of light above the aged wooden steps. In his tiny room, lengths of material were piled on tables and shreds of cloth littered the floor. Two daughters were bent over antique sewing machines. A gas fire puttered in the corner, and in the Turkish fashion a mug of water was hung by a wire hook from the fire-grille to stop the air from drying out, as if, I imagined, it might otherwise crack and fall in noisy pieces to the floor.

His name was Garbis Bey. He was an elderly, miniature Armenian with shock-white hair and kindly eyes crouching behind thick glasses.

'You're the fez maker?' I asked. All three, I noticed, were working on flat brimless hats made from a bright orange and blue patterned material of the sort that Fevzi Bircan had so disdainfully described.

Garbis Bey threw up his arms. 'In a manner of speaking,' he replied. 'These days, everybody – America, England,

Canada, Sweden – seems to want patterned hats like this. Or waistcoats of the same material. But, yes, I suppose I am still a fez maker.'

The younger daughter looked up from her work. 'Of course you are, Father,' she reassured him.

'Are you going to make fezzes today?' I asked him. I explained how much I wanted to see a fez being made, the fez that Fevzi Bircan's arthritic back had denied me, before they were made no more.

Garbis Bey looked apologetic. 'Come with me,' he said, placing a disproportionately large hand in mine and leading me along a chilly corridor. He stopped in front of a door and turned a large key in the lock. We stepped inside. As my eyes adjusted to the weak light, I could see that it was a fez repository. I had never seen so many fezzes in my life. They stood in wobbly stacks against the walls, fez stalagmites rising to the ceiling among lesser formations that strove for space at my feet. They lay horizontal along shelves, tubes of fezzes wrapped in brown paper which in some cases had split open and spilled on to the floor.

'You want to see a fez being made,' he said. 'You have been all the way to Konya to do so. And I want to see a fez being sold. Because of this' – he surveyed his massive overstock with concern – 'we have not made any for several months. Perhaps we shall not make any more.' Only as we reached the warmth of the workshop did I notice that Garbis Bey was still holding my hand.

'Will you be sorry?' I asked him, and he laughed.

'It is my main product line,' he explained, 'so of course I shall be sorry. But I was very young when the fez was abolished. And we Christians were among the first to adopt hats. I remember my father choosing a homburg. The flat cap was rather villagey for his taste.'

'Well, I for one like your main product line,' I remarked by way of consolation before I could suppress the sentiment. But it was too late.

Typically, Garbis Bey took my words as a lead to present me with a fez. He wrapped a tape around my head and dispatched his younger daughter to the repository with the measurements.

'But, Garbis Bey,' I pointed out as he placed the fez upon my head, 'I am your only end customer.'

'In which case,' he smiled, 'I must treat you with care.'

They bade me goodbye. I reached the bottom of the stairs and arrived at the entrance to the street. I hesitated. To remove it now would have shamed me. So I took a deep breath, pushed open the door, and for the first time walked out into Turkey with a fez upon my head.

I did not last very long. Within seconds I realized that I had never felt so uncomfortable on account of a hat. Heads in the crowd turned on every side. A policeman asked whether I was a tourist. I replied that of course I was. Why else would I be wearing a fez? More such questions and my room at the Pera Palas would soon come under suspicion and with very good reason, for it soon would harbour two fezzes and a *sikke*, and all in the hotel where Atatürk had stayed. Fearful of an incident to rank with Bursa's hundred and fourteen packages, I chose a quiet moment to remove the fez, and hurriedly concealed it in my bag.

I was just yards from the Pera Palas when a demonstration outside the American Consulate held me up. Hundreds of women draped from head to toe in black, wearing black *chadors* and carrying black umbrellas, were separated from the Consulate by lines of policemen with machine-guns. Slogans, picked out in white on the umbrellas, variously accused America of being the 'Big Satan', told her to stop interfering, to stop being imperialistic, and railed at Bush despite the fact that Clinton had been sworn in three weeks earlier.

'An all-female demonstration,' I remarked to the receptionist at the Pera Palas.

'The police might perhaps be inclined to behave a little differently if there were men among them,' the receptionist put it diplomatically.

'Why the trouble?'

'Bosnia,' he said. 'They're upset about Bosnia.' It was a prelude to the major rally planned for the next day.

I wandered into the hotel dining-room. Here, with only a few walls and not a hundred yards between them and the demonstration, another group of Turkish women were expressing their own antithetical interests, perhaps with less anger, but with equal fervour and certainly more dress sense. In a range of outfits that included orange hotpants, chiffon tops, and lacy shifts they cruised up and down the catwalk, their faces arrogant and beautiful, but it was as if only the thump of Western music from the banks of speakers kept the chants of 'America the Big Satan' at bay.

That night, modern Turkey's crusade would continue with a touristic entertainment at the Pera Palas, doubtless along the lines of the previous evening's show at the Ciragan, a luxury Istanbul hotel where once a Sultan's palace had stood. The Ciragan event, as reported in the daily newspaper *Freedom*, was captured in a single photograph that immediately reminded me of another. A young male tourist, French and stripped to the waist, stared into the eyes of a belly dancer as if to defy, and simultaneously enhance, the lurid provocation of her breasts jiggling inches from his throat. Of course, it reminded me of Atatürk and the old man of Amasya in the other photo, these two faces locked on each other across the photograph, a reminder served especially by the juxtaposition of turban in one case, and fez in the other.

Only this time, the fez wearer was a tourist and he wore it for fun. And the predicament of this fez, humiliated by its proximity to pseudo-oriental sleaze, would no doubt have delighted Atatürk. In the photograph, the fez has been press-ganged into serving a world it had always opposed, the same place that Fevzi Bircan was going. The fez had become a laughing-stock, it had finally become a silly hat, and as such its demise might now be considered official.

But when the fashion show packed up, the sound of

women in black railing at America could once more be heard in all its persistence beyond the hotel windows. It was a sound that would not go away, and in it I realized that the demise of the fez had not remade the people, not all the people, and much that the hat once stood for was still out there beyond the windows of the Pera Palas, stalking Turkey.

chapter fifteen

THE MORNING of the Bosnia Rally broke chilly and bright, light flooding in from the sea to span the brief day. Turks were gathering in their thousands in Taksim Square, where Istanbul's marches and demonstrations traditionally came to a head, often murderous and bloody.

But today, the fighting would remain elsewhere. Turks across Istanbul thought of Sarajevo, of that city's razed mosques and desecrated cemeteries. In their minds, they saw gun-toting Serbs wearing crucifixes and nationalistic young Russians signing up for the defence of Slavic brother Serbia. Bitterly, they reflected on how the West was failing them, and remembered Turkish *gastarbeiters* immolated in the towns, their factories now empty, of eastern Germany, and Turks across Istanbul left their homes and set out for Taksim Square.

A line of police in riot gear was frisking arrivals at the head of Independence Street. By the entrance to the square, hawkers were selling Turkish flags and scarves emblazoned with the words *Greater Turkey*. Islands of pragmatism in this sea of idealism, they were also selling the scarves of Beşiktaş and Galatasaray, two Istanbul football clubs who were playing each other that day. There were thousands here, perhaps not as many thousands as had been predicted, but whenever thousands of Turks forgo the grudge match, the big local derby, it is indication of how much they care. And the Turks of Istanbul had cared before.

On October 5 1908, Emperor Franz Josef of Austria had announced the annexation of Bosnia. The Austro-Hungarians had been administering the territory since 1880, but only under licence; it officially remained an Ottoman possession. Emotionally, as the people of Constantinople were forcibly to demonstrate, Bosnia remained Ottoman beyond dispute.

Autumn was already in the air on the day of Franz Josef's announcement. The plane trees along the Bosphorus were beginning to show the first indications of turning, the leaves tinkling brittle against the wind in which chill strains jostled amongst the fading notes of summer. Word of the Austrian annexation soon reached the quayside, where Ali the son of Mehmet was at work. Blockades, it was rumoured, were being organized outside the Austrian shops in Pera. Ali the son of Mehmet joined an incensed posse of dockers to march across Galata Bridge and lend their support to the blockades.

By October 8, all of the capital's Austrian shops had effectively been closed down. Once prospective customers discovered that shops were Austrian, they willingly turned away to seek their purchases elsewhere. Delivery carts with nowhere to go stood laden in the streets. On October 10, a proclamation cemented the blockade by calling on all Ottomans to embargo 'the loathsome goods of Austria'. Austrian stores were blacklisted on posters which were stickered to the walls of homes, offices, and mosques.

Depositors organized a run on the Bank of Vienna in Constantinople. Bosnian Muslims gathered above Galata Bridge and marched through Pera denouncing the annexation. Ali joined dockers and porters to prevent the *Galicia*, an Austrian steamer, from embarking six hundred passengers at the docks.

The anger ran deep. Ali had been a docker for many years but considered himself to have been an Ottoman for longer. He and his colleagues refused to work the Austrian cargoes even though their stand meant significant wage cuts; Ali's four children would go hungry that winter. One evening, in the depths of winter, he and his colleagues were approached by an Austrian agent offering them tempting sums of money to unload a cargo that lay stranded on the quayside. When questioned closely, the agent eventually admitted what the boxes contained. Contemptuously, Ali and his mates rejected the Austrian's bribe out of hand. In no circumstances would they unload fezzes.

Nine-tenths of all fezzes sold in Turkey at that time were imported from Austria. After sugar, the fez was Austria's second biggest export to Turkey. Soon, the people of Turkey were discarding their Austrian-made fezzes and replacing them with Turkish ones. As early as October 10, the fez factory at Eyup had dramatically stepped up production to make up for the anticipated shortfall.

In December that year, thousands of Austrian fezzes were torn to pieces in front of the Customs House at Smyrna. The boycott spread as far afield as Trabzon and even Beirut. The embargo, said to be costing Franz Josef's empire five thousand crowns a week, caused the Austrian fez industry to collapse. Settlement soon saw to it that the Austrians got to keep Bosnia but Ottoman coffers were handsomely replenished and Imperial pride restored. But not before Ali the son of Mehmet, who kept an Austrian fez at home for special occasions such as *bayráms* and the imminent circumcision of his second son, had taken it from a shelf one morning and carried it down to the docks. Strange how he normally wore this hat to demonstrate his Ottoman loyalties, he thought, as he took it from its bag and flung it into the Bosphorus. For a while, it floated upside-down amongst shards of winter ice before a wave scuttled it and sent it gently to the bottom.

Today history was repeating itself as the great-grandchildren of those same dockers, now with surnames, gathered in Taksim Square to carry the flag for Bosnia just as their forebears had done during the fez embargo. Above the heads of the Taksim crowd flew the green flags of Islam and the red flags of Turkey. Bosnia, placards proclaimed, was Turkish and Islamic. Bosnia belonged. English-language placards were articulate in spite of themselves: *We are all Probable Bosnians*, one read. *Serbs Shoot West Speak; Where are Human*

Rights; *How Many Auschwitzes have to be Witnessed*; *Attention America – there is oil in Bosnia*; and *We can Come suddenly. We die-for our Religion brothers*, said others. 'We die for Sarajevo', the chant went up from a group of young men, and the sound was carried to that distant city, ringed by Serbian guns.

But beyond the sound of those guns were the echoes of history. It was 1937. The writer and traveller Rebecca West was in Sarajevo on the eve of a visit to the city by the Turkish Prime Minister, Ismet Inönü, he whose new surname recalled his great victory in battle against the Greeks. The visit created a buzz of anticipation among Sarajevo's thirty thousand Muslims, who had always cherished their links with the Ottoman Empire and were anxious to demonstrate their loyalties to its young offspring. The night before Inönü's visit had been a busy one. The men could be seen queueing outside the fez shops among clouds of steam. When the turn of each came, his crumpled fez was clamped on to a fez-shaped cone heated like an iron. Another cone was laid on top of the fez and screwed down tight. Once the fez had been returned to pristine shape by the steam iron, the attendant released it with what West described as a 'motherly expression'.

The next day, thousands of Bosnian Muslims were to discover that the Prime Minister of Turkey had anything but a motherly expression for their fezzes. Accompanied by his War Minister, Inönü looked out over a sea of fezzes – wearing a bowler. The Prime Minister, whose country was busy making its ideological bed elsewhere, pointedly ignored the green flags of Islam flying from a nearby building, made no reference in his speech to the ancient ties that bound Bosnia and Turkey, and instead commended the Muslims of Sarajevo to the fledgeling Yugoslav ideal.

But by February 1993, that ideal had long since taken root, even briefly flowered, but was now being crushed on the wheel of vicious, competing nationalisms. In Taksim Square, the President of Turkey rose to the accompanying roar of the thousands gathered to hear him. As he spoke, it was as if he were making up for lost time, erasing the sentiments of the Turkish Republic's first Prime Minister half a century earlier in Sarajevo. Only three months later, Turgut Özal would die of a sudden heart attack. But today and despite the disapproval of his own Prime Minister, he stressed the ties that bound them, the people of Turkey and the Muslims of Bosnia, acknowledged Islam and history, the green and red flags flying on all sides, and for a moment it was as if he might finally make swansong mention of the fez, the hat that Inönü's bowler had summarily dismissed fifty-five years earlier.

The demonstration came to a head with relentless chants of 'Troops to Bosnia' and 'Embargo on Armenia', and I slipped away as the crowds broke up and streamed down the hill towards the ferries. Mannequins dressed like Europeans looked out from the shop windows. The anger of the demonstrators was lost beneath the first utterance of the muezzins cutting through the cold, smoky air as the light faded above Istanbul. The short winter day was over.

Spring

✳

chapter sixteen

THE HOTEL receptionist with rheumy eyes shook his head. '*Un chapeau turc*,' he pronounced definitively. Outside, dawn was breaking. Gusts of wind arrived without warning, rifling through the date palms.

'You're seriously telling me that this city has nothing to do with it?'

'*Pour les origines du tarbouche*,' he reiterated, 'for the fez, *il faut aller à Turquie*.'

'But I've just come from there.'

'*Tur-quie*,' the Moroccan repeated in a non-negotiable singsong, handing me a room key. He might as well have denied hamburgers in Hamburg, sherry in Jerez. I was in Fez, and in the namesake city nobody wanted to know.

Weeks earlier, I had rung the Egyptian Tourism Office in London with the same question.

'From Turkey,' the man had replied unequivocally.

'But the Turks did not introduce it until the 1820s,' I protested. 'You Egyptians were wearing it well before then.'

'No, no,' the Egyptian insisted, aghast at the idea. 'Definitely a Turkish hat.' And, by way of signalling the end of my enquiry, he offered to send me some brochures.

The *Encyclopaedia of Islam* agrees. 'A red cap worn by the Turks,' it states. 'A Turkish flat-topped cap', my dictionary insists. The traveller Charles Doughty described it as the 'Turkey Red Cap' during his travels through the Arabian Desert in the late 1800s. But modern Turkey blamed it on the Greeks, and the Ottomans had named it after a Moroccan city, which had never even been Ottoman. What was behind this Oriental denial?

For at its prestigious apogee, they would doubtless have squabbled amongst themselves to establish the origins of this hat as their own. Even as the Ottoman Empire had receded through the nineteenth century, the fez pushed on undaunted to colonize new territories. Not only was it established across the Maghreb, the Levant, and the Balkans, but also into Afghanistan and as far afield as India. In its heyday, the fez in Morocco extended far south beyond Marrakech, where there was a fez factory. Such was its popularity in Tunisia (there was another fez factory in Tunis) that the custom of the late nineteenth century was to collect fezzes and wear two or more at a time.

The fez penetrated into the heart of Africa on the heads of Arab traders who ventured inland across the deserts from the Maghreb or sailed south down the Red Sea and East African coasts before heading into the interior through modern Tanzania. The Ottomans introduced the fez to the Sudanis on their forays south from Egypt. Later the King's African Rifles, originally recruited by the British from Sudani tribesmen, adopted the fez as part of their uniform and rose every morning to the sound of the Turkish Reveille. In his *Historical Encyclopaedia of Costume*, 1888, Albert Racinet claimed: 'The majority of the native inhabitants of Timbuctoo are negroes, but alongside them live Arabs and Moors who stay in North Africa for business reasons. As a result, the local costumes are similar to those worn on the Mediterranean coast of the African continent.' There was a time, Racinet was implying, when the fez had been established at the figurative end of the world.

But today nobody was collecting fezzes, and the hat had come to such a pass that it was being denied in the city from which it had taken its name.

'But you admit that Moroccans wear it,' I persisted doggedly with the hotel receptionist as he sought refuge in his ledgers.

'*Pas beaucoup*,' he answered. 'Here in Fez, in Tetouan near by, and the surrounding area maybe. Elsewhere, no longer.' Above the reception desk hung a portrait of King Hassan. Fezless, he was dressed in sunglasses and T-shirt, and was holding a golf club.

Outside the hotel, spring rain clouds were trundling across the sky above distempered walls, flower pots, and filigree balcony railings. A man in a fez had hoisted his *jellabaa* gown up above his ankles and was stepping daintily between the puddles.

'But this is a curious subject, Monsieur,' said Aziz once I had explained my purpose. He was a smiling man whose tiny bones cracked when I shook his hand and whose thick eyebrows wriggled whenever he spoke, like impassioned bodies beneath bedclothes. He was a tourist guide, encouraged by the tourism ministry to wear the fez when working.

'Otherwise,' he said, 'I would never wear it, this fez, what we know as the *tarboosh*.'

'Even in Fez, the city where it all began?'

'You are sure of that, Monsieur?'

'I am no longer sure of very much, Aziz.'

'Well, let us go and find out,' said Aziz amid a climactic activity of eyebrows.

The walls of the medina, Fez's magical covered market, rose to swallow us. Suddenly, I was amongst people crowding in on all sides, and I was immediately aware of weathered stonework and cigarette smoke unfurling, and bewitching, layered smells in which nothing distinct could at first be identified.

According to the *Encyclopaedia of Islam*, the fez was so named because it was first manufactured here. More specifically, according to the *Britannica*, Fez had long had a monopoly on fez manufacture, 'for it was supposed that the dye which imparts the dull crimson hue of these caps and which is obtained from the juice of a berry which grows in large quantities near the town could not be procured elsewhere'.

'Close,' said Aziz as I tried to keep pace with him, dodging expertly between the swirling currents of market activity. 'But not quite. Poppies, not berries. But by the mid-nineteenth century, they were increasingly using artificial dyes anyway.'

'And the colour?' shouted Aziz above the hubbub. 'What does the colour mean to you?' In Turkey, I told him, it was considered to have originated from the slaves of North Africa's Roman colonies, who were given red caps on their emancipation as a sign of their freedom.

Aziz disagreed. 'Red has very positive associations in Islam, and Fez is Morocco's most religious and cultured city. That's what the colour means,' he told me with a guide's unwavering certainty. Perhaps he was right, but I was rather inclined to believe that proud Aziz did not like being reminded that Moroccans had once been slaves. Besides, in Turkey, the fez's old associations with liberty against a background of sartorial enslavement, made for splendid irony, and the theory was irresistible.

As we penetrated further into the medina, my senses focused and the smells began to disentangle. There were huge sheaves of mint for making tea, and fresh whitewash daubed against the walls. Cattle urine ran steaming from a puddle in a beaded line across the earth before being trodden into the dust. I caught the first whiffs of the gag-making stench of the tannery. I was tracking Aziz by means of his red fez, a beacon bobbing conspicuously above the crowd. I lost him in the thrilling moment I saw what I had come for. For a second, it seemed as if Aziz was everywhere; and then I understood that they were old men in faded fezzes on every side lingering by the spice stalls, grouped outside the mosques. Around the bases of their fezzes, I could see the discolorations caused by the sweat of summer, brown ripples set down as if by a receding tide.

A hand tugged at my arm. 'You should not stare, you know. At least, that is what you Europeans are always telling us. Don't worry, you'll see plenty more.' Aziz led me through a tinkling door into a half-lit shop. At *Berrada et Tahri, Fabrication de Tarbouch*, an elderly man was flipping through a ledger of invoices, a licked forefinger turning the pages. Motes of dust hung in the air. On the wall was a portrait of King Hassan, and this time he was wearing a fez, the only Middle Eastern leader to do so.

'Turkey, I believe,' the elderly man replied to Aziz's question.

'But it's named after a Moroccan town,' I objected.

'Not here it isn't. Here it's known as a *tarboosh*.'

The man at Berrada et Tahri had been making fezzes, just as his father had done, for forty-two years. Was his son likely to?

'Our monarchy is very well established,' he replied, 'and the signs are that the heir to the throne will continue in his father's traditional ways. That will mean wearing what you call the fez. So, yes, there will be work for my son.' So the king's endorsement would suffice to keep it going. On important occasions such as circumcision ceremonies aged five or six, the yearly feast to mark the end of the Ramadan fast, and on wedding days, many of Morocco's young men would continue to wear the Turkey Red Cap.

'But only on a handful of special days in the course of their lives?' I asked.

The man nodded. 'These elderly men you see in the medina, always they are being buried, and as the middle-aged men become elderly, fewer and fewer are wearing fezzes out of daily habit. Our younger customers are not likely to wear out their fezzes. We cannot, I mean, expect much repeat business.'

'And where do you make them?' I asked, in the hope that I might finally see a fez being made.

'Manufacture,' the elderly man corrected my verb, leaning across the table to a pile of cloths. They were felt pieces, mass produced and rough cut to size, which needed no more than shaping on moulds before the linings and tassles were attached. The felts came from factories in Brazil and Czechoslovakia.

The elderly man shrugged. 'The *tarboosh* may be old fashioned,' he said, 'but these days we make it in the modern world.'

'So,' said Aziz happily, our mission accomplished to his satisfaction. 'Turkey. Shall we go?'

But just before leaving, a man in a fez popped his head through the door at Berrada et Tahri.

'Hey, Abdul,' said the shopkeeper. 'There's a man here wants to know where *tarbooshes* came from.'

'Andalucia,' replied Abdul unhesitatingly. 'When we Arabs ran it.'

From then on, it went badly for Aziz. As the certitudes he thought to have delivered up to me haemorrhaged at every corner, he experienced something like a grievous loss of faith.

'Oh no,' another fez wearer exclaimed when we stopped him in the street. 'It came from Saudi Arabia with the Moors when they migrated this way in the ninth century. Definitely.'

'That's untrue,' said another. 'I heard it originated in military headgear when this was a Roman province.'

One hour later, Aziz and I collapsed over glasses of mint tea. We had now collected Turkey, Andalucia, Saudi Arabia, and the Romans as possible origins of the fez. To which we could add the Turkish belief that it came from the Greeks, and the claim – albeit apparently unwanted – of this the namesake city.

'Now,' I said, thinking back to Konya's dervishes. 'Do you want to hear my theory?'

Aziz shook his head. He had had enough of theories. The more we asked, the more obfuscated the origins of the fez became. The guide in Aziz was looking for digestible titbits of certainty.

'You do not have your answer, Monsieur,' he said, the bedroom activity of his eyebrows stilled for once as if he had failed me. But I patted him on the shoulder, thinking that perhaps I did, even if it was not the answer I had sought.

'Oh,' said the receptionist smugly as I checked out early the next morning. '*Vous partez pour le Turquie?*'

'Indirectly,' I replied, paid my bill, and walked down to the station. Dawn was breaking purple above the city as the train heaved and rolled gradually forward. The rain came down as we left the outskirts behind us, scattering among the leaves of the lemon trees and puddling on the mud-ochre earth. At the junction at Sidi Slimane, passengers bound for Tangiers disembarked while the train slid south-west towards Casablanca. Young men stood around in leather jackets. I heard one, wearing a T-shirt on which was printed the message 'Hard Rock Café, Orlando', discuss virtual reality in English with a friend.

A man stood at a distance, further down the platform, in the rain. He was not of the English-speaking world, of virtual reality and the Hard Rock Café in Orlando. The rain coursed off his old fez, returning the faded maroon to its original dark purple. I had come here to trace the fez's origins, but what I think I had discovered about this denied and marginalized hat were its imminent endings.

This was the hat that had once colonized Timbuctoo. The hat that Tunisians had once gone so far as to collect had gone into terminal decline. Generally, only guides and staff in the more touristy hotels still wore them. In Tunis, the *Souk des Chechias*, the Tunisian fez market, stood empty, a backwater amidst the currents of commerce. In Lebanon, where the fez was still manufactured on a small scale, its use was restricted to 'a few old whitebeards dreaming of happier times'. In Syria, it had been out of fashion since the late fifties and only remained the habit of some Muslim clerics who wrapped it with a turban, and some elderly notables including the President of the Union of the Syrian Chambers of Commerce. In Egypt, a few workshops were still making it for the tourist trade in Cairo's Khan el Khalili, the city's Grand Bazaar. From Libya came a few unconfirmed reports of a scarlet fez topped with a beret-like button of felt. Among the old colonial households of Kenya it was occasionally retained as the uniform of the servants. In Greece a long floppy fez with a thick tassle was used as part of the ceremonial military uniform. In Bosnia it was still used by clerics and, to a slight degree, among the more militant Islamic nationalists. And in Morocco, habitual use of the fez was giving way to special occasions, and in that retreat were intimations of extinction. Now the only Moroccan fez I had seen outside the medina of the city that bore its name was perched upon the grizzled head of an old man standing, uncomprehending, in the rain. I put him at eighty years old.

He too would soon be swept away, he and his fez, by the indifferent currents of history and progress. He would go the way of Island Castle, that Ottoman rockpool, haven of faded fezzes, *nargilye* pipes, and rose-petal jam that Patrick Leigh Fermor had stumbled upon at the point where Romania, Bulgaria, and former Yugoslavia met.

Not long ago, they had built a hydro-electric dam on the Danube a few miles downstream of Island Castle. The waters had risen, slowly at first but with an increasing appetite, until they lapped at abandoned tea houses and the empty mosque, seeped under the doors and rose to cover the windows. The water rose up the drainpipes and gathered in gutters that would never empty again, climbed steadily up the roof tiles, and rose until only the crescent of the minaret remained. And then that too was gone, leaving a confetti of rose petals and a few faded fezzes to float for some final moments above the waters of Western progress.

chapter seventeen

THE THREE had been at school together. Now that they were in their late thirties, only those friendships reminded them that they had once been children and the short holiday that they took together every spring grew in importance as each year passed. For a few days, they might laugh at the fading memories until they were returned to them as if new, and the laughter would soothe the rapid passage of the years.

For a few days, amiable Sadi would no longer feel lonely in the space of his Istanbul bachelorhood, with his wrecked head of hair and ballooning paunch. A generous light would fill Mustafa's proviso eyes and the pains in his chest that fed on worry and cigarettes would not trouble him. His two friends would tease him about his resemblance, with his thick black beard and hawkish features, to the gunmen of Beirut, but he enjoyed the teasing. Only when he was left to himself did the resemblance start to worry at him. Ismail would welcome his old friends from almost a thousand miles away in distant Istanbul, and in their company the *longueurs* of his life in a frontier town of south-eastern Turkey would be temporarily lifted. For the schoolfriends, summer was four spring days in Van.

It was a beautiful afternoon in May. In the obscurity of his ground-floor office, hemmed in by buildings and passing traffic, it struck Ismail that he had not heard the glockenspiel sounds of the *Aygaz* delivery van, the song of the Turkish winter, for days now. After the rigours of a winter at five thousand feet, he noticed these seasonal indicators. Like a flower with an instinct for sunlight, the darkness of Ismail's office had caused him to seek out the town's vantage points until he knew by rote every street corner with views beyond the city limits, every second-storey office and café where he could watch the snow on the mountains receding day by spring day, sidling up the valleys and screes as the sunshine pushed back the evidence of winter until only the high, sunless gullies offered it refuge, and mud smoked in the bright warmth, feeding roadside rivulets of melt.

Today his friends were in town and the vantage points were not enough. Ismail called up Sadi and Mustafa, and suggested an outing to the lake. They took Ismail's red pick-up. The radio played the theme from *Love Story* as they sped along the water's edge, and they let it play despite their suspicions that deep inside each might be laughing at the others for it. To the right, the lake ran to the distant feet of snow-capped volcanic peaks. To the left, the hills rose more gradually from the lakeshore, permitting a few snatched fields of yellow-green and spiky young trees in early leaf before the contours bunched together into a mean, unrelenting ascent.

I was standing at a nearby jetty a few miles down the road, eyeing a boat suspiciously. I was the only prospective passenger and the skipper was talking an extortionate price.

'I'll wait for some other passengers,' I told him.

'Not this time of day you won't,' he replied, flicking away the stub of a cigarette. 'They all come in the morning.' But just then three men drew up in a red pick-up from which sounded the tinkling notes of the theme from *Love Story*. One of them, I noticed, was fat. Another looked as if he had taken hostages in his time.

And so we met on the boat to Akdamar Island, a favourite escape for the people of Van. Now that summer was on the way they would soon take to the boats with their picnics and barbecues, and clamber ashore for a day in the sunshine. While the children swam in the icy water and the men smoked cigarettes and took their ease, the women would cook, turning kebabs on skewers in the shade of the almond trees.

The old cutter drifted towards the island across water in which was mirrored in perfect detail the mountains and the snow, and the lilac-coloured almond blossom partially concealing the sunlit terracotta ruins of a conically domed building. The prospect was so beautiful as to be highly improbable, as if the surroundings existed merely in dreams. We were crossing a great volcanic lake of a depth unknown but of waters so filled with mineral sodas that the clothes our helmsman trailed from the stern emerged transformed, bleached clean. Where the bows of the cutter disturbed the reflection, throwing out great ripples, we could see between them into a darkness without end in which we might lose ourselves. Lake Van did not have many fish, but cats that did not believe this were known to prowl the shore, with eyes each of a different colour. We stepped ashore among the whisperings of birds and insects, the air freighted with the scent of blossom. Once upon a time, they had called this place Vaspurakan. So unearthly was it that no other name would have done.

And then the plane came, so low that I did not hear its thunderous engines until it was overhead, casting over the island on its approach to the airport a black shadow that lingered chill long after the plane was gone. It was a military transporter; I could clearly make out the markings among its camouflaged, khaki-brown confusions. As it disappeared, reducing towards a black spot far down the lake, I sensed a reminder being served; that even amongst the blossoms of Vaspurakan, real life was liable to intrude.

I had flown into Van only that morning. Military transporters were parked on every side of the airport. As we walked towards the tiny terminal building, two distinct groups were taking shape on the tarmac. To one side, some thirty men were resolving themselves with an uncertainty, hoping that they might regard themselves as a welcoming committee but suspecting they should actually accept that they were there to be inspected. They were falling into line, running hands through their hair for the last time and patting at rumples in their jackets. Government department employees, they fixed their eyes upon a mandarin of apparent consequence and the attentive retinue that scraped and bowed its way across the tarmac around him. The mandarin reached the employees and worked his way down the line, cursorily shaking hands with each of them as they inclined towards him. And then he was gone, spirited into the warm interior of a waiting black Mercedes, leaving the thirty men to stand down and break into puddles of unmotivated manpower reaching deep into pockets for cigarettes, each wondering how his handshake had gone. And so their morning passed.

The other group was of younger men. They were conscript soldiers headed for military service. They had been issued with uniforms that did not fit too well, and with cropped haircuts, but their luggage remained pathetically their own. Some had suitcases with broken locks that were encradled with blue twine; others flaunted pirated status symbols such as Benetton holdalls. One forlorn character carried two plastic bags, one blue, one pink, with a single trouser leg hanging sorrowfully from the top of the pink one. They were waiting for nothing so much as a handshake, only the barked order from their commanding officer to board the transporter.

As they waited, two dead soldiers passed in front of them. A pair of green-shrouded coffins had been lowered from the hold of another transporter, shouldered by a duty of soldiers and borne slowly to a waiting military ambulance. As the coffins passed, all the fresh conscripts stiffened to attention as if by instinct, all except with the boy with the plastic bags, who bent respectfully to tuck away the errant trouser leg.

And so I wandered up the jetty at Akdamar, the place of Turkish forgetting. The island was a sunlit fairy kingdom, planted out with trees in blossom and tall headstones inscribed in an unfamiliar script. The friezes on the walls of the domed building standing on a shoulder of the island were like a text from a fabulous story that had nothing to do with the pathetic significance of handshakes in the pursuit of modest departmental preferment, or the coffins of young conscripts. Instead, there were lions, snakes, angels, and dragons, horses, dogs, gazelles, and oxen, eagles, turkeys, cocks, and bulls. But there was a problem in fairyland. The building, its pink sandstone walls absorbing the warm sunlight, was a church. And it was Armenian.

Even those around me who had recently ignored the military transporter, I thought, would surely have to acknowledge the awkward realities enshrined in this building. But jovial Sadi, whose portly presence accompanied me through the ruins of the church, taught me a lesson in forgetting.

'Selcuk,' he said, identifying the architecture of the building to his satisfaction. And with it, his mind was neatly delivered of any Armenian problem. By simple extension, the nearby headstones and the bodies which lay beneath them were no longer Armenian, and the town of Van no longer had troublesome Armenian connections. Sadi had airbrushed Armenia out of his life.

How had it come to this, that decent Turks like Sadi could refashion the evidence of bricks and mortar so that their absolving view of national history might prevail? The Armenians, perhaps three million strong in the nineteenth century, had lived under Ottoman sovereignty for hundreds of years. But their tragedy was to be located on the Ottoman periphery where the Christian Russians were always seeking to gain influence. In the nineteenth century Russia increasingly portrayed herself as champion of the oppressed Armenians. During the Great War there were those Armenians who intrigued to advance the Russian cause. The Russians captured Van and held it from 1915 to 1917.

Then the Bolshevik Revolution radically reshaped priorities in occupied Van. Suddenly, atheist Russia was no longer interested in old-fashioned notions such as Christian solidarity. Her new credo being workers, she promptly withdrew from Van, leaving the way free for the Turks to return, slaughter at their leisure what they saw as its fifth-column residents, and torch the place.

In my exasperation, I wondered what I could say to Sadi of all this: that well-documented charges against his country alleged that between 1915 and 1918 some one and a half million Armenians had been slaughtered by Ottoman troops in eastern Turkey. I guessed that Sadi was too well entrenched in his forgetting to acknowledge the testimony of surviving Armenians, those who had witnessed victims tied together as if in a necklace and thrown into eastern Turkey's fast-flowing rivers after one had been shot to become the millstone which would ensure, eventually, that all would drown. I chose not to tell him that the accounts of all those beheadings, those firing squads and rapes, were widely believed in the West. I did not tell him what was known of the deportations, forced marches through the Anatolian mountains to end in mass graves deep in the deserts of northern Syria. I only told him that the building on Akdamar was actually built three hundred years before the Selcuks. Besides, if he were right, perhaps he could explain why the Muslim Selcuks had built themselves a church. Assuming he accepted it *was* a church in which we were standing. After a long pause, Sadi nodded slowly. It was a church.

There is a conspicuous innocence in the Turkish spirit, a sincere belief in the highest of ideals that cannot countenance the possibility of such a holocaust. The Turkish refrain most sincerely expressed is 'We are all people', articulating a fervent belief in common humanity. 1915 is remembered as the year of Atatürk's defence of Gallipoli, the anvil of heroism on which the Turkish state was later forged. Turks find quite unpalatable the idea that in the same year the blueprint for the Final Solution was being fashioned at the other end of their country. And so Sadi and people like him have picknicked on Armenian islands until the island appears Turkish, and history is reordered to their satisfaction.

In libraries over the years, among travellers' diaries and

memoirs, mouldering pages of dog-eared print and sepia photographs, I had found unsensational accounts that had served to convince me. Not accounts that detailed atrocities against Armenians, but mere cameos compelling in their very ordinariness told by priests and adventurers, mercenaries and writers, painters and eccentrics, old soldiers and aristocrats providing a simple accumulation of unexceptional references to Armenians living their lives in nineteenth-century towns and villages all over eastern Turkey until the frequency of them led to the question: where, then, are the Armenians now?

For there was a time when Armenians lived all over Turkey, particularly in the east, as every nineteenth-century traveller remarked. There is the Armenian banker in the central Turkish town of Afyon, or Opium, who affronts the writer Professor Ramsay in 1883 by charging 5% of the value of a cheque to cash it (*Impressions of Turkey*, 1897). There is Frederick Burnaby's Armenian doctor in Tokat, educated in the States and speaking with a Yankee drawl; there is the peasant throwing a wedding party north of Van; the woman by the edge of Lake Van stitching a shirt for a passing sergeant; the young shopkeeper jailed in Erzincan for a married woman's love of him (*On Horseback Through Asia Minor*, two volumes, 1877). There is Lord Warkworth's Armenian host who suffers in his home near Erzerum the threat of a beating from a Turkish officer intent on interfering with his lovely daughter; there is his Armenian priest with his flowing jet-black beard (*Asiatic Turkey*, 1898). There is Edward Vizetelly's Armenian peasant helping the writer to a bag of wild duck on a bitter moonlit night by a stream near Erzurum; and his tall, gaunt Armenian, the landlord of a drinking den in the border town of Kars, wearing baggy breeches, bolero jacket, and a thread-bare fez selling Bain-Bruel Cognac which, with its spread-eagle label, has suffered a fortnight's journey on the back of pony or camel to reach the throats of his motley clientele (*The Reminiscences of a Bashi-Bazouk*, 1897). Then there is the Reverend Joseph Wolff's Armenian pipe maker's son who puts him up in a town of two hundred Armenians and two hundred Muslims and bemoans the fact that the town's Armenian schoolmaster has just packed his bags, leaving them with a school but nobody to teach in it (*Mission to Bokhara*, 1846).

All Armenians, peppered with the tellingly ordinary details of real life that combine to condemn. For now there were only the Armenian enclaves near the Syrian border and in Istanbul where I had found Garbis Bey and his daughters making a last few fezzes in a sweat shop, and an Armenian church on an island in blossom leading me once more to ask: where, then?

The boatman had made a fire from twigs by the water's edge and was brewing tea as we returned. His skivvy was offering up prayers to Allah in the shadow of the church. As we sat, Sadi told me his own story of Akdamar; the forbidden love of a beautiful girl called Tamara and a young swain whose efforts to reach her on the island were thwarted by those who stand in the way of high passion. It all came of course to an unhappy conclusion, the young man drowning from his efforts and sighing, 'Ah, Tamara,' as he disappeared under the waves, his last utterances supplying the island with its name. Even after his slow nod in the ruins of the church, Sadi evidently preferred his history thus.

They gave me a lift back in the red pick-up as night fell. Mustafa was trying out medallions of English on me, words and slogans such as his firm favourite, Camel Trophy Rally, with which to adorn his conversation. Sadi was murmuring 'Ah . . . Tamara,' and patting me between the shoulders. Every so often, Ismail would point out a new stand of streetlights and claim them as his own. In this way, I came to discover that Ismail was a lighting contractor. 'Mine,' he would say, 'mine, mine, mine . . .' of each and every streetlight standing proud and bright above the illuminated pools of road and pavement. On the outskirts of town he stopped to buy a bunch of white daffodils from a young boy at the roadside.

'For your wife,' I said. 'Your own Tamara. How nice.'

'For my wife?' exclaimed Ismail, laughing. 'For my office.'

Van looked unfinished despite Ismail's efforts. Lines of new buildings, incomplete shells through which you could see in one window and out of the other, rose on the outskirts of town. Ismail looked out, measuring distances and making estimates in his quest for new contracts. Concrete kerbstones were settling down with a sigh, as if drawn to the dirt they were supposed to combat. Newness did not survive long in Van. Scavenging packs of shabbiness hunted it down wherever it might be found, and finished it off in days.

When they picked me up that evening, an excellent mood prevailed. Mustafa's chest felt so good that he would be able to smoke continuously, all evening. Sadi had put the Selcuk church out of his mind, and Ismail was looking forward to a second-storey evening, with unrivalled views of his own illuminations, at Van's best restaurant.

The town's best restaurant was situated above the petrol station, but that incongruity only emphasized the sheer big-city style of the place. There was damask and ranks of cut glass. There were ice buckets and a man in dinner jacket seated deferentially behind an electric organ. There were beautifully interleaved menus, soft lighting, scrolls of butter, tomatoes sculpted to resemble roses, and vases of flowers. A posse of neatly waistcoated young men showed us to a table in the window. I understood how I should perceive the place; as a mid-town Akdamar, another rather more conveniently located place where Van's rich might forget.

As Ismail sneaked a fatherly peek at his streetlights through the windows, I saw mud-splattered lorries filling up on the forecourt. We drank to each other, to streetlights and to the bemused lorry drivers catching sight of our raised glasses as they pulled out into the night.

'You'll join us for a picnic tomorrow,' Ismail asked as salads, stuffed peppers, aubergine dishes, and plates of rice winged in from the outstretched arms of bestarched, meticulous waiters.

'I'd love to,' I replied, 'but I'm going to Hakkâri.'

Going to Hakkâri? They had not heard so strange a thing, they all agreed, in months.

'No,' said Ismail. He was not forbidding me, just telling me that I was wrong. I explained that I understood the drive to Hakkâri four hours south of Van to be extremely beautiful.

'Sure it is, but Hakkâri is disgusting,' complained Ismail. 'It will be like a pleasant walk to arrive at a toilet.'

Ismail's cousin joined us and was asked for his view on Hakkâri. 'I go there every month to sell sports shoes,' he said, and his tone told me that I could take it from him. But Ismail's cousin had no chance to push the point for he shortly froze, ducked, and turned to the others. 'My father is here,' he hissed, surveying the room for surreptitious escape routes from a crouched position just above the stuffed peppers. It was apparently a grave social offence to drink in front of one's father, the aged, balding gentleman posted at the far end of the room.

'I thought your old man's eyesight was going,' said Ismail.

'But you know how word gets round,' replied his cousin.

'Well, there goes his Saturday night,' said Ismail as his cousin disappeared discreetly down the back stairs. 'To fathers,' he announced, 'distant or dead,' and did the cousinly thing by making sure the missing man's quota of raki did not go undrunk.

We probably drank for everybody's cousins that night.

'Shameful,' said Ismail, swaying slightly in his seat. 'Shameful drinking, shameful looking at other women, shameful . . .' he hiccupped, 'going to Hakkâri.' When I aimed a bread roll at Ismail, Sadi stayed my arm and appeared offended. 'Bread is sacred,' he admonished me. 'Bread, the Turkish flag, and Mohammed.'

The trouble started while I was in the lavatory fending off the seductive advances of oblivion. By the time I got back, fortified by a douching of cold water, everybody was on their feet. It transpired that Ismail had provoked somebody at another table, and offence had been taken. Henchmen were gathered round the two antagonists as they circled each other, calming them down, interposing themselves where necessary, trying to make them see sense. But in this bristlingly aggressive war dance rival parties brushed against each other and the potential flashpoints started to multiply. Like the plane over Akdamar and the Selcuk church, reality had barged its unseemly way through the doors of Van's best restaurant. A whirling dance of insulted manhood worked its way down the stairs, rolling up shirt sleeves as it went. Worried Mustafa was rubbing his chest with great circular movements. 'One word,' he told me resignedly, 'and this.'

When the altercation spilled on to the garage forecourt, it promptly turned into a fight. The stifling manners of the restaurant, the ties, suits, and polite conversation it demanded, had clearly frustrated the menfolk of this frontier town. Now all pretence was abandoned, and getting into a fight on the forecourt of the petrol station was like coming home. Exhilaration was abroad. Men in flapping jackets and with ties draped over tight bellies were throwing fists at each other while friends and employees were attempting to bundle them into waiting cars. A man, face black with anger, swerved past me as he ran to thump another man, and apologized to the foreigner as he did so.

Then they were shepherding us upstairs again; it was adjudged that those in Ismail's party should consider themselves in danger, and take refuge in the restaurant until further notice. Tantalized, I asked Mustafa what that single word of insult had been, but he held up his hand as if to halt the traffic of my questions. So we sat as if in a bunker and smoked more cigarettes while a waiter supplied regular updates from the window. One man who had been hit in the stomach, he reported, was lying in a drunken stupor on the forecourt. A late-night petrol customer was standing over him, scratching his head. As things were, he could not position his car for petrol without running him over. Several cars had been circling, presumed to be waiting for Ismail. As we waited, a series of phone calls were made in which the unconditional withdrawal of the insult was negotiated. In what I took to be a moment of high tension, Mustafa caught my eye.

'You like George Michael?' he asked me.

Ismail had fallen asleep and was in no position to retract the insult. Eventually, exploratory phone calls made from the restaurant on Ismail's behalf went unanswered. Then it was noticed that reports from the window had dried up. The waiter there had also fallen asleep. The view from the window was of an unthreatening, sleepy town. Supporting Ismail between us, we carried him downstairs and dumped him unceremoniously into the back of the pick-up. As we sped off into the night, streetlights probed at Ismail's retinas and above the accelerating engine I heard his prostrate form mumble 'mine'.

Once more, I asked what had happened.

'Ismail called that man a pimp,' Sadi replied. 'I think he meant it as a joke. But there are people in this town who don't like Ismail.' Perhaps that was inevitable; illuminating the inky shadows where Van's hard men had always done their business undisturbed was never likely to win him friends.

We raced round a corner and came to a halt outside my hotel in a squeal of tyres. In the confusion, somebody had sat on those daffodils destined never to adorn Ismail's office; the sickly scent inside the pick-up was overbearing.

'Go straight inside and stay inside,' somebody told me urgently as if my life depended on it before kissing me on both cheeks. Never before had life felt so deliriously like a gangster movie. Next morning's bruises suggested I attempted an impulsive forward roll through the hotel door as if to avoid the inevitable gunfire.

I staggered upstairs, locked my bedroom door, and fell on to the bed. At the window, tyres skidded through the night.

chapter eighteen

I AWOKE TO a sensation that suggested I had ignored the regulations in a hard hat area to my cost. As I made for the bathroom, daylight at the window probed indelicately at the frayed nerve ends around my eyes, like protruding wires in the rubble of my personal demolition. As I bent to slake my thirst, the bathroom's cold tap coughed at me emptily.

How bad had it been? Did calling somebody a pimp invite a protracted vendetta in Van? Had Ismail's party gone into hiding until, by a series of negotiated settlements and concessions, honour was satisfied and one's safety was once again guaranteed on the streets? Should I await a cryptic message? Was it safe to leave? Or would I meet a besuited heavy on the stairs who, recognizing me as one of Ismail's boys, would puncture my solar plexus with a single well-aimed blow and whisper in my ear the Turkish equivalent of 'Compliments of the Captain'?

After the high melodrama of the previous evening, it was hard to accept that every offended party was most likely marinating in a raki-sweat sleep and incapable of remembering the insult, let alone avenging it. Instead, it was easier to remember that the English word 'horde' comes from the Turkish word 'ordu' meaning 'army', and to believe that I now knew why. Since I might not safely linger in Van, I tiptoed down the empty stairs, paid my bill, and fled to the bus station for the morning service to Hakkâri.

Hakkâri was not the most obvious place to flee to. Sanctuary has doubtless been sought more sensibly elsewhere. Hakkâri was the Kurdish town at the end of the road, with a reputation as an unlovely, desolate, and dangerous place. But even in my raki-thumping unease, I could not help thinking of a river called the Zab, even known sometimes as the Great Zab, and it wasn't every day a river was called that. When such a river flows south to a town called Hakkâri, what can you do but follow it, notwithstanding the claim of your host from the previous evening that it debouches into a toilet?

Moreover, it had been the intriguing habit of travellers, particularly those of the nineteenth century, to refer to '*the* Hakkâri', a strategic deployment of the definite article that conferred on the area an unlikely distinction comparable to the Punjab or the Serengeti. Colonial familiarity, in such cases, had probably prompted the definite article. But Hakkâri was different; neither colonial nor familiar, I guessed its use derived from a desire to lay boastful claim to a comparable kinship with these remote and inaccessible mountains, the subtlest kind of adventurer's name dropping that bespeaks intrepidity, in a place devoid of colonial cricket pitches or safari camps that had awed these travellers deep in south-east Turkey. (Or Kurdistan.)

No lesson had been more firmly impressed upon me than that the label 'Kurdistan' should only be attempted by those fully trained in the use of highly volatile and inflammatory linguistics.

'Kurdistan?' Istanbul Turks had bridled as I'd recounted my itinerary months earlier. 'You mean south-east Turkey.'

I honestly thought I'd meant Kurdistan, if only for the reason that there had been a time when KURDISTAN was writ large and ingenuous across these mountains on even the most official maps of an empire stretching from the Balkans to Baghdad. A time of nineteenth-century travel accounts such as Comte de Cholet's *Armenie, Kurdistan, Mesopotamie*; Ely B. Soane's *To Mesopotamia and Kurdistan in Disguise*; and A. M. Hamilton's *Road to Kurdistan*.

But now 'Kurdistan' had been Palestinized, stripped of its old traveller's poetry. To use it risked the ire of many Turks, who presumed offensive separatist sympathies. The cartographers who once laid out its letters in Ottoman map rooms now wrote ANADOLU (Anatolia) and TÜRKIYE (Turkey), as if to mark the territory as an inalienable Turkish birthright. The old names that once identified the various territories of eastern Turkey had meanwhile been deported. Armenia and Georgia were expelled east to the post-Soviet republics while Kurdistan went south to Iraq where, in spite of Saddam's inhuman savagery, the area was still known as such; Iraqi Kurdistan but Kurdistan nevertheless.

Relieved, I watched the outskirts of Van fall away behind us. The busboy eventually me brought me a bottle of much-needed water. Rows of veiled heads turned at my frantic, unchecked gurgling.

'The heat,' I explained, thinking that a raki hangover would not wash in this company. I pointed at where the sky would have been if the roof of the bus had not got there first. But the veiled women only looked at me blankly, for it was not very hot. In fact, when I looked towards the window and the treeless heights beyond, a light tracery of dismissive drizzle was falling against the glass.

I took refuge in my own map, where the final letters of TÜRKIYE and ANADOLU combined to form a pincer movement deep into the region. Lest anyone forget, was their message, but they also made the map hard to read, as if to suggest that outsiders anyway had no business here. It was, however, clear that bar an impossible track through border country to the south this was the only road into Hakkâri. The mountains crawling gradually up the window-panes either side of me threw a shadow across the map to reinforce the message that the Hakkâri region was remote indeed.

Such were the winter snowfalls here that villages regularly disappeared. The remains of fifty or sixty villagers might eventually be found strewn across a mountainside amid their broken homes and possessions long after the thaw had exposed them to the vultures, eagles, and wolves. Distances were long, winters were hard, and gradients were steep; in such a place the outside world existed beyond the neighbouring villages only as a vaguely heard rumour, and latterly as a strange entertainment of little relevance that reached them via their few television screens. The Kurdish fealties had always been to the village and to the valley. Trouble came from neighbouring villages short on grain or perhaps wives, from villages whose distinct dialects identified them as outsiders who were not to be trusted.

The Ottoman authorities in Constantinople and the feudal fiefdoms of Kurdistan had long enjoyed an untroubled working relationship. The Ottomans, cautious of aggravating what they saw as a strategic buffer against the Persian shahs to the east, largely left the Kurdish barons alone. For their part, they were happy to accept the notional authority of the Ottomans, largely paying the requisite lip-service as if by subscription.

As the Ottoman Empire strained at the seams in the late nineteenth century, however, so demands on the local barons to supply Kurdish manpower for the Sultan's wars against Tsarist Russia increased. But it was the emergence of the avowedly Turkish ideology in the early twentieth century that finally did for relations between Constantinople and Kurdistan. The Turks started priding themselves on their Turkishness, and took to calling their country Turkey. At this point, unsurprisingly, the neighbouring Kurdish villages started to view each other in a more favourable light. After all, they were all Kurds in a place called Kurdistan. Only since an aggressive notion of alien nationhood had started to lay claim to a geography and culture which had always been their own, did it seem to matter. And in that overlap lay seeds of trouble which have been germinating ever since.

In March 1993, a few weeks before my arrival in Van, the Kurdish guerrillas had declared a ceasefire. Perhaps no hatchets had been buried, but they had at least been laid down. Once reports suggested that the former war zone was now swarming with journalists, trades unionists, and even Finnish MPs, I guessed it was safe enough even for me.

Not far after the village of Headcastle (main feature: a castle at the head of the hill), the road for Iran turned off at New Bridge (newish bridge across the Zab). These names were unimaginative, but throughout my journey they had served me well; my habit of translating them wherever possible rendered them comfortingly familiar. But beyond New Bridge, I was on my own. Next stop was Hakkâri, with that exceptional circumflex sitting astride the second 'a' like a phonetic border post to make it read something like *Hakkqyari*. I could hardly pronounce the place, let alone guess how it translated.

At the first roadblock, a small soldier in green fatigues clambered from a chair outside his army post and shouldered his way down the aisle. He did the endearing thing of craning his head to different angles so that he might compare identification photos held up for his examination with the real thing. If you concentrated solely on his head and neck, you could convincingly make him resemble an inquisitive chicken. Thus does time pass on Turkish buses.

'England?' he asked of my passport.

'England,' I replied.

'Not Ireland?' he asked, narrowing his eyes. 'Bad people.'

'Good footballers,' I replied in an attempt to placate him.

'But terrorists.'

'Not all of them,' I said. 'And not on the road to Hakkâri.'

He nodded in understanding, said, 'London,' convincingly mimicked the noise of an exploding bomb, and returned my passport.

The road which had previously commanded broad views was now being funnelled into a gorge alongside a boiling river that leapt with a white-capped, melt-swollen fury. Every so often, the bus swerved to avoid neatly indented teethmarks in the tarmac where several yards of road surface had been swept away by the current to disappear among the rapids in a brown tide of uprooted saplings and hummocks. In slow time, it might have looked like a lava flow.

The sight was enough to coax from my recuperating brain a story that Sadi had told me the previous evening. At a nearby river crossing some thirty years ago, a wedding party in a lorry had left the road and disappeared into the spring current. There were no survivors. Since then, the locals had called the place Satan's Bridge.

'They never found the bodies?' I asked.

'They never found the truck,' replied Sadi.

His story-telling was improving. As I looked from the bus window at the landscape, I sensed all the anger contained within its contours. It was as if it had infected the people who lived among these mountains, along the valley of this river.

During the Great War, however, Turks and Kurds had co-operated enthusiastically in the annihilation of their arch-enemies, the infidel Armenians. A few years later, they dealt similarly with the Greek invaders, but the Kurds soon discovered that that final conflict was to be known as the *Turkish War of Independence*, and that no such co-operation would take place in the formation of a state called neither Kurkey nor *Turdistan*, but Turkey. Soon after, the new Turkish republic refused to recognize the existence of a language called Kurdish. Kurdish village names were banned. The Kurds were widely referred to as 'Mountain Turks'.

Why should it surprise me then that my Istanbul friends should not recognize a place called Kurdistan?

Kurdish grievances had finally come to a head in early 1925, six months before Atatürk would announce the abolition of the fez. A series of uprisings in February led to five thousand Kurdish insurgents laying siege to Diyarbakır, the regional capital. The local gendarmerie sent to quell the trouble threw in their lot with the rebels. In March, some Kurds actually infiltrated the city, such was their commitment to the cause, by means of the sewers, but were eventually repelled by Turkish cavalry regiments and by machine-gun fire.

With the dispatch to the area of eight infantry divisions, however, the government position was soon consolidated. As Turkish troops massed, the general staff requested a list of the towns and villages which had declared their fidelity to the republic. 'In order to have the fullest possible information before operations begin,' a report in the London *Times* interpreted the sinister request. Lack of national sentiment was no longer an option. If you were not prepared to declare as Turkish, then you were not on the list; you were Kurdish with all the attendant hazards implied.

When the government offensive came, the rebels were routed. In mid-April, the rebellion's leader, Sheikh Said, was captured; five months later, he and fifty-two of his followers were hanged in Diyarbakır. Another four hundred were hanged in Elâziğ to the north; rebel villages were burnt and their defiant peasants massacred. What had collided with the bold, bright idealism of the new republic?

On February 25, a *Times* leader writer had claimed that Kurds customarily lived on a high-calorie diet of killing: 'As the Kurds have no longer Armenians to kill, they have taken to killing Turks instead.' But even the Turks did not dare take such a line, claiming instead that religion was at the heart of the problem. They figured that the foreign powers might find much to excuse in the strong arm heroism of a young republic struggling to throw off the restraining shackles of reaction.

Certainly, there was a significant element of religious grievance behind the Kurdish revolt. At its head was a religious figure. The insurgents made repeated calls for the restitution of the caliphate. Officers and mandarins loyal to the old regime provided clandestine support to the uprising. And there was talk of *jihad*, a holy war against the infidel secularists in Ankara, who had abolished the caliphate only the previous year. The religious grievance was raw.

But there was another cause for Kurdish anger. What the Turkish press and the authorities did not much publicize was the fact that on the very day of the caliphate's abolition, 3 March 1924, all Kurdish schools, associations, and publications were also banned by decree. Was March 3 1924 just a busy day in the Turkish parliament or did the simultaneous abolition of the caliphate provide a convenient smokescreen behind which oppressive anti-Kurdish legislation might be passed? Was the problem Kurdish nationalism as much as religious reaction?

The rebels did not only demand a caliph-king, but a king of *Kurdistan*. Suggestions that the rebels were nationalists rather than Koran-thumpers drew a tellingly hysterical response from elements within the Turkish establishment. 'The rude, savage, and ignorant mountaineers of *Kurdistan*,' (my italics) one journalist wrote, 'are too uncivilized to have any possible notion about a national movement.' Beneath the journalist's invective a deep fear of Kurdish nationalism could be detected. Turkish nationalism underpinned the very legitimacy of the new republic's existence; it was the ideal by which the national entity was defined. Kurdish nationalism, however, with its large geographical overlap, was similarly the ideal by which the Turkish national entity was undermined. Kurdish nationalism called into question Turkey itself. But it was happening, the clear articulation of Kurdish nationalist aspirations, and the authorities were alarmed.

Perhaps it is because of this that other journalists have done a good deal of prison time for arguing the Kurdish case; perhaps this is why a travel guide which claimed there were Kurds in Turkey and a German magazine which included within its covers a map of Kurdistan were banned as recently as 1989; why some eight staff working for the pro-Kurdish publication *Özgür Gündem* (*Free Agenda*) died in mysterious circumstances during 1993, most recently a young correspondent, Ferhat Tepe, whose bruised body was found by a fisherman in a lake near Elâzığ on August 5 of that year.

Cliffs reared up on either side of the bus, blocking out the light. By the roadside lay mottled blocks of ice, glaciers the size of houses. Local men, rifles slung across their shoulders, had erected bivouacs from plastic sheeting and were coaxing fires into life for making tea. They were members of the village militias, paid by the government to carry government arms. In this, the poorest of Turkey's provinces, the men had no choice but to be in the pay of the government, if pay really meant pay, even if the affiliation branded them as traitors to the Kurdish cause and made them and their families prime targets for separatist attack. Every man has his price, and these beleaguered villagers were highly affordable.

The years since 1984 had seen a bloody litany of insurgent attacks on police posts and pro-government villages, the lynching of government sympathizers and Turkish teachers, and the torching of schools. They had also seen army reprisal attacks on PKK strongholds and on public demonstrations, and the gunning down of pro-Kurdish journalists. Since 1984, at least eight thousand civilians, insurgents, and soldiers had died.

An early October day in 1992 had accounted for some forty of them, all villagers, who had been attacked by one hundred guerrillas at a place called Walnut Mountain. I remembered the words of a witness to the aftermath, a young Turkish soldier I had met in Cappadocia the previous winter where he was on leave.

'It was still quite warm,' he told me. 'A beautiful time of year. I think they must have been approaching the end of the harvest. I remember noticing dust from the threshing in the air long before we arrived. That, and smoke at a distance. We'd been informed of the attack. And as we approached, you could smell the place, the oddest smell. We found most of the bodies within yards of the village square, and a few others elsewhere. From where and how they lay, you could see which of them had tried to run. You could tell who had had the quickest legs.'

Survivors told the soldier that the PKK had turned up and

persuaded the village's fifteen militiamen to lay down their arms so that they might more congenially talk to the villagers – Kurds to Kurds – in what passed as the village square. One of the insurgents gave a speech glorifying the PKK, and then they opened fire – Kurds on Kurds – without warning before torching a number of the houses.

Afterwards, the soldiers did what they could to help tidy up. A few of them offered cigarettes to the male survivors. Around them, burnt-out ruins smoked in the autumn air. The agonized keening of the women sounded over the corpses. In the middle of fields where the stubble stood starched and dry, secretaries from the judiciary sat at desks in front of type-writers, filling out reports. In front of one house, the washing was still out, and a white shirt was soiled by smuts. Machine-gunned oxen had fallen where they stood, in the yokes that attached them to their threshing sleds, the same sleds I had seen in Soapmakers and in Pomegranate; I could picture the beautiful flint patterns, embedded diagonally across the under-side of the bases, but smeared in this case with the blood and the viscera of murdered cattle.

It was meant to be a lesson, this massacre of Kurds by Kurds, to discourage others from accepting government arms. Village attacks of this sort happened with sickening regularity. Every Kurdish village was a potential Walnut Mountain. Forced to declare either for the PKK or the government, the villagers were prey to the faction they were seen to have rejected, and dependent on the protection of those who did not generally turn up in time.

At another road block, a soldier flipped through the pages of my passport, murmuring the names of distant Turkish resorts where he rather expected me to be.

'Kuşadasi, Istanbul, Antalya, Pomegranate . . .?' I merely shrugged, for the question was good.

And it became better as the bus meandered into Hakkâri, which I now learned best translated as building site. If you looked up, the shabby unfinished breeze-block walls with their obscene lips of long-dried cement protruding between the blocks like petrified waves gave way to sublime snow-covered massifs, reflecting light and sunshine like enormous mirrors. All that airy beauty only exacerbated the situation at ground level, where there was a strong sense of permanence about Hakkâri's unfinished state. On the second floor of a building where work had long stopped, only an ageing sofa in yellow chintz suggested that the foreman occasionally stopped by – comfort guaranteed – to supervise this stupefying lack of progress. It was as if the breeze-blocks and the aggregate, and the bags of cement piled in the shadows of such building shells, had become entrenched features of the landscape. If you looked closely, you could see that those piles of aggregate had settled down, become mossy over the years. The building materials represented an excuse that lasted for ever, the one that claimed the entire population of Hakkâri had only just moved in.

In the town square, Atatürk was mounted on horseback. Perhaps it was supposed to endear him to the Kurds on account of their fabled love of horses; more practically perhaps, it gave him the height he needed to ride with dignity the regular desecrations that were visited upon him, or maybe it simply allowed him to get away more rapidly. Whatever, the mount was rearing on her hind legs as if Hakkâri was a diamond-headed snake coiled at her feet.

I walked past the town's market, a series of tattered bivouacs spilling along the main street which in their appearance served notice of the shiny ghetto blasters, plastic trinkets, training shoes, and cigarette cartons on sale there. Nothing was made any longer in Hakkâri, not the kilims, the carpets, nor the saddle bags I had seen in the market towns elsewhere; nothing made but small fortunes servicing illicit consumer markets across Turkey's unguarded mountain borders with Iran and Iraq.

I noticed the intriguing word 'Turizm' and an attendant arrow had been scrawled in blue paint on a wall. Even without the aggrandizing 'office' or 'bureau', the message proved an economy with the truth; the arrow led me to a small room behind the bus company offices where a man entangled in lengths of blue twine was trying to tame a large cardboard box which had about it the suspicious look boxes have when they are destined for an unmanned border. I asked the man for a tourist brochure. He disappeared into a corner and returned with one that was dog-eared and creased. As I read, I soon became aware that I was in the presence of an awesome civic optimism. 'Hakkâri has important skiing possibilities,' ran the caption in English below a photo of the overhanging massif. This was to be translated to mean that although skiing was not currently possible – there was not a piste, not a ski-lift, not a pair of skis in or near Hakkâri – it did at least have snow-covered mountains. In the mean time, although the brochure did not say so, you were advised not to walk out of town for fear of being kidnapped or made to suffer a more permanent disappearance.

The town's second attraction as featured in the brochure had been given the heading 'Stock Farming in Hakkâri'. A motley and somewhat unfocused flock of goats was ranged across a yard. Dude ranching it was not. The third photograph, which acted as a promotional summary, had been taken from the lower slopes of the mountain by a photographer who had evidently chanced his life for the sake of his craft on a foray out of town. 'A General of Hakkâri,' the caption read.

Thinking to consider my recreational options over a cup of tea, I turned, waving the brochure in thanks as I left. But the Kurd looked up from his box in outraged astonishment.

'Where are you going?' he gestured angrily.

'For a tea,' I replied equably.

'Not with the brochure, you aren't,' he told me. 'You know where it is if you want another look.'

So I left the town's one brochure and took refuge in Hakkâri's one café, where the town's few, somewhat blunt-ened, young blades had gathered to smoke cigarettes. The room was dominated by a fountain, a large basin with a series of trickle-down rims below a fruit bowl full of apples, bananas, and oranges – made entirely of fibreglass. Somewhere inside the contraption a lightbulb glowed, giving the whole thing an eerie nacreous look as if it were alive. I skirted the edge of it uncertainly and sat down in a corner. When I looked up, I noticed that everybody was looking at me with an utter lack of expression which I took to be measured malevolence. I checked my fly. I ran the back of my hand across my nose. And still they stared. Where, I wondered, were all those observers and Finnish MPs when I sorely needed their steadying influence? Then one of the larger young men left his chair and walked slowly across the room towards me. I froze. When he got within reach and stretched out a hand, I shut my eyes and braced myself. He changed channels on the television perched just above my head.

Near by sat an old man wreathed in cigarette smoke. In heavily accented Turkish, he asked me where I was from. When I told him, he drew hard on his cigarette. He'd heard of England, he told me, heard of it on the television. But he knew more about Germany; plenty of Hakkâri men had been to work in Germany – Dortmund, Stuttgart, Dusseldorf – but not to England. He was too old to have worked in Germany, but he'd once been to Diyarbakır as a young man and had worked in Van some years back.

Van's sophistication had bewildered him. It had also made him uncomfortable; he was always getting into trouble for speaking Kurdish. I told him that I understood the laws had been relaxed in 1991. He snorted. 'In 1991,' he said, 'they told us we were free to speak our own language at home. Well, praise to Allah, as if we had not been speaking Kurdish at home for ever. They were only dropping a law they could not enforce. What we cannot do is to speak our language in public places or government offices. I worked as a waiter in Van. If the boss ever heard me speaking Kurdish to people, even Kurdish people, he would have sacked me.'

There existed, then, a strict linguistic dress code: speaking Turkish was like dressing for dinner, discarding the shabby garb that was Kurdish. Woe betide anybody who turned up in the wrong language.

The old man sighed, leaned forward, and took two cigarettes from my packet, one destined for his mouth, the other to lodge behind his ear. The future had never been there, reliable and dependable, allowing him to take the next cigarette for granted. 'Look at those young men,' he said. 'When I was young, the army left us pretty much to ourselves. But now they're everywhere. So what will these young boys do? I'll tell you what; Germany, if they're lucky, or Istanbul. Of those that remain, some of the older ones will take government money to carry government guns. Many of the rest will join up, because if they don't, the PKK will anonymously slip their names to the authorities as PKK sympathizers. The treatment they will then receive is pretty much guaranteed to turn them into PKK activists. The authorities don't seem to realize that they recruit for the PKK far more effectively than the PKK does itself.' He cackled merrily. 'And anyway,' he continued, 'many of them feel that PKK membership is preferable to the kind of treatment they can expect as Kurds during national service. If you're going to have to spend a couple of years getting wet and miserable in the mountains, better do it with your own people.'

I asked him if he supported the PKK.

'Of course,' he replied, not even bothering to lower his voice. 'Everybody around here supports the PKK.'

'In spite of what they do in the villages? In spite of Walnut Mountain?'

'They are all we have,' he said. 'We can hardly speak our language, we have to watch Turkish television, read Turkish newspapers, vote for Turkish political parties. The PKK may kill people in the mountains but they're the only voice we have. If they allowed us a political party, then perhaps fewer of us would care for the PKK.'

'Do you want to live in a country called Kurdistan?'

'I just want the same opportunities as the Turks. It is too late for me, but I'd like my grandchildren to learn Kurdish at school. That would be grand! I'd like to watch Kurdish programmes on television. And I'd like these fucking soldiers off our backs. For the rest, well, we might get some kind of autonomy one day but few of us really expect to get our own country. I mean, with neighbours like ours!' He pulled a fresh cigarette out from behind his ear, replaced it with another from my packet, and patted me on the knee as he did so.

He leaned forward into the flame of his match and allowed me the opportunity to look closely at his turban. It was a rough creation in the style I had occasionally seen elsewhere in Turkey. In Hakkâri, most of the old men wore them, a turban with a look decidedly civilian compared to what Hakkâri's defiant young men were wearing. Among the caps and the veils on the streets, they were distinctive in a paramilitary uniform with romantic flourishes, khaki boiler suit open at the front to a waist wrapped in a neat colourful cummerbund and a turban on their heads, a tightly bound, active-service item of headgear. It was the uniform of the PKK, but it was also a distillation of Kurdish national costume. The Turkish security forces regarded these young men suspiciously. Wearing the uniform was a calculated provocation that courted arrest.

When he became bold enough to stockpile a further cigarette behind his other ear, I returned the boldness by asking him about fezzes.

'Fezzes?' he replied. 'Turkish. No, we never wore fezzes here. Turbans, always turbans.'

'What happened then when the government banned them?'

'They banned them, did they?' he asked with the patience of one who was being amply supplied with excellent Western cigarettes. 'When was that?'

'Oh, about one hundred and sixty years ago.'

'And then they introduced fezzes in their place?'

'Yes.'

'So now those people think I should be wearing a fez?'

'Well, they actually banned them too.'

Hamdy Bey's 1873 photographic album of costumes supported the old man's argument that this had never been fertile fez territory. The nearest towns represented in the album were Mardin and Cizre to the west, and in 1873 at least neither featured a fez.

As I was leaving, my cigarette supply drastically depleted, I heard the old man telling a friend across the café that they'd banned turbans.

'Oh,' his friend replied. 'Why?'

'I don't know. And fezzes.'

There was a silence. 'What are fezzes?' And in that question was the thought that in coming to Hakkâri I had crossed linguistic and sartorial borders even if I was not deemed to have crossed a national one.

It soon became clear I had crossed a gastronomic one too. Tussling with the limpest, greasiest kebab it had ever been my misfortune to be drawn against, my teeth closed on an object hard enough to make me wince. It proved to be a brass screw, half an inch long. When I pointed it out to the waiter, he issued no apology but a Eurekan yelp, turning triumphantly to the chef behind the food counter. By way of explanation, he pointed enthusiastically at the large stainless-steel wall plate behind the vertical kebab spit, drooping forward from the top left-hand corner and the empty screw hole there. I think I was expected to share in the general celebrations. When the waiter proferred the screw, it was several seconds before I realized he was asking me to suck it clean of kebab gravy.

Later, I walked round the town, but did so with a deliberate purpose that masked my aimlessness. Ceasefire or no, there was a wildness about Hakkâri and not the merest hint of a Finnish MP. The semblance of order felt wafer-thin and I did not wish to attract attention to myself. But only when I started noticing the same faces did I appreciate that aimless wandering through the town was quite the done thing. Around me, everybody was doing it, the Hakkâri promenade, linking arms, fingering worry beads and patrolling for the next momentary diversion. We all stopped for a couple of boys skirmishing in the market, a few took notice of farm animals feeding off piles of rubbish in a back street. We gathered to watch another foreman supervise the removal of his sofa from one storey, now apparently completed, to the next one down. The delivery of a washing machine drew a considerable crowd of promenaders, and you could have sold tickets for a good view of the battered taxi which stopped in the main street with a puncture.

I woke during the night to a nearby clatter, and in my fevered imagination it sounded exactly like the sound ceasefires make when they break, and atrocities are committed on unfortunate tourists. In fact, the chest of drawers in my hotel bedroom had merely collapsed. The next morning, I breathed a sigh of relief as I clambered on board a *dolmush*; the van to Van. After a last 'General of Hakkâri', that sad, shabby town disappeared among the mountains for ever.

The ceasefire would last another two weeks. Then, one evening, over a hundred PKK guerrillas would set up several surprise road blocks near a Kurdish town to the north called Bingöl, or A Thousand Lakes. Later, it was reckoned that the PKK had been tipped off; among the buses they flagged down, one was carrying unarmed soldiers to their barracks. In the early summer evening, the Kurdish flag fluttering in the wind, the guerrillas delivered their customary propaganda speeches to a terrified audience, selected thirty soldiers, and marched them down to the banks of the Memdo River. There, they shot them all dead.

The ceasefire broke up in a welter of recriminations: the government, it was alleged, had shamelessly exploited it so as to consolidate its military positions in the south-east; the PKK had only respected its own ceasefire until it was ready once more to kill – unarmed soldiers by the banks of the Memdo River.

Soon, the murderous pattern was re-established with a vengeance. The PKK torched schools and lynched collaborators. Three hundred deaths occurred within a month, and army commanders vowed the total destruction of the PKK by the end of 1993. Then, for the first time, the PKK focused its attentions on the tourist resorts of western Turkey. A bomb went off outside Aya Sofya in Istanbul; another injured several people in Kuşadasi; and twenty-three people were injured in a series of four bomb explosions in Antalya.

'Kuşadasi, Istanbul, Antalya, Pomegranate,' I remembered the soldier's disbelieving refrain. But now that they had hit three of these places, the sound was no longer of water lapping against beaches and the hubbub of holiday bars but shattered glass, a moment of silence and the screams of terror. Even in these places Turkey could not escape itself.

�֍

chapter nineteen

FROM THE TERMINAL, a long concrete breakwater that fingered into Lake Van a few miles north of the town, I watched
the ferry lights approaching. For an hour, the throb of the
engines grew gradually louder as the ferry ratcheted her way
across the watery curvature of the Earth. Insomniac seagulls
hung around the single telephone wire above my head. 'Schedule?' the harbour master had dismissed my earlier telephone
call query. 'The ferry doesn't have a schedule.'

'But the train that it meets does.'

'Not a very good one,' said the ferry master doubtfully. I
heard him pull hard on his cigarette. 'But it will come,' he
assured me. And so would paradise, universal love, and
European union; the question was when.

'More difficult,' he replied. 'But I can make predictions.' It
was his best offer.

Until early in the twentieth century, imperial policy had
regularly been decided upon the various recommendations of
the Astrologer Royal, the Dean of the Chapter of Court
Horoscopists, and the Wizard in Ordinary to the Caliph. When
the Sultan's heavenly forecasters lost the imperial appointment
and their titular embellishments, they went private, taking
their soothsayer's advice to the streets and receiving inquisitive
clients in darkened rooms where the veils that covered their
faces also concealed the flashing electric lights draped among
their beards to reinforce the celestial impression. All life's
secrets were there, from love and longevity to revelations
pertaining to the promises of paradise. I wondered whether
this ferry master might have soothsayer's blood in him, and

inherited instincts intact enough to have a confident punt at the comparatively simple arrival time of a plain ferry. And, when I heard him say the word 'Midnight', I was not at all disappointed since I had half expected 'Thursday' or some such dreadful sound to assail me.

The waiting-room lived up to its name. It was not for the occasional irksome delay but for hard-core, uncensored waiting of the type with which the dock workers there were evidently intimate. They cast glazed expressions at the television film featuring a dubbed Burt Reynolds playing in the background. The room was heavy with cigarette smoke, distinct layers of it so thick you could almost read the stratified geology of the room's recent history in it to learn with a fair degree of accuracy who had smoked what, where, and when. The dockhands had settled into a semi-permanent debris of backgammon boards and tea trays containing tulip glasses, red and white plastic saucers, bowls full of sugar cubes, and spoons of a cheap alloy type which only that day had slit open one of my fiddling, time-consuming fingertips. From experience, the dockhands knew that the train would come when the train was ready, and that the ferry – for dignity's sake – would not bother to turn up until shortly before the train did. And until then they would drink tea.

The train came from the east, from Iran. The ferry came from Tatvan on the western shore of the lake, and the two met at the far end of the breakwater along which the railway line ran. Waves slapped below the rusty bollards as the ferry eased alongside, lining up the landside tracks with those upon her own cargo deck and shackling them together them so that they then ran, conjoined and unbroken, all the way to Tehran.

A few trucks and a *dolmush* lumbered off the deck. Foot passengers, roustabouts grimy with sleep and a single German tourist heading for Tehran, clambered into it. Then they loaded the constituent parts of a reconditioned tractor engine on to the roofrack and under the seats. The German was passed an old newspaper to drape across his lap before being handed an object which I heard him describe, quite correctly, as 'very oily'.

From my vantage point on the upper deck, I was aware of a stirring in the darkness. At first, all that could be seen was a beam of light, a hypnotic pendulum swinging above an approaching rumbling on the tracks. By means of a torch beam, a man at the front of the train was signalling to the driver at the back. As the train drew near the ferry deck, the motion of the torch slowed, the carriage slowed in response and rolled gently on to the ferry, and was shunted forward until the abruptly halted motion of the torch instructed it to stop. Then the proud carriages were uncoupled, the train was backed up, the points were changed and the process was repeated until by and by the entire train was broken up and installed on the ferry's adjacent sections of track. Finally, an errant taxi squeezed into a gap between two train carriages.

It was very clever, but more pointedly, it was perverse. Trains generally took to ferries only when they had to; this one had forsaken vast expanses of dry land to seek out the only navigable stretch of water for hundreds of miles. It reminded me of that strange species of fish which has unaccountably abandoned the water for dry land.

The answer lay in the geology. The train had taken to the sixty miles of water because it did not much care for the land around Van. Massive river valleys ran across the grain of the intended railway line, making track-laying a nightmarish prospect. Besides, it was a light-sleeping landscape, continually rearranging its contours in a never-ending series of mudslides and earthquakes that made no concessions to railway lines. In the area, I had seen short stretches of an old road running intact within a few yards of the new one. But elsewhere the same old road had disappeared completely and one could not trace where it had run. Indeed – such was the surrounding landscape – one could not see where the old road could *possibly* have run. A German general called Von Moltke, supervising military movements in the area, once declared with exasperation that nothing was flat in the area except the roofs of the inhabitants' houses. And Lake Van, Von Moltke would have added if he had had the strain-saving mind of a railway man.

The saloon was almost empty. I set myself down among dun brown plastic seats, cupboards stuffed full of old life jackets, and metal fittings that had developed a green tarnish in the salt air, and listened to the sound of the idling engine. So windless was the night that its reverberation travelled unspoilt from the heart of the ship, and you could almost hear it take a stairway, round a corner, and move down a few corridors, falling in with the step of the approaching ticket man, audible long before he arrived. A distant door slammed, a key turned in a lock, and a pair of feet were dragged down a long corridor. A key ring jangled from a belt. When the ticket man entered the saloon he lifted a single finger to indicate that he was ready for us.

And so we followed him to the ticket office. And waited outside while he unlocked the door, removed the wooden board to make a window where we might be served, and unlocked the drawer to sell each of us a ticket for five thousand Turkish lira. The combined takings from the passengers on board the ferry that night to Tatvan added up to just over £2. I felt like starting a kitty, so much so that when the ticket man opened up the snack bar, the same old wooden panels, the same jangling keys, I leapt up to buy a packet of stale strawberry-flavoured wafers that reminded me of school.

Only the increased reverberations through the seats on which we stretched out indicated that we were leaving. As we gently slipped our lines, swung to the west and kicked up a boiling wake, the engine seemed to leave the bowels of the ship and rise through the floors towards us. Our bodies were set a-judder as if with the first indications of illness. The ferry cut a swath through satin-black waters flat as death, carrying seven passengers, a taxi, and a train. It was shortly after midnight.

If the accuracy of the ferry master's prediction was

uncanny, then the mere seven passengers were the more so. Where was everybody? Where were the lolling heads, the incessant crunch of sunflower seeds, the cigarettes offered at dawn? The luggage falling from the racks to batter us on sharp mountain bends? The sound of a strangled tape expiring slowly on the bus cassette player? The collection from pale-faced passengers of bulging black plastic bags to be slung from the speeding windows?

True, the ferry had left late at night and, compared to the bus service to Tatvan, took its time. But it had struck me as an inalienable Turkish truth that you could pick out of a hat – brimmed or otherwise – a destination, a mode of transport, and a time of departure and be guaranteed a full load. Only a bicycle ever set out on a Turkish journey with seven or less passengers on board. Tractor trailers minding their own business, even those that attempted to slip surreptitiously away in the middle of the night, seemed to fill as if by magic with passengers. Transport on the move, buses, *dolmushes*, even donkeys, awoke a primeval instinct in these former nomads. They seemed to feel in their bones the sound of a distant revving engine, and it spoke to them, that to travel was the thing, the destination a secondary consideration. So where on earth was everybody?

On the earth, I suspected, with feet firmly rooted. Not on boats, anyway, not on the night ferry to Tatvan. Perhaps, since the lake had never played an integral part in their lives, it was simply that so much water scared them and they had turned away from boats. To them, it was only fearsome scenery, this accident of volcanic activity. No rivers flowed from it, and only the evaporation which sweated off it in the high heat of summer counteracted the effect of the melt-fed rivers that ran down to the lake. Its consequent saltiness, six times that of sea water, had always meant a sparsity of fish. The towns and the villages had kept away, holding back from the shoreline as if uneasy at too much saline watery proximity.

But such fear was strange for a people whose every routine

bus journey was philosophically accepted as a near–death experience, a people who were always throwing up when the terror and the motion on the high road bends combined, and the roadside skies were filled with discarded black plastic bags of flying vomit. What was it about the lake?

While awaiting the arrival of train and ferry that afternoon, I had idled away a few last hours with the three friends. On their last day together, they drove me down to the lakeside close to the ruins of the old city of Van. A long pebbly beach punctuated by scrubby plants stretched in an arc above wavelets on the foreshore. Ismail and Mustafa were snickering together, and remembering what they could of the fight outside Van's best restaurant.

But Sadi looked out across the water, to the silvery peaks of the old volcanoes and said it was the most beautiful place in the world. Even as he did so, however, I saw him shiver. It was not the warmest day but nor was it shivering weather. I bent to trail my hands in the water and where the teaspoon had nicked me my finger stung, not the sweet ache of salt water but a sharp pain that the water's sodas, acids, chlorides, and sulphides inflicted; Lake Van made me shiver too. In all this great expanse, only a few hardy fish had learned to survive its poisoning effects. It was beautiful, but it was also malevolent.

We walked that afternoon through the ruins of Van's old city razed by the upheavals of geology and of mankind. Among the fallen masonry, mounds of grass–covered rubble now, was indexed the tragedy of a place where three peoples, three nations, overlapped and failed to find a way of living with each other. All that stood amidst the expanse where homes and streets once had been was the minaret of a fourteenth-century Ottoman mosque, and in that surviving monument was Turkey's triumph over Armenia and Kurdistan.

But it was triumph at a price so terrible that it was as if the combined tragedies of these three nations had infected the place and turned to poison the waters of the lake. It was not, only the tragedy of Van itself, the Armenians slaughtered where we were standing, among these very ruins, by vengeful Turks and Kurds after the Russian withdrawal in 1917, and not only tethered corpses clogging the rivers that ran down to the lake, but also the tragedy of the eight thousand soldiers and insurgents, villagers and teachers, women and children, Turks and Kurds who had died among these mountains over the last decade, the neat bullet holes in the bodies of thirty unarmed young soldiers lying by the banks of the Memdo River. It was everybody's tragedy. And if you looked into these depths, looked further than you perhaps might care, you might see the secrets they hid; like the hundred local dissidents sewn into sacks and thrown into the lake at the end of another Kurdish revolt in the summer of 1930, but also in the glimpsed hair of a drowned bride waving among the reeds, among the bodies of a wedding party and of a marriage that was never consummated except in the icy embrace of a poison lake, evidence of nature itself turned malign. And what you saw, standing by the shores of the lake, might finally make you shiver.

I awoke to a drenched dawn. Low clouds had been torn to shreds to soak the ferry and Tatvan's approaching wharves, the sheds, the rusted railway lines, and the few hazels and poplars that lined the track into town. Puddles were settling in the potholes.

I stayed in Tatvan long enough to have breakfast in a cake shop. They brought me small cheese-laced rolls, honey, and tea while the remnants of the rainstorm at the window were gradually tidied away by an emerging, methodical sun. It was a good place for breakfast but not, it was said, for much more than that; Tatvan had long had a reputation as the most down-at-heel of eastern Turkey's towns. Tat was not one of Atatürk's post-Independence War honorary prefixes; whatever it actually meant, it hurdled the language barrier with ease.

After Hakkâri, however, I knew better. I enjoyed my view from the window of the cake shop. In Tatvan, I was reminded of what I had always admired about life in Turkey. Everywhere was evidence of lives being lived, a continuity through the generations in the deep-worn steps where endless feet had fallen, the dark-stained seats where succeeding generations of local bottoms had sat, tarnished counters old with transactions, accumulated traces of work and life, hands oily and calloused, splintered and ingrained with dirt adding up to a kind of honour. There was redemption in it, and until a better redemption came along, it would have to do.

The hundred-and-thirty-mile bus journey west to Diyarbakır took all morning. I slept most of the way, waking only for snatched glimpses of the passing countryside, an old man kicking at his unresponsive motorbike, soldiers gathered at a barrack gate shaped like a rifle, complete with trigger and bayonet which lifted skywards when a soldier leaned his belly on the butt.

'There's danger in Diyarbakır,' Ismail's wife had told me as she and her husband, immaculately sober and scrutinizing the nightscape for illuminable areas of darkness, had dropped me at the ferry terminal the previous night. I knew of the shootings that plagued the area's major city.

'You should stay in after 8.30 p.m.,' she'd said. Tell that to your husband.

But as we approached the city's outskirts, I could see that the fabled black basalt walls no longer kept any danger at bay. Diyarbakır had burst out of her defences and spilled over the plain on almost every side in a succession of unplanned suburbs, market gardens, hospitals, and cement factories until the old city seemed like a comparatively tiny core, the original enclosing instinct lost at the heart of an uncontrolled sprawl.

The day must have come when, despairing at the lack of space, a pioneering inhabitant of the city first contemplated life beyond the walls, as if time and change were finally rendering them redundant. Who had been first to make his home beyond their protective shadows? And more importantly, why had he waited so long? For since every warrior clan worth its salt including Romans, Selcuks, the splendidly named Black Sheep Turkomen, and the Ottomans had invaded and occupied Diyarbakır over the years, it did not appear that the walls had been entirely effective.

So it was with my converted caravanserai hotel, built in the early 1500s but with impressive defences of its own that ignored the protection provided by the city walls a mere fifty yards away, much as one might supplement the feeble financial fortifications of a state pension. A strong gateway and high walls enclosed a large courtyard with rooms off on all sides.

The Selcuk sultans had revitalized the caravanserai system in the twelfth and thirteenth centuries. Regularly built within a day's walk of the average camel from each other, the traveller could rely upon a Selcuk caravanserai. Inside, he could attend to his camel, eat, wash, pray, and sleep while the scent of opium and the sound of song filled the air. In the late twentieth-century version, he could watch CNN, fax, and use the mini-bar. But until they filled the pool, he could not swim. And since there was no plug, he could not wash his clothes in the basin. No object as the plug is quite so objectionable to the Turk, who regards washing in stagnant water as an offence against cleanliness and Islam. Running water is always provided outside mosques. Nor, however, is any object as the plug quite so essential to the cheapskate Western traveller. So I customized the vegetable tray from the fridge. And as I washed my pants in a place designed for tomatoes, I thought how strange it was, my lack of plug, while incomprehensibly instant images and sounds were transmitted into my hotel room from a satellite high above the earth.

I stepped outside and was hit by a blast of history. I was within yards of the Mardin Gate, where Sheikh Said and fifty-two of his followers had been hanged in the aftermath of the Kurdish Revolt of 1925. Not that anybody was going to remind me. Diyarbakır's new face was represented by two young men in suits, the directors of Mezopotamya Export and Import Agent Ltd Co, who hijacked me as I wandered past their shiny offices. Among modern word-processors and type-writers, they installed me in a chair and laid a draft letter in English before me. The business of Mezopotamya Export and Import Agent Ltd Co, they explained, was to facilitate the aid work in Iraqi Kurdistan of organizations like Médecins sans Frontières and Save the Children. Could I cast an eye over their letter of introduction? '*We have set up our company to help your all your need,*' it read. '*We love your helping, postal transaction, representation, import and export, guides, all agency kind work. And translation.*' As I put their letter straight, they demonstrated how much they loved my helping by bringing me a cup of tea. Feeling increasingly helpful, I pulled up a typewriter and started to type up my improvements. But the letters on the keyboard were in the wrong places. There was no 'x' for 'export', no 'w' for 'We'. It was a Turkish typewriter. Laughing, they directed me across the office to an English one. But as I typed, I mused on how it had all started and on the letter that the offices of the Department of Alphabet Reform in Turkey must have written to Remington Rand Inc in the United States in late 1928:

Dear Remington Rand Bey,

Greetings,

Please forgive the use of nib and camel-hair brush.

You may be aware that our exalted leader, Mustafa Kemal Atatürk, has introduced a new alphabet now in mandatory use throughout our country. All citizens, from children in the schools to their grandfathers, have been learning the new characters for the past few months. We, the Republic's civil servants, have sat exams in the new alphabet.

Our new alphabet, closely modelled upon that in use in your country and elsewhere in the Western world, replaces the Arabic script formerly in use in these regions. Dating from the Ottoman period and adopted for its religious associations, the Arabic script was not suited to the phonetic needs of our language and has consequently delayed our progress towards enlightenment.

Now that we have adopted the new alphabet, whose twenty-nine characters ensure that the spelling of every word in our language can be correctly ascertained from its phonetic make-up, we are anxious to upgrade our office equipment accordingly.

So that we need no longer write to persons such as you with nib and camel-hair brush, could you please design keyboards to suit our alphabet, a copy of which is enclosed, and send three thousand typewriters forthwith.

On leaving the grateful management of Mezopotamya, I walked straight into a funeral. The coffin was being borne along at such a pace that to have called it a cortège would have lent it a misleading sedateness. Tiring bearers were constantly being relieved as new candidates emerged from the crowd of mourners, leaned their shoulders under a corner, and supported the corpse of their friend along the crowded street, past the stalls of melons and tomatoes, to the distant cemetery.

Upon the coffin was draped a green shroud on which the swirls of Arabic calligraphy were picked out in gold. Only here, it seemed, at the margins of life, did the old alphabet endure.

'I think the dead person is a teacher,' a voice mused in English at my back. Three young boys were smiling at me. 'I think this,' the speaker continued, 'because there are so many young students following.' He nodded to himself, satisfied with the theory. 'My name is Kasim. How do you do?'

Kasim clearly had long since progressed from the one-line school of English I had encountered elsewhere in Turkey. He and his friends trawled the streets every afternoon after lessons at the *lycée*, looking for tourists on whom they might practise.

They often bagged engineers and soldiers from the American military-base near by, backpackers from Canada, France, and Finland, and now they had caught me.

'Like a fish,' one of them said. 'Are you mind if we join you?'

'"Do you",' I corrected him, my old teaching instincts activated by the boys' enthusiasm. There was a flurry of activity and grabbed notebooks as the boys went into emergency session, identifying the mistake and prescribing the treatment.

'What are you doing in Diyarbakır?' Kasim asked me once linguistic order had been restored.

'What is your business here?' a friend put it. When I told them, feverish conferring followed.

'I think,' said Kasim, 'we go to the flea-market.' Three fourteen-year-old boys led me among old men immersed in piles of leather jackets and *shalvar*, the baggy trousers popular here and to the south. From the blank expressions our enquiries generated, we might have been quizzing the old men about more obscure items of ancient history, but eventually a shaky trail emerged.

'We go back to the big street,' said Kasim.

'Main.'

'Main, yes, main.'

On the main street, we found the hat maker, seated amongst flat caps and rolls of grey worsted and brown checks, who eventually raised an eyebrow as if a memory had been stirred.

'There was a man made fezzes,' he said, 'but he died two years ago. His shop was four doors up.' Four doors up was now a cheese shop, and any memories were submerged among great drums of oily white goat's cheese. 'In my opinion,' said Kasim, 'no fezzes are made in Diyarbakır any more.'

'Yes,' said one of his friends. 'They no longer make fezzes in Diyarbakır.'

These Kurdish schoolboys were not interested in questioning the sense of my investigations. All that mattered to them was their pursuit of the key, called English, to a better life. And they brought to that pursuit a single-minded devotion, spooning up words, figures of speech, and scraps of grammar with a ravenous appetite.

Kasim's father was a bus driver for the municipality – Kasim's word. He had six children and earned £150 a month, and Kasim was not prepared to settle for that. But he was also an adolescent. 'An American airman from the base recently taught me dick,' remarked Kasim, apropos of nothing. 'But then an English tourist told me the word was cock. Which one is right, please?' I was rescued by the sight of a fez-wearing ice-cream salesman who told me he had bought his fez several years ago at what were now the cheese premises.

'It's the tradition,' Kasim explained. 'Ice-cream sellers often wear fezzes, but only when they are at work. Now then, dick or cock?'

When the boys dragged their highly prized English speaker back to school the next morning, I did not imagine the questions could get harder.

The *lycée* was a modern block fronted by a basketball hoop among the sprouting constructions of Diyarbakır's latest suburbs. On every side stood foundations made from yellow-fresh baulks of wood and shiny steel rods protruding like straws from deep draughts of concrete. The fifty-odd pupils in Room 2a clapped furiously on my arrival.

'Ask him questions,' said the teacher, setting them free. They rose to their feet in great clamorous waves, like heroes climbing from the trenches, arms flailing to catch my attention, asking their questions, absorbing the answers, thanking me for them, and sitting down again. But even as they sat, there were always more fresh questions to replace those I had repelled with my answers.

'What do you think of Turkey?', 'Are you interesting in fashion?', or 'Do you like dance Michael Jackson?' I could handle. And even if they laughed, I could tell them that my favourite football teams were the Destroyer of Christians Pistachio and the long-relegated whirlers of Konya. I was just beginning to feel in control of the situation when an earnest young girl with her hair in bunches penetrated my defences and overwhelmed me.

'Are you working class, middle class, or upper class?' she asked. I wanted to tell her it was an impossibly candid question to ask of an Englishman.

'And are you wearing knickers?' I might have replied. Instead, I embarked on a long explanation that was designed primarily to deflect the question. That, if they wanted to learn English they should perhaps know something about English customs, and it was not the practice in England to refer to one's class in public. In fact, whatever one's thoughts, one was publicly dismissive of the whole class notion.

The girl in the bunches waited patiently until I had finished. 'So,' she said entirely undiverted, 'what are you?' And I took shameful refuge in the forest of straining hands that surrounded her.

The other difficulty arose when a young boy, who had been quiet for much of the lesson, asked whether I was hell. I could see that he had drawn on finite reserves of courage to participate, and as a former teacher I knew how desperately he needed encouragement. But until Kasim explained that an American serviceman had visited the school a few weeks earlier and used little but variations on this confusing expression, I did not even know what the boy meant.

By the time the class had finished, I felt inspired by the enthusiasm and motivation of these children. It seemed to lift the city up, up above the resignation of the taxi-drivers who no longer bothered avoiding the potholes on the roads and did not care that their mayor spent all his time by the distant banks of the Bosphorus. The example of these children liberated the city from the cares of its people who no longer troubled themselves to complain about harassment from the security forces deliberately selected from western Turks, but just bowed their heads to the cuff of the palm. Even Kasim's thwarted future plans, heartbreakingly recounted, could not break the spirit that the children embodied. 'I wanted to be a pilot,' he told me as he and his friends accompanied me back to my hotel after class, 'until I discovered that Kurds did not become pilots.'

When the boys wished me well and turned to go, I asked them whether there was anything they needed, an English dictionary perhaps.

'We have English dictionaries,' Kasim replied. 'What I want is an English typewriter.' Pilotry or no, Kasim would fly.

For while his forebears had tentatively learned the alphabet of the foreigner, Kasim was set on learning his language. July 30 1929, when a freighter of the Fabre Line left New York docks bound for Constantinople, was the day that could be traced triumphantly to Kasim. In the freighter's hold was a consignment of boxes on which the words Remington Rand Inc were stencilled, containing Turkey's first three thousand typewriters. The freighter passed through the Straits of Gibraltar, skirted the North African coast past Algiers whence Aimée, the French Sultana, had once set sail, and past Tunis where a Grand Admiral had once found fezzes to delight his Ottoman Sultan. And so, weeks later, the latest innovation from the West was unloaded at the docks in Constantinople.

In spite of all the obstructions and humiliations that would confront him, Kasim was set on improving himself. This was the better kind of redemption I had been waiting for, and in Kasim's example, I realized that some good things came by water. Perhaps the Turks need not be scared of boats.

chapter twenty

ON THE ROAD to Adıyaman, before we were beyond the
outskirts of Diyarbakır, I found myself checking the age of my
road map. It was four years old. Never before had I checked
its age; never before had I felt the need to. I had always felt it
safe to assume that Turkey's roads, which had linked Asia
Minor's ancient cities since time began, were always going to
be there. What was a negligible four years against the venerable
lineage of these thoroughfares?

This complacent presumption had first come under fire
only ten minutes earlier when the ticket man at Diyarbakır bus
station had described a route to Adıyaman that seemed
unnecessarily long.

'The bus goes south,' he explained beneath eyebrows where
entire colonies of Anatolian insect species as yet undiscovered
might have hidden. 'South almost as far as Glorious Urfa and
then north and west on the new road to Adıyaman.'

A *new* Turkish road? What was this strange thing?

'But that's much longer,' I insisted, shoving my map, aged
four, beneath his nose. 'Why not take this road, Road 59,
direct to Adıyaman?'

He pushed at his glasses until they disappeared beneath his
eyebrows and replied, 'Because that road is no good any
more.'

But never before had that deterred Turkish drivers. Most
eastern Turkish roads were permanently 'no good', it came
with the territory but they were usable nevertheless. Roads
deteriorated but their deterioration was generally gradual so
that local drivers, already experts in the evasion of potholes,

had plenty of time to adapt to the contours as they developed and to warn each other between shifts when sections of road retired from service without warning.

'By no good,' I enquired, 'do you actually mean potholed?'

The driver tossed back his head, raised his eyebrows, and clicked his tongue in the emphatic Turkish negative.

'A landslip?' I pressed him, but neither was that the problem. 'Or is it simply,' I asked him, my finger snaking out as if to prod him, 'that your drivers prefer the new road even though it causes delay to their passengers?' For perhaps that was it; the irresistible temptations of virgin tarmac. The ticket seller wearily pushed me a glass of tea and offered me a cigarette. There was something ominous in the magnanimity of all this that should have prepared me.

'Your Road 59,' he eventually said, 'is not potholed. Nor do the drivers take to the new road by choice. Road 59 is under water. And will remain so.'

The road, it transpired, had recently been submerged along with a number of villages under the rising waters of the Euphrates as it backed up behind a great dam, the centrepiece of the Southern Anatolia Project. The dam was expected to potentialize an enormous irrigation project in the parched border country to the south-east, to generate massive amounts of hydro-electric power, and to bring employment to the area's separatist malcontents. 'So if you still want your road back,' said the ticket seller, 'go argue it with the Atatürk Dam.'

I fingered my map fondly. This was change so rapid that I was being asked to replace it before its time, before the accumulated holes, rips, and stains of any map worth its salt signalled that retirement had finally been earned. Vast tracts of land that had not changed in centuries were suddenly raising the country's cartographers from a sleep untroubled since the forced removal of words like 'Kurdistan', as new roads appeared all of a sudden, and old ones disappeared under new lakes.

According to the old man in a turban who sat next to me, the weathermen were being kept as busy as the cartographers. Ever since the lake had started to fill behind the dam a few years back, he explained, the weather had been thrown out of kilter.

'*Bozuk*,' said the old man in summary as a grey veil of rain swept across the bus. The word meant broken, but in the grey light I might instead have heard 'bollocks' and he might have been a cantankerous pensioner on a London bus cursing rain-clouds over Hackney. But then he wound himself up, stared at the sky, and claimed it was all Allah's doing, wrath at human interference on a scale that He had never intended, and I thought no more of Hackney.

The bus eventually turned on to the new road, and as if to mark the sheer smoothness of the ride the driver lit a cigarette and flipped on a cassette of Arabesque music. His body snaked in sinuous response as we headed through the pistachio trees and the vines punctuating the mocha earth, among masses of wind-blown poppies and cornflowers, and beyond them the silvered evening expanses of the lake.

Below the dam, a small town had been built to serve the numerous construction and maintenance teams. Lines of pre-fabricated huts and a petrol station gave way to huge banks of electrical plant squatting behind barbed wire before the open road headed north, and gleaming pylons, like great navvies, marched off towards the horizon in every direction with cargoes of volts to power an infinitude of unshaded Turkish light bulbs.

So grand was the scale of the constructions that even the old man forgot his reservations, and told me how the dam was marvelled at by people across Europe and America. But the excited movements of his head were causing the turban to unravel, and rather than disenchant him of the notion that the dam was exclusively the Western topic of the moment, I only wished to halt his frenzied movements before the entire creation fell apart.

'What a reputation,' I agreed admiringly, and the old man sat back, honour satisfied and turban rescued from collapse.

Not many years ago, rainfall rituals had often been enacted throughout this area to save a drought-threatened harvest. Hanging a scorpion from a tree was said to help. So was burying a snake alive. But the most effective method of ensuring rain was to write a prayer on a dog's head and throw the poor mutt into the river. Water, if not dogs, had always been regarded as a sacred gift. In the earlier years of the twentieth century, those about to be executed, even fez-wearing reactionaries, were offered a glass of water along with an olive as a sign of peace. Now, the latest rainfall ritual was to build an eight-turbine rock-fill dam, the fifth largest in the world, so that water, no longer sacred, was finally cornered and could at last be taken for granted.

But as it collected behind Turkish dams, those who depended upon it in downstream Syria and Iraq regarded it as increasingly precious. For Turks and Arabs had shared very little ever since the Ottoman overlords had been kicked out of Arabia and Mesopotamia during the Great War – except water. That the Arab countries received water which had already been used by the Turks was an unwelcome reminder of their former subservience. Iraq and Syria may have won their freedom, but the Euphrates and Tigris rivers still rose in the mountains of eastern Turkey, still passed down the gullets and through the systems of Turks before flowing south to humiliate them. They felt like children dependent for sustenance on the capricious whim of a brother tall enough to turn a tap beyond their reach.

What the Arabs did with their water had never greatly concerned the Turks. They did not damn Syria for damming the Euphrates to create Lake Assad, named after the country's president, in the seventies. But in January 1990, when the river waters upstream were first witheld behind the great Turkish dam near Adıyaman to create a lake named after the local hero, Syria and Iraq were incensed. Filling Lake Atatürk was projected to take anything between five and ten years, during which time the flow of water to Syria and Iraq was likely to be around half its usual level. Damascus and Baghdad pointed out that water might be the future cause of war in the area. The reaction of the god-fearing old man on the bus did nothing to suggest otherwise: 'What are they complaining about?' he fumed. 'They've got oil, haven't they? Do they want to swap water for oil, barrel for barrel? We'd be happy to.' And everybody on the bus laughed.

I had come this way, however, even if via this unexpected diversion, for another reason entirely. I wanted to see the remains of a two-thousand-year-old civilization perched high in the mountains, safe from the rising waters behind the Atatürk Dam. In truth, I was surprised at myself. I have never been drawn to truly old things. Perhaps it is because I have never in my imagination been able to breath life into them, the complex relationships between ancient civilizations. The Hittites, Romans, Greeks, Persians, the Assyrians, Lycians, Phrygians, and Neo-Hittites, the Pamphylians and the Lydians, the Medes and the Cimmerians, they all seemed so remote as to be entirely unconvincing. All that stone, all that hieroglyph was of a world that could be coldly interpreted but never sensed, a world beyond reclamation. Until now, my own journey had largely been through the manageable past, the nineteenth and early twentieth centuries. It was a past chronicled by crinkly letters in spidery handwriting or the impressions left by the keys of the earliest typewriters, by fading daguerrotypes and even the living memories of the very elderly, lives you could reach out to and touch where history was still warm, still alive. And I was not sure what was drawing me to the old bones, history's charnel house on Nemrut Mountain.

Adıyaman was dark by the time we arrived. It wore the standard-issue uniform of Turkish towns: shabby concrete, brightly lit signs advertising, despite a missing bulb here and there, banks and garages alongside the shacks of tailors and mechanics whose roofs were held in place by piles of old tyres as new wiring spread in ivy tangles over defunct growth hanging in loops outside the windows, and deeply shadowed alleys where the deeper shadows of veiled women moved silently. But that was not all: there was over-embroidered decorative evidence of the recent civic prosperity that the dam had brought; new Mercedes cars cruised around, and I glimpsed sophisticated foyers and bright apartment buildings. Street lights glittered with newness; street signs stood subaltern-erect, not yet victims to the inevitable collision that would tear the concrete base from the pavement and bend the signs double at the midriff where rust would quickly set in.

It was all so impressive that I was not prepared to defend myself against the approach of a young tout who entrapped me despite my long experience of such things with that single polished sentence of English delivered irresistibly: 'Hi. If you're looking for Nemrut Mountain, perhaps we can help you.' And he walked away without awaiting my response, confident in the knowledge that I would not be far behind.

And so I came to be on the minibus, along with a Danish blacksmith, his wife, and a veterinary scientist from Australia, that rattled into the mountains the next morning. The sun was shining and it was warm. Allah had clearly relented on dam building.

We were untalkative as the minibus clambered up the track, each leafing through the jottings of our own expectations. The outside world had not known of the ruins on Nemrut Mountain until 1881. Few visitors had come here until the seventies, but since then they had come with great regularity, during the summer months when the mountain was accessible, and usually at sunrise, establishing it as probably the greatest tourist draw in all of eastern Turkey. We had seen the brochures, but our silence suggested that we still hoped to be surprised by Nemrut Mountain.

The peak of Nemrut Mountain was the geographical and spiritual heart of the Commagene kingdom, established a few decades before the birth of Christ as a buffer state between the Roman and Persian empires. The Commagenes were a one-hit wonder, the Kajagoogoo of Anatolian kingdomlets, but evidently the Commagenes did not think of themselves as such. By means of vast funeral mounds, monuments to the power of posthumous publicity, they set out to be remembered.

It was obvious from the surviving evidence, however, that nobody else expected the Commagenes to last. It was, for example, an ominously Roman bridge, not a Commagene one, which carried us across a tributary of the Euphrates and into the Commagene heartlands. Built while they were in power, the Commagenes might have thought to ask themselves, if they had not been so preoccupied with the mounds, why the Romans were prepared to invest in the transport infrastructure of a region not their own. Somebody in the Roman Ministry of Roads and Bridges, they might then have realized, had been quietly tipped the wink to the effect that the Commagenes might call themselves a dynasty but were to be limited rather to a short period. And so it proved when the Roman Emperor Vespasian cursorily incorporated the region into the province of Syria in AD 72, and the Commagenes were history, much of it forgettable, without so much as an independence movement to their credit. This was perhaps because they had not yet given their country a name, and an independence movement in a country without a name is unlikely to have a prayer.

But in their own way the Commagenes quite refused to be forgotten. In death, at least, they would make mighty names for themselves. Nobody had told them their glory might in any way be limited, and they thus behaved as if divinity were their absolute due. At Arsameia, the ancient capital of the Commagenes, I trekked up the path with the Australian veterinary scientist past fallen statues and bas-reliefs. The valley below us was full of yellow and red flowers and hawks hovered, as if they had been hung out to dry in the warm sunshine.

Just before the scattered ruins of the town stood a relief showing Mithradates, the founder of the Commagene short period, shaking hands with Hercules. Forgetting the fact that he is naked, Hercules reminded me of a celebrity in the paid endorsements business posing for a publicity shot. Perhaps he is opening the Commagene equivalent of a supermarket. But what nobody has told him is that, cast in stone, he will pose naked with this Commagene nobody for ever. Nor can he have guessed, such are the twists of history, that the site of his ill-advised endorsement will come to be one of the most visited in Turkey. Hordes of twentieth-century visitors will witness his humiliation. Next to the two figures stands a huge inscription in Greek, which forcibly suggests itself as a classic, early instance of unread contractual small print. Certainly Mithradates, with the added advantage of being fully dressed, looks to have pulled off quite a fast one. I found myself drawn to these people as scraps of Commagene character were conveyed across the millennia. Perhaps there was life in the annals of ancient history after all.

The minibus wound up the mountain between banks of old snow. Peaks rose on every side. In this ancient kingdom digested by Romans, by Persians, by Ottomans, and by modern Turks, we each found ourselves thinking of our own countries and the issues of absorption and national identity as the Danish couple were reminded that it was their referendum day back home on ratification of the Maastricht Treaty on European Union. They had registered 'no' votes before leaving for Turkey. For his part, the veterinary scientist told me that most Australians had had enough of their junior relationship with Britain and were becoming increasingly republican. The minibus came to a halt where the road ran out below the funeral mound of King Antiochus of the Commagenes, son of Mithradates.

The anti-federalist blacksmith had poor legs and hired an expensive mule to carry him to the top while the rest of us set off up the path. As we climbed, I considered the life of

Antiochus who had died young, possibly from one of those violent delusions of grandeur to which he was habitually susceptible. Antiochus apparently spent much of his time assembling the family tree and ended up, on the basis of spurious evidence, with an ancestry far more exalted than was actually the case, doubtless a syndrome widely recognized by genealogists today. In Antiochus's case, it was Alexander the Great of the Greeks on the one side and Darius of the Persians on the other. In 40 BC, you couldn't claim more illustrious antecedents than that.

Unless, that is, you claimed kinship with the gods. I reached a large stone terrace running along the eastern side of the mountain. The great peak of gravel and stones where Antiochus was believed to be buried towered above me. Huge decapitated figures were seated along the terrace to guard and honour Antiochus's memory. Their fallen heads stood six foot high at their feet while a chill wind whistled amongst them. They looked out among stone lions and eagles and scraps of fallen masonry, to the mountains on every side. If you could match the bodies with their heads you would see four gods, Apollo, Fortuna, Zeus, and Hercules, with Antiochus sitting imperiously between them.

Antiochus's research of the family tree connecting him so indubitably to Alexander and Darius had fitted conveniently into the guiding principle of the time, which was to forge the equivalent gods of East and West into single figures so as to provide a cultural bridge between the various peoples, and thus combat ethnic, sectarian, and religious frictions. Furthermore, the combination gods on the terrace – the Sun God Apollo was also Mithra, Helios, and Hermes; the local Fertility God was also Fortuna and Tyche; Zeus was Ahura and Mazda; Hercules was Artagnes and Ares – allowed Antiochus to make shrewd room in the confusion for a statue of Himself, and Himself uncombined.

Into this bombastic magnificence rode the Danish blacksmith on his mule. 'God,' he bellowed, forgetting referendums and the petty aspirations of nations, and for a moment the great heads seemed to prick up their stone ears as the single word echoed round the mountain. A great gust of wind came from somewhere, and a single shivering hawker grabbed at his postcard stand as it skittered towards the mountainside. I walked round the back of the funeral mound to the western terrace, a mirror image of the eastern one where I noticed further reliefs which featured Antiochus shaking hands – a family trait, this – with Apollo, Zeus, and Hercules. The same five stone figures, Antiochus and the flanking divinities, lay fallen in banks of deep snow. *I Antiochus*, my guidebook translated a relief for me, *caused this monument to be created in commemoration of my own glory and that of the gods.*

I looked away. I could see the Euphrates like silvered thread working its way down the valley until it was lost in the distant cobalt-coloured suggestion of water backing up behind the Atatürk Dam. The five stone figures looked west towards Ankara, Istanbul, and Europe; beyond them and the burial mound at their backs their eastward-facing counterparts looked towards Iran and the heart of Asia. And as I looked at them, their faces battered by the frozen winds of almost two thousand years, framed by the carved curly locks of hair, I came to notice their hats which, it gradually dawned on me, were what had brought me here in the first place.

The stone heads on Nemrut Mountain were wearing fezzes. Not all of them; Fortuna was garlanded with vines and fruit, Apollo's hat was rather too flattened to be a fez, but the other figures were prototype fez wearers all. I checked, and sure enough there was evidence of tassles at the back of each hat. Here were fezzes in the heart of Turkey, a thousand years before the dervish *sikke* was ever invented. In the expanses of past, I now realized, I might never find the origins of this hat. But in knowing that, I also understood that the pursuit of the fez to its beginnings was no longer the point, and I was glad to abandon it. For the first time, I realized, all that mattered was what the fez meant. And now, in these fez-wearing ancient Anatolians, that much was clear; for they were looking both ways.

Over the centuries, succeeding generations may have caused the fez to represent whatever best suited them, made it variously masquerade, according to the times, as the badge of Westernization, of Orthodox Islam, as symbol of Ottoman loyalty, and even as a poor toy of tourism. But here on the side of a desolate mountain, its true meaning was revealed as a hat that reconciled the disparate heads beneath it, that looked both ways. Ancient history had astonished me.

Antiochus may have been a stickler for flashy send-offs. His father may have shaken hands with naked gods. But there was something that this pickaninny potentate had understood. He had placated the Eastern and Western cultural elements that were at variance in his society, melding into single unities gods, beliefs, and value systems, so that what emerged was neither Eastern nor Western, and both Eastern and Western at once. Sultan Mahmud II's words upon the introduction of the fez echoed around the ruins: 'Henceforth, I recognize Muslims only in the mosque, Christians only in the church, Jews only in the synagogue. Outside those places of worship, I desire every individual to enjoy the same political rights and my fatherly protection.' This was the way forward: that neither West nor East might prevail, but that the two worlds might coexist, and their conflicting ideologies might no longer collide in the wreckage of car bombs and detentions, language laws and burnt-out hotels.

On Nemrut Mountain they were at last looking both ways, the Highway Code for the Turkish journey. Perhaps I had found it, that better redemption still.

✵

chapter twenty-one

THE EXPRESS COACH left Adıyaman at midnight, travelling so fast as to dump me in an unlit bus station at three thirty in the morning. The option was the late-night post train from the nearby town of Gölbaşı, or Lakehead, reputedly of a speed so slow that the guard and his assistant were presumed to disembark at every tiny junction and collect by hand the mail from surrounding farm houses and hamlets. Which suited me fine; I would wake at eight thirty, and climb refreshed from the train into the full light of morning. That at least was the idea.

So I abandoned the midnight express coach at Lakehead and walked down to the station. The spring sky had bloomed cold with haloed night lights. Ghostly outlines of freight trains stood idle among the sidings. Through a soft-lit window I could see the station master slumped at his desk. His peaked cap had fallen forward like the snowplough front of a winter train. When I knocked at the glass to check departure times with him, his head rose as if from the depths of a swamp, he regarded me with a sleepy but withering indifference, and then he settled upon the cushion of his other cheek.

I had not appreciated what it meant to be a post-train traveller. Post-train travellers were not entitled to make irksome demands of the station staff. They were here on sufferance, the disenfranchized, travelling underclass, expected to sit patiently in the waiting-room until a brusque face appeared at the ticket window. Then the queueing was dutiful and obedient, as if we were in line for the soup kitchen. We were welfare travellers, buying tickets that were vastly cheap even by

Turkish standards. Mine cost 30p, which to pass the time I calculated at 5p per travelling hour. In the waiting-room, the spitting of nut husks, the flare of matches, and the gentle burr of the stove combined to perform the distinctive soundtrack to cut-price Turkish life.

Five pence per hour was certainly cheap, but did not prove good value. When the post train finally hauled up at Lakehead with those sacks of personally collected mail at three o'clock in the morning, it also delivered a full complement of passengers packed into cramped carriages foul with the smell of post-train feet. Only the kindness of a stranger provided me with a seat when a child was hauled upright to make space for me, father and son changing places so that the boy might not slump against the stranger. The boy had been sleeping long enough for sleepy dust to have formed along his eyelids. Above us, fully grown men had taken to the luggage racks. I sat wedged between two men so close that our arms were pinioned, interfering with the passing of nuts, grapes, cigarettes, and scraps of conversation. In this position, I free-fell into sleep.

I awoke entirely unrefreshed to daylight, and rainwater showering me through a window that yawed open with the rhythm of the train. The men either side of me had disembarked during the night, but in sleep I had remained in my tucked-up position, like a mummified parachutist surrounded by acres of untenanted space. I gently cracked the mould of my bones, stretched up, secured the window, and looked out. We had left the mountains for the rich rain-green of the lowland plains. In coming to an end, the geology of Anatolia was giving fifth-column indications of approaching Syria. We were heading towards *tarboosh* territory.

A little later, a branch line carried me south into a low landscape so distinct with its date-palm skyline and the oily sea dark with shoals of fresh rain that I might have expected a border. But as I looked from the window there was no such thing, only a bedraggled child chasing a cat through puddles and a huge steel foundry dissolving in the mist. A young soldier opposite me picked his nose with an assassin's deliberation, and discarded the bogey down the barrel of his gun. In such a context, it seemed odd to find myself thinking of Steven Spielberg.

In the last Indiana Jones movie, a scene opens to a background of foliage, mosques, and minarets gilded in the dawn light above the caption: REPUBLIC OF HATAY. Spielberg's movies are crammed with fancifully titled imaginary settings such as this; it just so happens that the Republic of Hatay is not one of them. The Republic of Hatay actually happened, and at that moment my train was moving south across its old border and entering the former republic on the way to the port of Iskenderun. Now, where guards, flags, and border posts once stood, were only the sodden cotton fields of the Turkish province of Hatay, and a bogey drying in a gun barrel, a scene that owed nothing at all to Steven Spielberg.

Instead, the dour descriptions of an early merchant called Peter Mundy came to mind. 'It is very unwholesome,' he declared of Iskenderun, 'by reason of the huge hills hindringe the approache of the sun beams, until nine or ten a Clocke in the mornings, lyeing in a great marsh full of boggs, frogs, and foggs.' In the 1820s, disease was so prevalent in the town that it was known as the Bane of the Franks. Iskenderun's tombs were said to be more numerous than its houses. Ships that moored here during the summer regularly lost a third of their crews to disease. The agency factors based here were described as having 'a languid air, yellow complexion, livid eyes, and dropsical bellies'. And they hadn't even arrived by post train.

So when we arrived at Iskenderun station forty minutes later, far from the Indiana Jones version, with its period Levantine buzz, the monkeys and parrots, the befezzed merchants and porters, I was quite resigned to the train's mundane lurch to a halt, the measured removal of a finger from a soldier's nose, and a walk through puddles into town.

When Spielberg chose as the plot engine of his movie the

rediscovery of the Holy Grail, Iskenderun was an obvious setting. For the city was the ancient gateway to the Holy Land, landfall of Crusaders and pilgrims alike. In Spielberg's version, the chase for the Grail begins when it is discovered that a passing Crusader knight of the eleventh century apparently concealed it in the area. 1938, meanwhile, was presumably selected by Spielberg as a prime year for Nazis. With all the Grail chasing and Nazi bashing, it is no surprise that Spielberg's characters failed to realize just what an interesting time they might have had in Iskenderun in 1938 by simply stepping out of fiction.

In the version according to Spielberg, Hatay's 1938 leader dressed as an oriental potentate, all decked out in spangle, glitter, robes, and turban-wrapped fez. In fact, the President of Hatay favoured a suit, tie, and homburg. At the time, no more effective means of expressing secular, reformist, pro-Turkish tendencies was available. The President would not have been seen dead in a fez. Rather than a mere sartorial slip, Spielberg's version served to miscast the President's fundamental ideology. Had this version held good, had the President actually been a fez wearer, then history might have followed a quite different path. The forgotten border that I had crossed that morning most likely would still exist and in my passport a fresh stamp would read Republic of Hatay, or even the Syrian Arab Republic.

In the aftermath of the Ottoman Empire, Hatay was slow to resolve itself upon a chosen future. This littoral twenty miles wide by seventy long was Ottoman by tradition but by geography Syrian. Hatay belies Turkey's rectangular integrity, a nub of land protruding hernia-like from its southern underbelly. As a territorial enhancement, Turks are quite sanguine about their spoilt border symmetry. Not so the Syrians, who regard the loss of Hatay not only as a grievous wound in the neat square of their own geography but as a national humiliation. On maps drawn in Damascus, Hatay is still depicted as Syrian.

Iskenderun, meaning Alexander's City in Turkish, was

founded by Alexander the Great after his victory over Darius's Persians at the nearby Battle of Issus in 330 BC. Under French mandate between the wars, it was known as Alexandrette and even at that time was considered a significant strategic prize. It was remembered how, in the late nineteenth century, Iskenderun had been proposed by the British as a terminal for a railway to India, and even for a canal system linking with the Euphrates and thence to the Persian Gulf that would rival Suez. During the Second World War, the port was an important disembarkation point for troops and equipment destined for the Egyptian Front. Fearful as her mandate drew to an end of offending either Syria, the natural claimant to the territory, or Turkey, the influential regional power, France dodged their respective tackles by granting Hatay independence in 1937. But that independence would not last; the Commagene brush with autonomy would prove to be positively dynastic by comparison.

I found a hotel on the corniche where the Mediterranean swilled noisily around the bay. But little else stirred except the lank strand of hair in front of Hassan Bey the receptionist's nut-brown eyes which seemed to be in perpetual motion, unwinding like a telephone left to hang by its cord. He was standing in front of a shiny array of conspiciously undisturbed room keys. The hotel felt rather too big for the two of us. I asked him how business was.

He spread his palms wide. 'Where do you want to start?'

'The Gulf War?' I suggested.

'Before then, well before then,' he replied gloomily. The war in Lebanon and strained relations with Syria, he told me, had already sidelined Iskenderun before Saddam's war forced the Turks to close the lucrative Iraqi oil pipeline terminal at the nearby town of Dörtyol, or Crossroads. Sanctions on what Iraqi trade remained had put the local hauliers out of business.

'And what you see,' said Hassan Bey, running his fingers through the tinkle of unused room keys, 'is the result.' He turned to write down my passport details.

'English,' he said, noting my nationality. 'Turkish,' he then added, jabbing at himself with his pen.

Only in Iskenderun, it struck me as I stepped outside, might a Turk need to remind himself of his nationality. For on the recognizable stream of Turkish that passed me in the street floated the distinctive gutturals of Arabic. I, who had not seen churches since Istanbul, now walked past Catholic, Orthodox, and Armenian ones. Old men in spats and tortoise-shell glasses, true Levantine dandies, walked back streets that were not named, but numbered in the Parisian fashion. The clock on the justice court, a building which looked to have been transplanted here from the deserts of *Beau Geste* Arabia, was made by Charvet of Lyon. In the restaurants, they were eating hummus, the chick-pea paste of the Levant which I had encountered nowhere else in Turkey. There was a dentist called Alfred Beyluni. An export company on the waterfront was called MacAndrews & Forbes whose business was exporting bails of Turkish and Afghan liquorice for use in confectionery. Alexander's great city may have become a town over the years but its Levantine spirit, commercial and cosmopolitan, evidently remained intact.

As early as 1581, the Levant Company, a major trading organization, had been founded in Iskenderun. Peter Mundy may not have liked it, but for traders such as himself it was the only place to be. By the late 1600s, they were alerting Aleppo to the news of merchandise arrivals at Iskenderun by carrier pigeon, which covered the sixty miles in as little as two and a half hours.

Given all this, Spielberg may be said to have redeemed himself by correctly suggesting in his movie a marked presidential soft spot for the kind of expensive foreign motor car in which the Nazis pay court to the local potentate: 'Rolls-Royce Phantom II,' Hatay's President purrs. 'Four point three litre, thirty horsepower, six cylinder engine, with Stromberg downdraft carburettor. Can go from nought to a hundred kilometres an hour in twelve point five seconds. And I even like the colour.' Over the years, the people of Iskenderun had acquired a taste for the good things that come from across the sea.

And so it is that Spielberg's President gets the Rolls and the Nazis get the archaeological run of Hatay in return. In fact, a shady deal was brokered here in 1938, but it involved not Rolls-Royces, a befezzed potentate, and Germans but territory, Frenchmen, and Turks. As the Nazi threat loomed, the French reasoned that possession of Hatay might bolster Turkish vulnerability against Hitler's honeyed whisperings. So France contrived the circumstances by which a Turkish annexation might appear legitimate. Since 1939, the Turkish flag has flown over Iskenderun.

As I wandered through the town, however, I noticed that it did not hang alone. A sodden Union Jack was strung limply to the flagpole above a surviving Ottoman mansion whose blossom-filled garden ran down to the corniche. Brass door-plates variously advertised the building as home to the local Lloyd's agent, Catoni's Maritime Agencies, and the British Consulate. I remembered how Freya Stark had come here in the fifties and succeeded in wangling the consul's car for a day to explore the battlefield at Issus. Her example beckoned me through the doors.

The British Honorary Vice-Consul to Iskenderun sat in a large, bright office whose windows overlooked the geraniums. The consul was female, Christian, and largely Syrian by origin; like Iskenderun itself, Hannoud Alexander did not conform to the Turkish pattern. Her story, like her surname, was in many ways that of the town. The languages she had spoken since childhood, French, Italian, Greek, Turkish, and Arabic, were the languages of this Levantine port, and her work as a shipping agent was the pulse which had brought it prosperity. In her hands was entrusted one of the town's eight foreign consulships; the names of the other consuls, Makzume, Levante, Boutros, and Glyptis among them, sounded as un-Turkish as her own.

When Turkey annexed Hatay in 1939, non-Turkish

elements who did not wish to become naturalized were given the right to opt for Syrian or Lebanese nationality within six months. Those who stayed included Hannoud Alexander, who adopted a Turkish pseudonym, Hind Koba, for use when required by Turkish officialdom. Since she was at ease in five languages and could make a case to argue that she was composed of several different nationalities, the imposition of a second name was never going to trouble her.

Hannoud had worked for Catoni Maritime Agencies for forty years. The Catoni family, whose origins lay in France and Corsica, had established their agency in Iskenderun three hundred years ago. In 1885, Augustine Catoni was appointed British Consul and became Lloyd's agent for the town at the same time, sixty years before the same appointments were made in Beirut, Lattakia in Syria, and Mersin to the north in Turkey, all ports which have now far outgrown Iskenderun. As Catonis served British interests in Iskenderun, so the consulship became ever more closely linked to the family name. When, finally, there were no more Catonis, consular positions fell to long-serving Catoni employees such as Hannoud.

Hannoud showed me round the old house. In the upstairs rooms, items of furniture appeared stranded in space, and the air was musty as if it had not been disturbed in weeks. Cobwebs were beginning to colonize the spaces above the doors. Official consular visits, Hannoud told me, were increasingly rare these days, and the consul chamber was gathering dust. There were the first signs of leaking, brown discolorations advancing across ceilings, and chunks of plaster cornicing which had fallen like Christmas cake icing to moulder on the floors of uncurtained rooms.

The venerable shipping agency had fared as poorly as the building which still housed it. The staff had shrunk, shutting off unneeded rooms as they retreated towards redundancy. When Hannoud had joined Catonis in 1953, the agency employed forty people, and eight hundred British ships alone visited Iskenderun annually. Now there were just five employees, the once-sizeable British community was now numbered at six, and the port statistics for 1992 revealed that just 1,605 ships in total had visited Iskenderun in 1992. In the port, they had once loaded silk, cotton, and yarn from Aleppo, carpets and rhubarb, and muslin from the caravans that came overland from India. And unloaded, I imagined, Rolls-Royces from Gravesend and railway track from Hamburg. Nowadays it was coal and grain, steel and fertilizers, and nobody seemed to know nor care which way these grey commodities were headed.

When I returned to the hotel that evening, Hassan Bey was still standing in front of his brightly shining room keys. As he reached up for mine, he deliberately swung his hands through the surrounding keys to set them jangling as if with the hope of renewed activity.

'Did you know there was a film, very famous in the West, set in Iskenderun?' I told Hassan Bey, thinking that the town might profitably sell itself on the Indiana Jones connection. But Hassan Bey only lifted a finger and said, '*Midnight Express*.' Like most Turks, Hassan Bey did not much expect Western films to supply positive portrayals of Turkey.

Ever since the film's release in the 1970s, Turks have taken great exception to *Midnight Express*. The film, which recounts a young American's stay in an Istanbul prison after attempting to leave the country taped to a considerable amount of secreted hash, reveals its stance in a few bald lines: 'Justice in Turkey is like asking bears to shit in a toilet'; 'They have special classes for corruption at night school'; 'For a nation of pigs, it sure is funny you don't eat them.'

But *Midnight Express* was only the most recent episode in the litany of insults that the Turks have suffered at the hands of the West. Hassan Bey and many others like him wondered how Westerners could still consider them 'barbars', or barbarians. In the sixteenth century, Martin Luther had prayed to be delivered from the World, the Flesh, the Turk, and the Devil.

For the Turk was Terrible, and Turning Turk was the final heresy. 'Nose of Turk' was one of the ingredients that went into the witches' cauldron in Macbeth along with such pleasantries as 'finger of birth-strangled babe'. Out of a contempt that masked fear, the British had called their dogs Sultan and their pubs the Turk's Head ever since the days of Ottoman supremacy. Before the days of coconuts, the British had shied at wooden Turk's heads in country fairs.

But when Hassan Bey told me what had so enraged him about *Midnight Express*, I discovered to my surprise that it was something far more specific. 'In *Midnight Express*,' he said, 'somebody pisses on a portrait of Atatürk, no? And,' he added, barely containing himself, 'they actually dress Turkish people in fezzes.' For Hassan Bey, this was the final insult. For that hat was what those Arabs wore. Unforgivably for Hassan Bey, the film had confused Turks with Arabs. *Tarboosh* or tar brush, his words reminded me how ubiquitous is prejudice.

Hassan Bey had not seen *Midnight Express*, in which incidentally nobody pisses on Atatürk's portrait, nor is anybody made to wear a fez. But his fury about fezzes persuaded me to drop the Spielberg connection. For there are plenty of fezzes in Spielberg's Iskenderun, historically accurate as it happens. For Hatay was not yet Turkish in 1938, and the fez was still legal in this distant corner of what Atatürk considered the Turkish birthright.

The fez would not last. Iskenderun would soon become Turkish, and subject to Turkish law. But if you listened to the accounts of Hatay's absorption into Turkey you could hear voices from behind Iskenderun's faded French shutters that cried foul. France had betrayed them, the voices said. As late as 1936, they explained, Syria's claim to Hatay had been widely accepted. Even when the French compromised by granting independence to Hatay in 1937, the republic was linked by customs and monetary agreements to Syria.

But as the threat from Nazi Germany increased, the voices

continued, the French became increasingly compliant to Turkish demands. The imminent elections gave the Turks a pretext to propose that their troops might usefully maintain order in the young republic until the poll results were published. The French assented.

Moreover, as the elections approached, eastern Turks were said to have been bussed into Hatay to bolster the pro-Turkish vote. The voting commission comprised three Turks and a Frenchman in charge of an exclusively Turkish corps of registration officers. In response, much of the non-Turkish population boycotted the elections in disgust. Unsurprisingly, the election results indicated that the local population favoured accession to Turkey. Soon, the belated design of the Republic of Hatay's flag was announced. It would be a white crescent and star on a red background. It could be distinguished from the Turkish flag, it was brusquely explained to those who dared query it, by the fact that the star would be outlined in white.

One afternoon, I walked through town beneath clearing skies. I could hear the mingled sounds of church bells and muezzins, of Arabic and Turkish. On the doorways of the apartment blocks, I noticed the eclectic names of a disparate people inscribed, and I wondered how long they might last, these Levantes, Boutroses, Makzumes, and Alexanders before they made way for rows of Özturks, the 'Pure Turks' so popular when surnames were introduced to Turkey but in which was contained an exclusive, in-bred idea of nationalism that would only offend cosmopolitan Iskenderun.

On the waterfront stood the town's statue of the Father of the Turks surrounded by the sculpted figures of his sons and daughters, the soldiers, peasants, and workers of the Turkish Republic. The sheer size of the glistening black monument suggested that Turkey's claim on Iskenderun and the surrounding province of Hatay was non-negotiable. It was also built, I figured, with more practical considerations in mind.

Late one Monday night in 1960, just before Christmas, those who did not consider themselves Atatürk's sons and daughters had blown the previous statue to pieces.

The rains had washed free of dust the tender, translucent leaves of the lemon trees, and the air was bright, vibrant with the sense of imminent heat. Children were playing football on rutted tracks amongst new washing and the ferreting of chickens. I could hear carpets being beaten. I reached a whitewashed archway and stepped inside the town's French military cemetery.

Two boys on a bicycle were weaving between the graves where cypresses threw long shadows. The dead were mostly marked by single stones, rounded marble headstones inscribed in black with a cross, name, regiment, number, and a date. Among them were graves marked simply with the words *'soldat français inconnu'*. Soldiers of the French colonies, hundreds of riflemen from Algeria and Senegal, lay in mass graves below inscriptions that only recorded their numbers.

Between 1919 and 1921, these nine hundred soldiers had been landed at Iskenderun to play their part in the Allied attempt to suppress the emergence of modern Turkey. Less than twenty years later, the ground in which they lay would be absorbed into the country whose birth struggles they had tried to smother.

In the spring of 1938, a few months before the Hatay elections, Atatürk set out in ailing health from Istanbul by train, ostensibly to attend a series of military parades close to the border with Hatay. In celebrating Turkish victories over those same forces whose dead lay in the dappled shade of the French military cemetery at Iskenderun, the Gazi publically reinforced his claim to Hatay. The French hastened negotiations over the territory in Turkey's favour.

Little more than a year later, on June 23 1939, two documents were simultaneously signed. One, a Declaration of Mutual Assistance signed in Paris between France and Turkey, effectively foiled Axis attempts to woo Turkey. The other, in

Ankara, provided for the cession of Hatay to Turkey. The Germans and Italians, seeing a potential ally morally committed to neutrality, furiously described the agreements as an 'infamous bargain'.

But Atatürk had not lived to see Hatay incorporated into Turkey. The spring heat of that train journey to the south the previous year had exhausted him. On his return to Istanbul, he could hardly make unaided the short walk from the train at Haydarpasha down to the presidential barge waiting to ferry him across the Bosphorus. The Gazi was in the advanced stages of terminal cirrhosis. Except in death, he would never leave Istanbul again.

He died in Istanbul on the morning of November 10 1938. They carried his body in state across the Galata Bridge and down to a Turkish warship which ferried him across the Sea of Marmara to the town of Izmit. There, his cortege boarded the presidential train and Atatürk was carried to his beloved capital while his people mourned him.

Atatürk had, however, lived long enough to know that the outcome of the Hatay business was assured. When Turkish troops had marched into Hatay at five minutes past midnight on July 3 1938 that summer to oversee the elections, Atatürk did not expect them to leave. And during the last few days of his life, as the winter cold gathered in his bones, perhaps he will have thought of that distant littoral, the final piece of the jigsaw poised to complete the Turkish picture. And in his dying thoughts, he may have looked forward to the day when his followers among Hatay's population would finally tear reviled fezzes from the heads of those that still chose to wear them.

It was so entirely about hats, it struck me, as I lingered amongst the graves. I thought how strange it was that the French should have appointed to lead the Hatay negotiations one Monsieur Bonnet, the aptly named Mr Hat. How strange even that they should call this place *Hat*ay, whatever its indistinct meaning in Turkish.

Perhaps this was how Atatürk's life had ended; a valedictory vision of the people of Hatay, Turkish and Arabic, Muslim and Christian, watching as their beloved red-felt hats, whether they chose to call them fezzes or *tarbooshes*, were stamped into the summer dust. And time to hear in the crowing slogans proclaiming Hatay to be Turkish, the serving of the death warrant on the lessons of compromise and cosmopolitanism that had been passed down to the people of Iskenderun from that distant mountain where Antiochus lay. Time to muse on the thought that the final few fezzes would soon be ground into Iskenderun's dirt; that he had at last achieved all he intended, positioned the final piece, and the Turkish jigsaw was complete.

✳

epilogue

A WEEK LATER, I sat under a tamarisk tree in a Turkish village square, listening to cicadas chiselling holes in the drowsy quiet of the afternoon. Summer had arrived and I could smell pine, heavy and resinous, and oregano. Children were playing along the foreshore. A man was painting the upturned hull of his fishing boat a deep maroon. Chickens pecked at the dust. Two children steered cattle through the village. On a wooden balcony, a couple were mending fishing nets. A man in an apron occasionally emerged from the nearby tea house to collect glasses off the tables. And above the village, an old man was working a small plot of land.

It was May 19 again. The year had come full circle but this time I was some distance from Pomegranate, perhaps four hours west by bus and maybe twenty years away. It felt as if I had returned in time, and the man in the field above the village might have been Mustafa Yildirim, the old farmer of Pomegranate who had never understood his surname, and Turkey's problems were banished as I sat in the shade of my tamarisk tree.

From a distance, I watched the old man as he worked. Eventually, he wiped his brow, rested his hands on his hips, dropped his hoe, and walked down the path into the village. As he approached, he caught sight of me and nodded. He shouted for a glass of tea, sat down near by, and said that he hoped I was enjoying my time in Turkey.

'You are travelling around?' he asked. 'A tourist?'

'Yes,' I replied. 'A tourist looking for fezzes.'

'Ah,' he said. 'A student of history. Or did you find any?'

I had found fezzes for tourists, I told him. In Pomegranate, I told him, I had found them in the shops and on the head of a man outside a restaurant. In Istanbul I had seen them in the hotels, on the heads of mannequins in the museums, and on gravestones in the cemeteries. I had seen some in the trinket shops of Sivas, and one on the head of an ice-cream seller in Diyarbakır. And I thought for a moment to have seen one on the head of a man his age in Kastamonu.

'Thought for a moment?' the old man asked.

'Well, I thought it was a fez. It was felt and red, just like a fez. I remember the man walking past the vegetable stalls in the market but he disappeared and I never had a chance to ask him. But when I asked others about it, they told me it was no such thing.'

'Well, of course they told you that!' the old man exclaimed. 'We are not so proud of our fez wearers. But a fez is hard to mistake. If you think you saw a fez in Kastamonu, then I should say that you did, especially if you came for no other purpose than to find one.'

As he spoke, I began to understand more clearly why I had come. Looking back, I realized that the fez had been the means to an end, no end in itself, for I had failed to trace this elusive hat to its origins. But now it seemed that to have done so would have been to pin it like a butterfly to a board, and I preferred to let it drift free in a distant, uncertain past. The end had been Turkey herself.

The fez had guided me to the divisions that modern Turkey denied, the divisions that would always leave Turkey at odds with herself but that made her intriguing, endlessly different, and, finally, the country she was. All she could do was heed the example of the fez and strive to balance herself above the oppositions that claimed her.

Still, it meant something, that one genuine Turkish fez sighting finally confirmed, for it was perhaps the last one. Soon, it would go the way of the others but when it had, I could at least say what I had seen, defiant and unbowed, that day on the snow-trudged streets of Kastamonu.

'And now,' asked this inquisitive old man, the first Turk to have admitted fezzes might still endure in his country, 'what will you do?' The question would do for Turkey. What would come of this country torn by ideologies where they ruthlessly ploughed under the past only for it to germinate in the present? A country where every action spawned a reaction; where the hanging of fez wearing religious reactionaries led by turns to the car-bomb deaths of bare headed secularists; the erection of statues in every square and the explosions that destroyed them, and the erasure of saintly faces from Cappadocian frescos; a country where they bared their breasts or shrouded themselves in veils; lost themselves in the banal Western blandishments of Pomegranate or prepared for the law of the Islamic *sheriat*. What would Turkey do?

'I don't know,' I told the old man, thinking I might linger for a few days. 'I can't decide.'

'Hah!' the old man exclaimed, rising to his feet. 'You can't decide, and neither should you. Whenever we Turks decide, we seem to injure ourselves. We hurt each other. Indecision,' he said, thumping the table in front of me. 'Indecision, not ideology; that's the whole point of being Turkish.'

The man arrived with the tea to the sight of the old man standing over me, waving a cigarette, clearly exercised.

'Hey, Mustafa *amja*,' the tea man admonished him. 'Leave the tourist alone. Is he disturbing you?' he then asked, turning attentively towards me.

'Not at all,' I replied. 'He's explaining the whole point of being Turkish.'

As the evening muezzin sounded over the village and the sun set, turning the water to mica, I called out for two more glasses of tea.

✳

bibliography

The following are publications to which I have referred, or am otherwise indebted. Dates given refer to first London publication unless indicated otherwise.

Allom, Thomas, *Character and Costume in Turkey and Italy*, 1839

Armstrong, Harold, *Turkey and Syria Reborn*, 1930

Barber, Noel, *Lords of the Golden Horn*, 1973

Bean, George, *Turkey's Southern Shore*, 1968

Blanch, Lesley, *The Wilder Shores of Love*, 1954

Buchan, John, *Greenmantle*, 1916

Burnaby, Frederick, *On Horseback Through Asia Minor*, 1877

Byron, Robert, *The Road to Oxiana*, 1937

Chaliand, Gerard, *A People Without A Country: The Kurds and Kurdistan*, 1993

Childs, W. J., *Across Asia Minor On Foot*, 1917

Dalrymple, William, *In Xanadu; A Quest*, 1989

Darke, Diana, *Guide to Eastern Turkey and the Black Sea Coast*, 1987 edition

Doughty, C. M., *Arabia Deserta*, 1928

Ellesmere, Earl of, *The Two Sieges of Vienna*, 1861

Franck, Harry A., *The Fringe of the Moslem World*, New York, 1928

Garnett, L. M. J., *Mysticism and Magic in Turkey*, 1912

Glazebrook, Philip, *Journey to Kars*, 1984

Halid, Halil, *The Diary of a Turk*, 1903

Hamdy, Bey, *Costumes Populaires de la Turquie*, Vienna Exhibition, 1873

Hotham, David, *The Turks*, 1972

Kelly, Laurence, *Istanbul; a Travellers' Companion*, 1989

Kemal, Yaşar, *Mehmet My Hawk*, 1961

Kinross, Lord Patrick, *Atatürk: The Rebirth of a Nation*, 1964

Leigh Fermor, Patrick, *Between the Woods and the Water*, 1986

Lewis, Bernard, *The Emergence of Modern Turkey*, 1951

Lewis, Geoffrey, *Modern Turkey*, 1974

——, *Turkey*, 1965

Linke, Lilo, *Allah Dethroned*, 1927

Loti, Pierre, *Aziyade*, 1927

Luke, Sir Harry, *The Old Turkey and the New*, 1955

Magris, Claudio, *Danube*, 1989

Mango, Andrew, *Discovering Turkey*, 1973

Mansel, Philip, *Sultans in Splendour*, New York, 1988

Newman, Bernard, *Turkish Crossroads*, 1951

Orga, Irfan, *Portrait of a Turkish Family*, 1950

Pardoe, Julia, *The City of the Sultan*, 1837

Pereira, Michael, *East of Trebizond*, 1971

Pickthall, Marmaduke, *With the Turk in Wartime*, 1914

Ramsay, Sir William, *Impressions of Turkey*, 1897

Robins, Philip, *Turkey and the Middle East*, 1991

Searight, Sarah, *The British in the Middle East*, 1979

Settle, Mary Lee, *Blood Tie*, New York, 1977

Slade, Sir Adolphus, *Records of Travels in Turkey*, 1833

Sole, Robert, *Le Tarbouche*, Paris, 1992

Toynbee, Arnold, *Turkey*, 1917

Toynbee & Kirkwood, *Turkey*, 1913

Vizetelly, Edward, *Reminiscences of a Bashi-Bazouk*, 1897

W'arkworth, Lord, *Asiatic Turkey*, 1898

Waugh, Sir Telford, *Turkey, Yesterday, Today and Tomorrow*, 1930

West, Rebecca, *Black Lamb and Grey Falcon*, 1955

Wolff, Reverend Joseph, *Mission to Bokhara*, 1846

Wood, Alfred, *A History of the Levant Company*, 1935

Yeats-Brown, Francis, *Golden Horn*, 1932

I am also indebted to Patricia L. Baker's essay 'The Fez in Turkey:
A Symbol of Modernization', which appeared in *Costume Magazine*,

and to the following newspapers: *The Times*, the *Independent*, the *Daily Telegraph*, the *Guardian*, the *Financial Times*, all London; the *New York Times*; the *Egyptian Gazette*, Cairo; the *Turkish Daily News*, Ankara; and *Dateline*, Istanbul.

THE NEW HARTFORD MEMORIAL LIBRARY
P.O. Box 247
Central Avenue at Town Hill Road
New Hartford, Connecticut 06057
(860) 379-7235